CARACOLEANDO AMONG WORLDS

CARACOLEANDO AMONG WORLDS

Reconstructing Maya Worldviews in Chiapas

SILVIA SOTO

THE UNIVERSITY OF
ARIZONA PRESS
TUCSON

The University of Arizona Press
www.uapress.arizona.edu

We respectfully acknowledge the University of Arizona is on the land and territories of Indigenous peoples. Today, Arizona is home to twenty-two federally recognized tribes, with Tucson being home to the O'odham and the Yaqui. Committed to diversity and inclusion, the University strives to build sustainable relationships with sovereign Native Nations and Indigenous communities through education offerings, partnerships, and community service.

ISBN-13: 978-0-8165-5432-4 (hardcover)
ISBN-13: 978-0-8165-4755-5 (paperback)
ISBN-13: 978-0-8165-4756-2 (ebook)

Cover design by Leigh McDonald
Cover art by Antún Kojtom
Typeset by Sara Thaxton in 10/14 Warnock Pro with Ernestine Pro and Helvetica Neue LT Std

Publication of this book is made possible in part by the proceeds of a permanent endowment created with the assistance of a Challenge Grant from the National Endowment for the Humanities, a federal agency.

Library of Congress Cataloging-in-Publication Data
Names: Soto, Silvia, 1973– author.
Title: Caracoleando among worlds : reconstructing Maya worldviews in Chiapas / Silvia Soto.
Description: Tucson : University of Arizona Press, 2024. | Includes bibliographical references and index.
Identifiers: LCCN 2024004835 (print) | LCCN 2024004836 (ebook) | ISBN 9780816554324 (hardcover) | ISBN 9780816547555 (paperback) | ISBN 9780816547562 (ebook)
Subjects: LCSH: Maya literature—Mexico—Chiapas—History and criticism.
Classification: LCC PM3968.85.C54 S68 2024 (print) | LCC PM3968.85.C54 (ebook) | DDC 897.42709—dc23/eng/20240415
LC record available at https://lccn.loc.gov/2024004835
LC ebook record available at https://lccn.loc.gov/2024004836

Printed in the United States of America
♾ This paper meets the requirements of ANSI/NISO Z39.48-1992 (Permanence of Paper).

CONTENTS

PREFACE

Shapers of the Land

Cada quien conoce su rumbo, su modo y su tiempo.

Each of us knows her way, her mode and her time.

—ZAPATISTA WOMEN'S OPENING ADDRESS AT THE FIRST INTERNATIONAL GATHERING OF POLITICS, ART, SPORT, AND CULTURE FOR WOMEN IN STRUGGLE

I come from a lineage of shapers of the land, descending from the Sierra region of Zinapécuaro, Michoacán, México.[1] My *abuelito* Salvador, maternal grandfather, was a pottery maker whose practice he passed on to his wife and children. He shaped the earth into practical cups, plates, and cooking pots. He was also a corn grower who worked the land following the three-sister system of corn, beans, and squash. Tender of his own food, he liked the idea of providing the family's needs and sustainment. As children, my mom, aunts, and uncles nurtured the corn ears piled up at home during the harvest season, and shapes of clay in various stages of the pottery making process in the backyard. They learned from this interaction responsibility, care, and respect for the land that provided for them.

My fraternal *abuelito*, Marcelino, grew up as an orphan and with little access to land. Once an adult, he rented a small plot to work and support the family. Zinapécuaro is a Sierra region covered with pine trees. My *abuelito* Marcelino tended these pine trees on the land he rented and extracted the tree resin to sell. This was profitable labor; while nothing abundant, it was enough to support his wife, my *nañita*, and their four children. He knew the Sierra and the trees he cared for and relied on for sustainment. When my *abuelito* Marcelino died at the young age of forty-three, my eighteen-year-old father was forced to seek labor *en el norte*. Working the fields of Texas and California's Central Valley, my father continued that love and respect for the land that he had learned from his father, my *abuelito* Marcelino.

A small plot of land came into my family's responsibility with my dad's hard-earned dollars in *el norte,* and although as a migrant worker my dad was never able to tend to it, my mom assumed responsibility of managing the chunk of land. During harvest season the corn ears would take over the corridor of our small house in Zinapécuaro, as my mom fervently pursued state outlets to purchase the harvest in bulk. From the teachings of her father, my *abuelito* Salvador, my mom would keep several of the best corn ears to use for the next planting cycle. She would also keep some of the corn to feed the family, not a lot, just enough to teach us the life cycle of the maize and its power in sustaining our families for generations.

My *abuelito* Salvador died when I was barely seven, and my *abuelito* Marcelino died over two decades before I was born. There are very few photos of them, but the stories of their kindness and giving ways are numerous. Postrevolutionary Mexico identified them as campesinos, corn growers. And as corn growers, they were caretakers and shapers of the land who understood life cycles, reciprocal relations, and the power of love in all that is life giving. These stories have nurtured me, and these knowledges continue to inform my place in the world, my intellectual curiosity, and my pursuits.

I am a Mexican immigrant and Chicana scholar in Indigenous studies, who, for three decades, has maintained a research focus on the Maya region of Chiapas. Importantly, the legacies of *mestizaje* situate me as a mestiza when I am moving about the world and traversing the various spaces of my ethnographic work in Chiapas and in Mexico at large.[2] I am the product of this colonial project. I was born in Zinapécuaro, Michoacán—P'urhépecha region—and can trace my roots four generations back on both sides of the family. Zinapécuaro is what anthropologists have labeled a de-Indianized town, which means that the expansion of colonial projects shattered Indigenous lineage relations.[3] I do not claim a P'urhépecha identity, and I state this position in recognition of my fractured connections and relations to the communities. This stance is in line with the Maya communities I have been working with in Chiapas, where language, traditional *traje,* and relation to the community are tied to their identities. This is the position also shared in Native American and Indigenous studies, where discourse on issues of self-identity is tightly linked to the importance of community recognition and belonging.[4] My fractured relations to my family's Indigenous past are tied to complex histories of *mestizaje* that do not place my identity in a linear and direct position as colonizer.[5] Our histories are more complex than these fixed binary relations. And, in understanding my place in the world, I continue to pursue the stories that address our multifaceted histories of *mestizaje* and discourses that navigate nonpolarized identity relations. Such is the power that family stories carry in the making of our histories.

Waking Up to a Revolution

This book's inception story began in the fall of 1993. At that time, I was completing my first semester at the Universidad Nacional Autónoma de México (National Autonomous University of Mexico or UNAM) as a participant of the University of California Education Abroad Program, during my junior year as an undergraduate at the University of California, Davis. On New Year's Eve 1994, the Zapatista Army of National Liberation (EZLN) burst onto the world's stage. As the Indigenous insurgency was shaking Chiapas, Mexico, and the world, UNAM was deep in its own revolutionary actions in solidarity with the EZLN. Classes were interrupted for weeks as lectures and discussions circled back to the uprising. In addition to the EZLN's published communiqués, my broader introduction to this historic uprising came from the panels UNAM organized to analyze the uprising from an economic, social, historical, and cultural perspective. The auditorium in the Facultad de Filosofía y Letras (School of Philosophy and Letters) played a series of films on the representation of Indigenous peoples in this art form, the School of Economics hosted roundtables on the impact of neoliberal policies on the uprising, and UNAM's main quad became the center of artistic and musical performances. The organizers of UNAM's caravan to Chiapas collected donations of dry goods at most of these events. Scholarly analysis, art, music, activism, and the fervor of students and faculty communities at UNAM were my introduction to the Maya regions of Chiapas. And I joined in this enthusiasm and commitment in solidarity with the Indigenous insurgency.

The EZLN disrupted the course of Mexico's history. The uprising shook Mexico's infrastructure and forced the nation to look into the depths of Mexico *profundo*.[6] When Mexico and the world looked into the Maya region of Chiapas, communities were ready to share their stories rooted in Maya cosmovision—relation to place, affirmation of identities, and spiritual and cultural practices that sustain communities' relations. And I followed their stories of the formation of the insurgency; the denouncement of exploitation, oppression, and denials; the construction of autonomous communities; and, most importantly, the reaffirmation and redignification of Maya identities. In my interest to further root the EZLN within Indigenous worldviews, I followed my intellectual curiosity into the contemporary Maya literature of Chiapas. This book speaks of these relations, the shared languages of the EZLN and the contemporary Maya literary movement in their different trajectories, but with one shared vision of reaffirming their Maya worldviews.

The book project itself closes a cycle for my *acompañamiento* of the EZLN. In March 2018, I was one of over five thousand women of all ages who gathered in the Caracol of Morelia, Zapatista autonomous territory, for the First International Gathering of Politics, Art, Sport, and Culture for Women in Struggle. My participation was significant and resonant of my first journey to Chiapas, in August 1994, to attend the Democratic National Convention, the first international gathering hosted by the EZLN in the newly established Aguascalientes (center for political, social, and economic activity in Zapatista territory) of Guadalupe Tepeyac. I was then one of about six thousand national and international members of civil society participating in dialogues with and alongside the EZLN. Among the many topics of exchange was the EZLN's position on exploring new directions for democratic state action inclusive of Indigenous peoples, gender-balanced relations, Indigenous autonomy and self-determination, and the construction of a future for all peoples of Mexico (EZLN communiqué, August 3, 1994).[7] The women's gathering twenty-four years later also spoke to this vision, as well as to one of the philosophies of the Zapatistas, *lento pero seguro* (slow but certain), which the women astutely demonstrated with the organizing and successful gathering.

These are the connections (family relations, activism, and academic research) that inform the narrative that unfolds in this book and that have guided my research into the Maya regions of Chiapas. The teachings from my parents, informed by their parents and generations before them, resonated with my journeys alongside Maya communities of Chiapas—journeys of learning, listening, and reciprocal relations with the communities. I am living in Northern California now, homelands of the Coast Miwok and Southern Pomo peoples, reflecting on these trajectories. Political borders separate me from the lands my *abuelitos* tended and cared for most of their lives, but I carry their stories, teachings, mindfulness, and sense of connection to and respect for all that is life-giving.

ACKNOWLEDGMENTS

The completion of this book project is the result of the collective efforts of mentors, colleagues, friends, family, and institutional assistance. I am grateful for the support, *acompañamiento,* and love through these processes.

Thank you to my parents, Matias and Elena Soto, for teaching me how to question and look at the world with a critical eye; my sisters, Guadalupe, Olivia, Martha, Lilia, and Lorena, for grounding me; and the next generations, my niece Sofia, my nephews Julian, Eztli, and Rio, my great-nephew JJ, and my great-niece Ariella for sharing their growing curiosity and luminosity. *De mi corazón al suyo, gracias!*

Thank you to my mentors and friends from the University of California, Davis (UC Davis)—Inés Hernández-Ávila, Stefano Varese, Victor Montejo, and Bettina Ng'weno—for their unremitting guidance and encouragement that continue to be a blessing in my life's work. I am grateful as well to my friends, colleagues, and mentors from the University of Illinois at Urbana-Champaign (UIUC)—Robert Warrior, Jenny Davis, Anna María Escobar, Krystal Smalls, Korinta Maldonado, Veronica Paredes, and John McKinn—for believing in my work and encouraging its continuation. And at Sonoma State University (SSU), thank you to my dear colleagues Natalia Villanueva-Nieves, Daniel Malpica, and Ronald Lopez for carrying me through the last steps of this project.

The SSU School of Arts and Humanities, SSU Office of Research and Sponsored Programs, UIUC Office of the Chancellor, UIUC Center for Latin American and Caribbean Studies, UC Davis Hemispheric Institute on the Americas, UC Davis Humanities Institute, and UC Davis Chicana/Latina Research Center, as well as collaborative projects funded by the University of California Mexus-Conacyt and the Pacific Rim programs, have all backed the development and completion of this manuscript.

I am eternally grateful to Kristen Buckles, University of Arizona Press (UAP) editor in chief, for her endless support from the moment we started discussing the vision of this book. Thank you, too, to the anonymous reviewers of the manuscript for the gift of reading my work and presenting me with such invaluable feedback, and to the rest of the team at UAP for making this publication happen.

To my *semilla* friends: Lisa Gonzalves, Yazmin Garcia, Margaret Roberts, Michelle Bloomberg, and Patricia Segura. Thank you for walking this trajectory with me, steady, strong, and supportive. And Lisa Gonzalves, thank you for the time, persistence, and care you gave to reading and editing sections of the manuscript. Your support means the world to me.

Last but not least, I am grateful for the invaluable work of the poets, writers, and artists who are the spine of this book. My dear friends Daniel Ochoa, Irene Nich, Enriqueta Lunez, and Roselia Jimenez, thank you for opening the door to your homes and hearts during the various stages of this project.

A NOTE ON TRANSLATION

> Translation is more than just moving from point A to point B. Translation is an art. The translation process is interactive, it is an exercise between the translator and the text. Connected to this act is an art, it is what's in the heart, in the mind that guides this process.
>
> —NICOLÁS HUET BAUTISTA, "THE ART OF TRANSLATION"

The Maya literature I examine in this book has been published in Spanish and the authors' Maya language: Ch'ol, Mam, Tojolabal, Tsotsil, or Tseltal. For these contemporary authors, trained within public school systems that follow a "Spanish-only" curriculum, their process has been to first write in Spanish and then translate the literature into their Maya language. As a native Spanish speaker, I worked with the Spanish version in my analysis of the literature, then proceeded to translate from the Spanish version into English. After I completed the translation, I worked with both English and Spanish versions of the literature, until the analysis was complete. Moving among the languages created a constant flow, exchange, and reflection that nurtured my literary analysis of the Maya authors' work during the writing process of this book. The English translations of the poetry and quotations from the literary works are all mine, unless otherwise noted. In deciding to include the Maya and Spanish versions and English translation of the poetry alongside one another, I want to affirm the authors' work and the power and value of the respective languages. This is also the first time that the literary work of the majority of the authors is presented in English, and, as such, the bridging of languages has materialized. It is critical that the work of the Maya authors as originally published is honored by remaining intact.

CARACOLEANDO AMONG WORLDS

Introduction

Buried Knowledges of Maya Indigenous Consciousness

In the summer of 2014, the Centro Estatal de Lenguas, Arte y Literatura Indígenas (State Center for Indigenous Languages, Art, and Literature, CELALI) celebrated its seventeenth anniversary by organizing several events in San Cristóbal de las Casas and other surrounding communities, including lectures, recitals, and theater performances.[1] I attended the opening ceremony, hosted in its office space in San Cristóbal, which included a photography exhibit on the history of CELALI. While reading the captions of the photographs, I paused for a moment longer to absorb a photograph of Enrique Pérez López, then director of CELALI, addressing a panel of Zapatistas and non-Zapatista officials (I identified the different affiliations based on those wearing the black ski mask that characterizes the Zapatista Army of National Liberation [EZLN]).[2] Their faces may have been blurry, but the photograph revealed a strong engagement between the panelists and Pérez López. Moments after I paused on this photograph, the 2014 ceremony started. Pérez López's opening remarks recalled that earlier moment when he had addressed the EZLN and representatives of the government during the dialogues of San Andrés in 1996.[3] "Ustedes siguieron su camino y nosotros seguimos el nuestro" (You followed your path just like we followed ours) were the words he shared with the EZLN, emphasizing the importance and necessity of both sides' understanding and respecting each other's way.

Pérez López (2008) has explained the establishment of CELALI as the result of decades of organizing of Indigenous intellectuals in Chiapas, Mexico. "Nosotros no somos dueños de nuestras vidas. Necesitamos un espacio en donde diseñemos, creemos, y planeemos ese destino" (We are not the owners of our lives. We need a space where we can design, construct, and plan our destiny). Indigenous intellectuals of Chiapas had been discussing the development of a center for them and by them that would nurture their intellectual endeavors. The EZLN uprising and the San Andrés dialogues provided the space to negotiate and push the government to finance the establishment of the center. This is how CELALI came to be a distinctive space, Pérez López stated, a space that followed a path envisioned by and for Indigenous peoples.

This book project was born from my years of accompaniment of the EZLN, since their early steps in 1994, and my objective of rooting the EZLN within Maya worldviews.[4] In pursuing my interest in elevating the voices of Indigenous peoples of Chiapas and unearthing the buried knowledges that have raised Maya Indigenous consciousness, I followed my intellectual curiosity and turned to the Indigenous literary movement. This book focuses on the contemporary literary movement of Maya writers of Chiapas. At the heart of this examination is a journey into the trajectory of this literary movement and its connection to the EZLN insurgency: two movements, developing alongside each other, following different paths, but rooted in shared visions of rescuing, reclaiming, and recentering Maya worldviews. This shared vision emerges in this book through my analysis of selected pieces of the contemporary Maya literature of Chiapas—poetry, short stories, and what is considered to be the first novel written by a Maya Tsotsil writer of Chiapas—and close readings of the EZLN's six declarations of the Lacandon Jungle and selected communiqués.[5] The themes that emerge from the literature reveal essential elements of Maya worldviews, such as relation to ancestral places, epistemologies that inform their worldviews, and cultural and spiritual practices that sustain these worldviews.

Focusing on the creative work of Maya writers and artists of Chiapas, the book brings into conversation literature that, most of which, has been translated into English (from the Spanish version) for the first time. This approach places various generations of Maya writers of Chiapas in discussion through their literary works, and positions them alongside other Native American and Indigenous scholars. Further, rooting these experiences to place brings into dialogue the EZLN insurgency and its own trajectories, as captured in the six declarations of the Lacandon Jungle. Although I bring into my analysis the scholarship of Maya writers of Guatemala and the Yucatán Peninsula, the book concentrates on the Maya literary movement of Chiapas. Using an applied methodology, the book follows the trajectories of this contemporary literary movement and the EZLN. The methods I apply to the study of contemporary Maya literary production in this book (1) engage with the local, theorizing from within; (2) traverse beyond political borders to dialogue with counterparts of the Global North, putting into action the hemispheric approach to Native American and Indigenous studies; and (3) expand even more, beyond the limits of the Americas, drawing from current discourse shaping global Indigeneities.

On Methodology

Drawing from inter/transdisciplinary methodologies in Native American and Indigenous studies, the book creates a critical dialogue and bridge among literary productions of Maya writers of Chiapas and Native American and Indigenous scholarship. The trajectories of the Maya literary movement in Chiapas are framed within research methods that U.S. Native scholars—including Leslie Marmon Silko (1996), Beth Brant (1991), N. Scott Momaday (1999a, 1999b), and Simon J. Ortiz (1992, 1998)—have been applying for decades to the process of rescuing hi/stories, such as oral tradition, memoirs, and reframing methodologies. In the rescuing process, these authors have tapped into stories nurtured through generations and impressed in familial and community memory, affirming, as Silko (2010) attests, that in the telling and writing of hi/stories, gaps are filled. This rescuing process also speaks of a responsibility to communities to share their stories, which are rooted to place and time (Ortiz 1981) and which affirm the continuity of Native and Indigenous peoples (Momaday 1999a, 1999b). Its methodologies follow the notion of theorizing from the cultures themselves (Talamantez 1990) and grounding research within communities' knowledges, practices, and peoples (Smith 2005). Importantly, these methodological practices are all decolonizing research methods.

This framework is also developed within a hemispheric approach to Native American and Indigenous studies that recognizes the shared experiences of survival and persistence of Indigenous peoples, as well as the uniqueness and transnational nature of these experiences (Forbes et al. 2002). This hemispheric approach is in dialogue with Chadwick Allen's (2012, xiv, xv) trans-Indigenous methodologies, where he suggests moving away from the traditional binary approach of "*ands* and *comparative*." Recognizing the disparities that emerge when working between English and non-English literary productions and the tension that can arise from the seeming asymmetry in the literary relations of these geographic areas, Allen emphasizes the importance of the dialogues of "unexplored possibilities" that a trans-Indigenous methodology offers. I apply Allen's trans-Indigenous methodology to my analysis of Maya literature and expand on this method to encompass the reading of Indigenous literatures published both in Spanish and in authors' Indigenous languages.

The methodology that I utilize is relational, rooted to place, and engaged in the value of learning and praxis. This position is in dialogue with the work of Osage scholar Robert Allen Warrior (2005, 182) and the concept of "intellectual trade routes," which refers to ideas that travel "literally across geographical or cultural space." Intellectual trade routes emerge through dialogues among and with texts, "a connection between things that had seemed disparate" but that come together through dialogue. These are the connections explored through the literature analyzed in this book, which highlights the reemergence of Indigenous knowledge production as the writers reconnect with their histories to recenter their Maya Indigenous worldviews.

In my analysis of the Maya literature of Chiapas, I also engage with the position of Acoma scholar Simon J. Ortiz (2006a, xii), who states that the writer is never too far removed from their work. In the production process, writers' work must be driven by an Indigenous consciousness as Indigeneity cannot be taken for granted in the making of the literature. My introduction to the body of literature central to this project was through the authors themselves. The literature as presented and researched was always an extension of the writers' identities, cultures, and relation to place. "Mi poesía soy yo y yo soy parte de mi poesía" (My poetry is me and I am part of my poetry) is the way Tsotsil poet Enriqueta Lunez explains this relation (pers. comm. 2023). Such association is informed by the authors' ongoing connection to their ancestral lands and ongoing interactions with their environments. The close relationship of the author and their work guides my literary analysis in this book.

In addition to the literary methodology, other research methods utilized here include ethnographic work, archival research, participant observation, and formal and informal interviews with some of the writers and artists. My trajectory since 1994 as an activist in solidarity with the EZLN also informs my analysis of the contemporary literary productions. I collected the majority of the literature in the summer of 2008. Additional research trips included a three-month stay in Chiapas in 2011, six weeks in 2012, and four weeks each in 2016 and 2018. Most of the literature central to this project has been published by CELALI, and all the writers and artists have an established (but not exclusive) affiliation with the center. Such close engagement with the varied layers of literary production nurtures and sustains my analysis of the visual and textual literatures.

Analyzing the contemporary literary movement of Maya writers of Chiapas in relation to the EZLN insurgency centers the connection of literary productions to place—social, cultural, and political life. I refer to this approach as an "ethnography of literature," building on what anthropologist Zuzanna Olszewska (2015, 6) refers to as "an ethnography of poetry." Olszewska gives life to this methodology through her work with Afghan refugees in Iran, where the analysis of the literature is intricately rooted to the political, social, and cultural relations of those communities. The literature is the poets' response to their condition as refugees in their local communities and a way to claim their sense of identity and sense of place in relation to the larger dominant society. In Chiapas, social, cultural, and political life was greatly transformed after the 1994 EZLN uprising. As the eye of the world was captured by this insurgency, the contemporary literary movement grew within this gaze and flourished. Situating the visual and textual analysis as an ethnography of literature highlights the growth of these two movements and the development of their intricate connections.

The Growing Disciplinary Field of Indigenous Literatures of Mexico

I taught my first class on Native American and Indigenous literatures as a graduate student at the University of California, Davis, in spring 2009, Native American Studies 5: A Hemispheric Approach to the Literatures of the Americas. At that time, I relied on the three-volume work of Carlos Montemayor and Donald H. Frischmann (2005–7) to use as part of the curriculum on Indigenous literatures of Mexico, but mostly, I relied on my own translations of the literature from Spanish into English. Since then, the growth in this literary field has opened knowledge exchanges. Throughout my analysis of the contemporary literary production of Maya writers of Chiapas, I also bring into conversation recent studies on Indigenous literatures of Mexico. The concepts and methods employed within these works further contribute to the trans-Indigenous methodology that frames this project. The next few paragraphs showcase the various works that inform my analysis.

To begin with, the field of Indigenous language revitalization in Mexico affirms the efforts of contemporary Maya writers. *Like a New Sun: New Indigenous Mexican Poetry* (2015), edited by David Shook and Victor Terán (Isthmus Zapotec), and *Chiapas Maya Awakening: Contemporary Poems and Short Stories* (2017), edited by Sean S. Sell and Nicolás Huet Bautista (Maya Tsotsil), underscore the importance of Indigenous languages by placing them alongside Spanish and English translations. The inclusion of the poetry in the authors' native tongue in these publications supports efforts to articulate Indigenous worldviews.

Paul M. Worley's *Telling and Being Told: Storytelling and Cultural Control in Contemporary Yucatec Maya Languages* (2013) underscores the oral tradition that emerges in the methodology of contemporary Maya writers. Worley illustrates the power of the oral tradition that the storyteller carries in relation to Yucatec Maya epistemologies. He further develops this position in his collaboration with Rita M. Palacios in *Unwriting Maya Literature: Ts'íib as Recorded Knowledge* (2019). The recognition of the power of the storyteller decenters text as the source of archival knowledges. In drawing our attention to other sources of knowledge, Worley places Indigenous peoples as carriers of archival wisdoms. Such an approach speaks to the practices of contemporary Maya writers of Chiapas, who, in the process of rescuing their epistemological trajectories, tap into the stories housed in their communities and carried through the oral tradition of their elders.

Gloria E. Chacón's *Indigenous Cosmolectics: Kab'awil and the Making of Maya and Zapotec Literatures* (2018) deploys carefully crafted concepts of *kab'awil* and cosmolectics to explore the literary production of Maya (Chiapas and Guatemala) and Zapotec writers. The concept of *kab'awil* (*doble mirada* or double gaze) recognizes interactive sources of knowledge, a revolutionary approach affirming that, for Indigenous peoples, knowledges do not move linearly. In other words, in the process of affirming Indigenous knowledge systems, contemporary writers who follow a *kab'awilian* practice unearth generational knowledges from the communities to inform and affirm their present. This approach is clearly visible in the literary production of female Indigenous writers who are rescuing knowledges on gender balance relations central to stories of origin to realign their presence as writers and members of their communities. Chacón's concept is essential in my analysis of the poems in this volume, such as that of Diego Torres Sánchez (Tseltal), who, through literature, rescues the role of women in history and reclaims the Tseltal gaze in his telling of the 1712 Tseltal Revolt in his hometown of Cancuc.

Arturo Arias, in his two-volume *Recovering Lost Footprints: Contemporary Maya Narratives* (2017–18), presents a decolonial approach to the study of Maya literatures of Mesoamerica, particularly selected Yucatec and Chiapanec Maya writers. Arias places the literatures in a historical context of social and political turmoil that speaks to the persistence of these communities and their intellectual efforts. The writers, in this way, emerge as extensions of those histories of place, the ancestral lands that continue to nurture their worldviews. Such an approach further affirms Arias's argument on the value of Indigenous literatures in our ongoing understanding of Latin American literatures and histories. My engagement with his work is rooted in the close connection that he establishes with the power of histories and literatures.

Worley and Palacios's *Unwriting Maya Literature* (2019) presents a decolonial methodology through the deployment of *ts'íib,* a concept used to read Maya literary productions of Guatemala and Chiapas beyond the Western-centered lens. *Ts'íib* is an interactive source of knowledge and a recorded knowledge that recognizes orality, textual productions, performances, textiles, and visual narratives as expressions of Indigenous epistemologies. Worley and Palacios critique Western-based genres of literature and methods that fall short in the analysis and understanding of Maya literatures by excluding nontext productions. *Ts'íib* as a concept facilitates the study and understanding of Maya worlds and the relations that emanate from the cosmos that are essential elements of Maya knowledge systems.

Lastly, Hannah Burdette's *Revealing Rebellion in Abiayala: The Insurgent Poetics of Contemporary Indigenous Literature* (2019) contributes to this growing field on Indigenous literary productions by bringing into dialogue social movements in Latin America in the last thirty years and the literary production that has emerged from these histories of social unrest. The analysis is carried on through her introduction of the concept of "insurgent poetics," which connects to the idea of literature as something that emerges from spaces of social unrest and that is weaponized during social movements. This position is shared by Indigenous writers, both in the United States and in Latin America, whose work has historically shown that in moments of social unrest, poetry and other literary expressions emerge and circulate widely. The connections that I make between the Maya literary movement of Chiapas and the EZLN insurgency speak to this concept of insurgent poetics, but only in the way the insurgency sheds light on Indigenous intellectual mobilization in Chiapas. Although the literary movement did not emerge from the specific period of social unrest the EZLN created, it did unfold alongside this unrest, the turmoil of the insurgency bringing attention to and solidarity among all Maya peoples of Chiapas.

Caracoleando as a Methodology

The Indigenous voices that emerge in the literatures analyzed in this book are in a constant process of defending Maya ways of life by critically rescuing, restoring, and reclaiming knowledges buried in their communities and ensuring the continuity of their peoples. Captured in the literature, these efforts focus on: the recuperation of time and long memory grounded in Indigenous cosmology; the recuperation of space and sacred geographies of knowledge related to biospace; the recuperation of language as carrier, creator, and reproducer of knowledge; and the recuperation/reconstruction of the social, political, and cultural project both present and future (Varese, Delgado, and Meyer 2008). Their voices also express that this is a journey to their past, a validation of their present, and a reconstruction of their future.

The dialogues the literature creates move across time and place. I propose here, then, a concept that has emerged from the work itself and that is rooted to time and place: *caracoleando*.[6] The concept emerges out of the symbol of the *caracol* (conch shell), which the EZLN has been strategically using to depict the course of its insurgency. The infinite and nonlinear symbol of the *caracol* invites the gaze to expand and retract, to move inward and outward, and to travel away from the center and back again. The depiction of the *caracol* resembles the auricle, which also speaks to the EZLN's philosophy on the significance of listening as central to dialogue and understanding. The speech scrolls in Maya codices, or textual records of the Maya, also resemble this spiral movement of the *caracol* and connect to the emphasis on communication and the value of exchange. So too do the many textile designs that carry the symbol, representing the multiple mediums Maya peoples explore to communicate. The movement behind this symbol leads me to think of this noun (*caracol*) as a verb (*caracolear*), and even more precisely as the gerund *caracoleando* to capture the magnitude of the generated process it encompasses. The concept is inclusive and collaborative because the symbol itself is continuous.

Caracoleando refers to the nonlinear and indefinite actions Maya peoples have followed for the last five centuries, as well as to the ontology of Maya peoples—the ways of being and the production of new ways of being that draw on old ways, or the idea that the new Maya man/woman is informed by the old Maya man/woman but is in a constant process of change. *Caracoleando* also demands a venture into liminal spaces, leading to affirmations of Maya identity and the creation of new processes of thinking and enacting Indigeneity. *Caracoleando* captures the actions of the EZLN and Indigenous intellectuals of Chiapas, placing these actions in the long trajectory of insurgencies and mobilizations in the Maya region of Chiapas across the last five hundred years.

The concept of *caracoleando* is reflective, and is in dialogue with Māori scholar Linda Tuhiwai Smith's (2005) call to conduct research in dialogue with communities and in recognition of the contribution of the peoples in these communities. This is a dynamic and introspective approach that anthropologists Stefano Varese and Guillermo Delgado (Aymara), as well as Rodolfo Meyer (2008, 388) have also applied to their work in the Andes. These scholars call for the recognition of cultural markers to identify a culture's values, such as different relationships to the land and different relationships to beliefs grounded in nature that fall outside the frame of "Euro-American notions of time, space, and the *subject*." Miguel Rocha Vivas (2021) captures these approaches in his concept of "oralitegraphies," which stresses the value of multimedia usage in Indigenous scholarship that includes textual, oral, and visual narratives. Understanding the difference in these relations is vital to an integrated approach to research. U.S. Native scholars share this position when they write about the cosmovision of Indigenous peoples in a way that speaks to human and other-than-human perspectives on the world, recognizes millennia-old systems of moral economy at the center of Indigenous communities, and acknowledges Indigenous peoples' relation to place, time, culture, art, artifacts, and language. Indigenous autonomy and Native sovereignty are at the base of this body of work.

The Literary Movement of Chiapas

In Chiapas, the contemporary intellectual movement can be traced to the late 1970s, when Indigenous intellectuals engaged in a reframing of the ways Indigenous peoples related to the state project of Indigenismo.[7] Their approach was a reawakening in response to ongoing abuse, exploitation, and oppression of Indigenous peoples through state-imposed projects. As Indigenous intellectuals began to meet one another and reflect on the current state of their communities, Tsotsil scholar Jacinto Arias Pérez was their guide to developing a literary tradition in the state of Chiapas (Pérez López 2008).[8]

Arias Pérez did not achieve this leadership position randomly. He is believed to be the first Tsotsil to leave Chiapas and Mexico to pursue graduate studies in the United States. His 1973 master's thesis from Catholic University, "The 'Numinous' World of the Maya: Contemporary Structure and Change," published in Mexico in 1975 under the same title in Spanish, *El mundo numinoso de los mayas: estructura y cambios contemporáneos*, is considered to be the first ethnographic work on the life of the Tsotsil Maya peoples of Chiapas by an Indigenous scholar in recent history. Focusing on the everyday life of the Tsotsil community in San Pedro Chenalhó, Arias Pérez engages in a critical analysis of the lives and cultural and spiritual traditions of this Tsotsil community. His work reveals struggles but also, more importantly, the continuity of ways of life of Maya peoples of Chiapas.

In addition to the leadership of Arias Pérez, the development of the literary movement in Chiapas is also linked to the 1974 Indigenous Congress in San Cristóbal de las Casas, where Indigenous intellectuals of Mexico came together to discuss the conditions of their communities (Collier and Quaratiello 1994). The organization of the meeting fell under the bishop of the Diocese of San Cristóbal, Samuel Ruiz García. The relationship of Bishop Ruiz with Indigenous communities was established under the teaching of liberation theology, which spread in Latin America after the publication of *Teología de la liberación* (1972, published in English as *A Theology of Liberation* in 1973) by the Peruvian priest Gustavo Gutiérrez. This theology was developed in line with the philosophy of Brazilian scholar Paulo Freire, who writes in *Pedagogy of the Oppressed* ([1968] 2000) on critical pedagogy, empowerment of peoples to transform their lives, and awareness raising (Ferm 1986; Hennelly 1990). These philosophies were in the air at the 1974 meeting, as the gathering in honor of the five-hundred-year anniversary of the arrival of Fray Bartolomé de las Casas (the Spanish Franciscan historically considered a defender of Indigenous peoples) quickly turned to dialogues on the dire condition of Indigenous peoples of Mexico. Though the histories of Indigenous organizing in Chiapas predate this gathering, the event affirmed new directions of organizing rooted within Maya worldviews (Hernández-Ávila 2017, 5–6; Soto 2015).

In the early 1980s, young Indigenous writers formally trained as grade school teachers within the state-run school system began to meet and discuss the current state of their communities. Recognizing their responsibility as leaders, they not only questioned the assimilation projects they were expected to perform as teachers, but began to develop ways to transform the system of oppression from within.[9] This was a process that, according to Pérez López (2008), entailed digging deep into their memories, meeting with the elders of the communities to recount and piece together their histories, and rediscovering one another. Indigenous intellectuals emerged from this process with a sense of recognition and responsibility to their communities. They learned that the way out of their state of oppression was inside them, inside their communities, and inside their languages, cultural practices, and histories. Thus, they began to pen their stories, stories that they had heard all their lives, stories that were born and nurtured in their communities and that, once shared, elucidated the knowledges that sustained them. All these activities to assert their sense of being led to Maya intellectuals pushing for the establishment of a center that would provide the space to continue this work.

CELALI's purpose—to offer a space for Indigenous peoples, managed by Indigenous peoples, and reflective of Indigenous peoples' vision—makes it unique, but it is not the only space to have been established for Indigenous intellectualism in Chiapas. In 1982, Sna jtz'ibajom or Casa del Escritor (House of the Writer) was founded in San Cristóbal as a space for creative production—theater, art, literature, and song. The writers' cooperative was established with the help of U.S. anthropologists affiliated with the Harvard Chiapas Project, in collaboration with local communities.[10] In 1994, Isabel Juarez (Tseltal) and Petrona de la Cruz (Tsotsil), the two foremost women in the cooperative, left to establish the all-woman theater group Fortaleza de la Mujer Maya (Empowerment of Maya Women, FOMMA) (see Hernández-Ávila 2017, 7).[11] Since FOMMA's establishment, its activities have expanded to include writing workshops and performance studies. In 1991, the Unidad de Escritores Mayas-Zoques (Union of Maya-Zoque Writers) was also established as a space to support, promote, and disseminate Indigenous literary and art production. Members of and visitors to these centers interact and are in conversation with one another's efforts.[12]

One notable early contribution of CELALI to the trajectories of Maya literary production in Chiapas was the publication of *Palabra conjurada: cinco voces, cinco cantos* (Conjured word: five voices, five songs) (López K'ana et al. [1999] 2012). The book, one of the earliest publications by CELALI, brought forth the poetry and short stories of five writers: Josías López K'ana (Tseltal), Juana Karen Peñate Montejo (Ch'ol), Ruperta Bautista Vázquez (Tsotsil), Nicolás Huet Bautista (Tsotsil), and Enrique Pérez López (Tsotsil). This publication was a watershed moment in the trajectories of Indigenous literary production in Chiapas. With this book, poetry and short stories rooted within the authors' Maya worldviews expanded into the writers' creative process, giving meaning to their worldviews (Arias 2017–18, 2:221; Chacón 2018; Lopéz K'ana et al. [1999] 2012, 9–13). The publication marked a new direction in the Maya literary production of Chiapas and the role of CELALI in these trajectories.

At the national level, Indigenous intellectuals came together formally through the foundation of Escritores en Lenguas Indígenas Asociación Civil (Civil Association of Writers in Indigenous Languages, ELIAC) in November 1993. The headquarters of the association, Casa de los Escritores en Lenguas Indígenas (House of Writers in Indigenous Languages), was established in Mexico City (Hernández-Ávila 2003, 36). ELIAC brought together Indigenous intellectuals who had been trained and educated through the projects of Culturas Populares (Popular Cultures) and had been organizing in their own communities since the early 1980s.[13] The wide range of activities of ELIAC has opened spaces for Indigenous writers and artists at a crucial time in history (see Hernández-Ávila 2003, 2017). Enrique Pérez López's work as director of CELALI is in line with these legacies of community organizing. The paradigm shifts that unfolded through the establishment of these spaces for intellectual growth were not isolated occurrences.

Following a trend among Latin American countries, the Mexican state began to pursue a neoliberal agenda that culminated with the approval of the North American Free Trade Agreement (NAFTA) in 1993.[14] Referring to the "neoliberal multiculturalism" model from anthropologist Charles R. Hale, Shannon Speed (2008, 119) writes that "[in this] model, recognition is a part of the new logics of governance that predominate in the neoliberal state." The

1992 revision of Article 4 of the Mexican Constitution, which recognizes the plural composition of the state—along with Mexico's 1990 ratification of the International Labour Organization's (ILO) Convention 169, which "sets forth a broad range of economic, political, land-related, social, and cultural rights for indigenous peoples"—was part of this agenda (Stephen 2002, 341). The paradox of these developments is that as states aligned behind the neoliberal agenda, they opened spaces for the manifestation of Indigenous peoples' rights. These manifestations, however, did not materialize in any constitutional changes or policies that may affect state governance (Moksnes 2012; Speed, Hernández Castillo, and Stephen 2006, 204).

The pursuit of neoliberal policies in Latin America in the 1980s, along with the changes to the Mexican Constitution and ratification of ILO 169, shifted the relation of Indigenous peoples and the state, giving way to more dynamic exchanges. This was reflected in the 1990 gathering of over 120 Indigenous nations in Quito, Ecuador, to "celebrate the continental meeting '500 Years of Indian Resistance'" (Varese, Delgado, and Meyer 2008, 391). The resulting Declaration of Quito reaffirmed Indigenous peoples' stance in defense of their ways of life since the day after the arrival of the Europeans. The declaration also rooted Indigenous mobilization in the Americas and recognized the demand for Indigenous autonomy and self-determination as essential to affirming Indigenous ways of life.

The Quito meeting led to mobilizations in various parts of the Americas on October 12, 1992.[15] In San Cristóbal de las Casas, this action involved marches led by high-ranking members of what was then the underground EZLN insurgency (Harvey 1998; Montemayor 1997; Tello Díaz 1994). These demonstrations against the atrocities of five hundred years of oppressive colonial power were test practices for the EZLN uprising, Zapatistas would later reveal (Pérez López 2008). In other words, manifestations such as those that followed the 1990 Quito meeting tend to exist in relation to changes within the state.

The establishment of CELALI followed these histories of Indigenous mobilization and coinciding changes in state laws and policies that forced the state to recognize its plural constitution. This recognition, however, did not imply direct action in support of Indigenous causes. CELALI's establishment was the result of pressure the EZLN placed on the state, but its continuance as a center in support of Indigenous cultures, languages, arts, and literatures is the result of an ongoing defense of these efforts, particularly with regard to funding and its impact on the center's activities.[16] The center continues to provide a space for artists and writers to produce, publish, and circulate their work, and to strengthen networks of support in collaboration with cultural centers in the communities of the Chiapas Highlands. The complex interconnections of CELALI and the EZLN bridge these two movements (intellectual and insurgent) that have transformed the Indigenous presence in Chiapas and Mexico at large.

Histories of Indigenous Rebellions in Chiapas

The Zapatista Army of National Liberation emerged out of the Lacandon Jungle in the early hours of January 1, 1994, denouncing centuries of imposed silence and marginalization. Zapatistas mobilized through the streets of seven cities in Chiapas, including the touristy city of San Cristóbal de las Casas, occupied them with the use of armed force, and declared war on the Mexican Army. The triumphant pronunciation of the First Declaration of the Lacandon Jungle from the balcony of City Hall after the takeover of the city of San Cristóbal defined the goals and directions of the EZLN. Through the declaration, the EZLN (1994a, 1994b) placed itself within the long history of resistance against systems of oppression in Mexico. The articulation of "ENOUGH IS ENOUGH!" launched the EZLN to the forefront of revolutionary movements at the end of the twentieth century.

When the 1994 EZLN insurgency is contextualized against previous revolts in the Maya region of Chiapas, two main rebellions dating back to the eighteenth century are widely referenced: the Tseltal Revolt of 1712 in San Juan Cancuc and the Tsotsil Rebellion of 1867 in San Juan Chamula. Together, these three movements encompass three key eras in Mexican history: the colonial (1717 revolt), postindependence (1867 rebellion), and postrevolutionary (1994 EZLN insurgency) periods. The historical circumstances were reflected in the course of each rebellion and the response of those in power. The violence exerted against Indigenous rebels, however, varied little between events.

The central themes in the Tseltal Revolt and Tsotsil Rebellion were religious practices and land rights. Related to these were forced cultural and religious transformations, forced labor, evictions, and physical attacks (Bricker 1981; De Vos 2011; Gosner 1992; Stephen 2002; Womack 1999, 80–82). In the organizing process of these rebellions the idea was not to overthrow the oppressive colonial power, but to reinterpret the social, cultural, and religious systems and make them more relevant to Indigenous experiences. The central idea of these insurgencies resonates with the position of the EZLN, whose interest lies not in obtaining electoral democratic power, but rather in securing a more inclusive system of power. This position, according to Dylan Eldredge Fitzwater (2019), is grounded in the philosophy of the Zapatistas' Maya languages. Drawing on research with the Tseltal language in Zapatista communities, Fitzwater explains that the EZLN's teachings of autonomy and self-determination include the key concepts of *ch'ulel* ("the body's other" [33]), *o'on* ("collective heart" [xv, 32]), *pask'op* ("struggle" and "to make the word" [10, 30]), and *ich'el ta mu'k* ("to carry oneself to greatness" [9]). His fieldwork and study of the language lead him to conclude that the language itself encompasses a philosophy toward the making of a better world, and a balanced world in relation to the self and all that inhabits the cosmos. The ongoing defense of autonomy and self-determination (in the words of the EZLN), or the defense of social, cultural, and religious systems that are more relevant to Indigenous experiences (as articulated in the 1712 revolt and the 1867 rebellion), is in line with those philosophies steeped in the language.

Mariana Mora Bayo (2017, 127), drawing on her extensive work with Zapatista communities, addresses these philosophical relations when she interprets the concept of *lekil kuxlejal* as a daily aspiration to live in a dignified matter. "The struggle for *lekil kuxlejal* has as a central pillar the collectives' relationship to a physical locality, which connects them both to their ancestors and to the possibility of future generations," she writes, highlighting the complexity of the term. This is the aspiration of the communities that found in these rebellions the route to achieve their worldviews, and so the trajectories of these historical rebellions informs the themes that emerge in the literary production of contemporary Maya writers of Chiapas. Such is the case of La Guerra del Pajarito (Pajarito's War) of 1911, discussed below, which is also part of this history but is excluded from most narratives on the histories of uprisings in Chiapas.

At the core of the Tseltal Revolt of 1712 and the Tsotsil Rebellion of 1867 was the mobilization of communities in response to increasing tributary demands by the church, poor harvest cycles, and continuous exploitation by the colonial order. The rebellions' shared goal was the recuperation of spiritual practices and sacred relations, and a realignment with their belief system. But mostly, the Indigenous peoples wanted to lead life on their own terms. The leader of each rebellion was a young woman, which also situates the mobilizations within Maya philosophies of duality and gender balance realignment. This is a position shared with the EZLN, in which women have a participatory role at all levels of the insurgency. Despite the centuries separating these rebellions, the shared characteristics epitomize Indigenous peoples' constant efforts to defend their ways of life.

Chapter 3 presents a more extensive narrative of the Tseltal Revolt and the Tsotsil Rebellion in order to contextualize the interventions made in the official histories of these rebellions by Tseltal poet Diego Torres Sánchez and Tsotsil poet Luis López Díaz. What follows here is a more summarized narrative of these histories. The 1712 revolt began in San Juan Cancuc, when news circulated that a young woman, María de la Candelaria, had witnessed an apparition of the Virgin with the request to build a hermitage for her adoration in the community. The shrine was built, and within days followers of the Virgin began arriving with offerings. Once news of this newfound faith reached the church, its leaders ordered the destruction of the shrine, but their order was ignored. At this time, María de la Candelaria delivered yet another message from the Virgin: "to start the rebellion against the Spanish rule." She added, "believe me and follow me, because there is no more tribute, or king, or bishop, or district magistrate, and do no more than follow me and believe this Virgin" (Womack 1999, 85). The message of liberation ignited a revolt of at least thirty-two villages against Spanish forces. The leaders were persecuted but violent confrontations continued for months, until the better-armed Spanish were finally able to put this insurgency to rest (Bricker 1981; Gosner 1992).

The participants of the 1867 rebellion in San Juan Chamula met a similar fate. The beginning of this rebellion can be traced to the moment a young Tsotsil woman, Agustina Gómez Chechev, declared that "three sacred stones had fallen from the sky and communicated with her" (Bricker 1981, 119; Stephen 2002, 93–94). A shrine for the stones was built, and the number of followers who traveled to visit the area rapidly increased. A hermitage was erected, and the peoples of Chamula, as well as communities nearby, began delivering offerings to the sacred stones. The church and ladinos (non-Indian mestizo people) mobilized and openly attacked the communities that were adoring the stones. The violent battle that ensued left several hundred people dead. However small or large the number of followers of the stones was, any act of rebellion against the interest of the church and ladinos was viewed as a threat to their economic status, thus the need to violently repress the movement (Stephen 2002, 94).

Unlike the Tseltal Revolt and Tsotsil Rebellion, the story of Jacinto Pérez Ch'ixtot, better known as Pajarito, is not mentioned in the literature on the EZLN. The story is recorded in a CELALI anthology edited by Enrique Pérez López, *Memoria indígena de la revolución en Chiapas* (Indigenous memory of the revolution in Chiapas, 2010), which rescues stories housed in Indigenous communities on the role of Maya peoples of Chiapas during the Mexican Revolution of 1910. In the volume, Pajarito's War emerges as remembered by both Tsotsil and Tseltal communities during this historical period. Pajarito's story is simple: during the revolution and amid a struggle for state power, he joined the faction seeking to move the state capital from Tuxtla Gutiérrez to San Cristóbal. Amid these battles, Pajarito decided to rebel from within, rising up against the *kaxlanes* (non-Indigenous peoples, outsiders to the community, and those with economic and political power).[17] Indigenous soldiers joined him as he pledged that if they won the battle "they would be free of taxes and would get rid of all the ladinos in their towns" (Pérez López 2010, 39). The ladino troops from both local factions rallied against him, and he was caught in a bloody exchange that put an end to his life and to the rebellion. The Pajarito rebellion fought in defense of a homeland free of *kaxlanes*, abuse, and exploitation—a world where they could gain a piece of land to farm and could care for their families (Pérez López 2010, 40, 60–61).

At the base of these rebellions was a realignment with Indigenous worldviews: not a reclaiming of the past, but a community's attempt to piece together fragments of their past to affirm their sense of dignity as Indigenous peoples in their present (Warren 2001).[18] Such revolutionary ways of engaging with histories involve, far from nostalgia, new approaches of learning and sustaining knowledge systems. This position is in line with the EZLN's stance on autonomy and self-determination, and its demand that the Mexican state see Zapatistas as both Mexican and Indigenous. The fight for land, reestablishment of relation to place, and realignment with Maya identity are also themes that emerge in the literature (poetry, short stories) that constitutes the body of analysis in this book. By retelling the histories of these rebellions, I want to highlight that in all cases, the realignment of power Indigenous peoples were seeking was the result of inward reflection and the communities' quest to unearth and center their buried knowledges.

Outline of the Book

In this book, I examine the Maya intellectual movement of Chiapas and the Maya insurgency of the EZLN: two movements following different paths with a shared vision of the reconstruction and reaffirmation of Maya worldviews. Chapters 1 through 3 focus on the Maya intellectual movement as articulated through literary production. Chapter 1 more specifically analyzes the importance of presence and recognition as central themes in the poetry of Maya writers of Chiapas. The acts of speaking and writing unfold within the poetry, revealing new visions of Maya worldviews. Chapter 2 expands the literary analysis to short stories, visual narratives, and the first novel written in Tsotsil. Through this literary production, Maya writers and artists reveal the essential elements to rebuild their worlds and, in the process, rescue fragments of their Maya epistemologies in order to restore their relations within Maya worldviews. Chapter 3 presents an analysis of two narrative poems of Maya writers of Chiapas historicizing their Indigenous and Maya experiences in relation to the 1712 Tseltal Revolt and the 1867 Tsotsil Rebellion. In the aftermath of the 1994 EZLN uprising, scholarly analysis of the insurgency was contextualized against these two historical rebellions. The publication of these poems presented for the first time a reading of the rebellions from the perspective of Tseltal and Tsotsil members of the communities. My analysis of these narrative poems reflects new directions in Maya literary production and new approaches in the recording of the communities' long histories of rebellions against the colonial project. The chapter offers a useful transition into chapter 4, which presents a close reading of the EZLN's six declarations of the Lacandon Jungle released to date. The declarations reveal goals, philosophies, and periods of trial and error in the trajectory of this insurgency. In my analysis of the six declarations, I trace the connection between the EZLN's philosophy and Maya worldviews, which in turn reveals the EZLN's worldviews. These worldviews emerge not just as an extension of the communities' Maya past, but also as a process of recapturing fragments of the past to shape their future. The conclusion, finally, traces present and future trajectories of these two movements (literary and insurgency): the ongoing growth of Maya literary production, the increasing circulation of the works in English, and new directions of the EZLN.

CHAPTER 1

Rebuilding Maya Worlds

Awakening, Presence, and Possibilities

From the moment the Zapatista Army of National Liberation (EZLN or Zapatistas) burst into the public eye, it stated its position and vision as an organized guerrilla movement through the release of the First Declaration of the Lacandon Jungle of January 1, 1994, published in its newly established paper, *El Despertador Mexicano* (Mexican Awakener), and made available online.[1] The media surrounded the Zapatistas as they declared control of the city of San Cristóbal de las Casas and six other cities in the state of Chiapas (captured in the special coverage by Canal 6 de Julio), bombarding them with questions about their uprising, despite their position having already been clearly stated. In the years since this New Year's uprising, Zapatistas have released six declarations and hundreds of communiqués stating the philosophy of the movement, giving rise to what they call the power of the word, which has allowed them agency in the narrative of their movement. As books, films, music, and art about the EZLN continue to be produced to capture their struggle, their stream of communiqués stating the position and direction of the movement grants them control of their histories.

The contemporary Maya literary movement of Chiapas unfolded alongside the EZLN's initial steps of underground organizing, with Indigenous intellectuals at the time reframing the ways they related to state projects of Indigenismo.[2] Enrique Pérez López (Tsotsil) (2008), former director of the Centro Estatal de Lenguas, Arte y Literatura Indígenas (State Center for Indigenous Languages, Art, and Literature, CELALI), refers to this period of time as a reawakening of Indigenous peoples of Chiapas. The strides made by this Indigenous intellectual movement coincided, too, with shifts in Mexican policy toward a neoliberal agenda; changes to Article 4 of the Mexican Constitution, recognizing the plurality of the state; and the state's endorsement of the International Labour Organization's (ILO) Convention 169, which recognizes Indigenous rights in addition to labor and economic rights. In the late 1970s, these Indigenous intellectuals (young men and women who had mostly formally trained as teachers) had begun organizing by engaging in a shared reflection on the current state of their communities. The focus of these intellectuals was on education, the rescue and teaching of histories, reading and writing, and song and art rooted in their Maya belief system. There was no initial systematic application of this vision; instead, they were simply a group of people coming together to reflect and dialogue on new possibilities in their own relationship to their Maya worldviews.

Thus, in the last four decades, these two movements have flourished parallel to each other, crossing paths in different stages along the way. Local languages, Maya and Spanish, are central to this process. Orality and the written word are the guiding forces in the articulation of their positions. Such action connects to the Nahuatl concept of *in xochitl in cuicatl* or *floricanto* (flower-and-song), which captures the way that poetry and poetry's metaphors unlock the mysteries of life and dreams that are central to a Nahuatl worldview (León-Portilla 1990a, 75). The EZLN has strategically and powerfully used this approach to deliver its flowery word through the written, audio, and visual release of communiqués. This approach is captured in its fourth declaration—further developed in chapter 4—which declares that "the flower of the word will not die," in relation to the war Zapatistas are waging in defense of the rights of Indigenous peoples of Mexico (EZLN 1996a, 1996b).

In this chapter I examine the poetry of three Maya writers. The first section of the chapter centers on four poems and the ways the poets engage with the writing process of the poetry, allowing the written word to take center stage: "Sts'ibujon: Yo escribo" (I write) by Tseltal poet Adriana del Carmen López Sántiz, from her poetry collection *Jalbil k'opetik: Palabras tejidas* (Woven words, 2005); "A'yej: Discurso" (Speech) by Tsotsil poet Andrés López Díaz, published in the anthology *Sbel sjol yo'nton ik': Memoria del viento* (Memory of the wind, López Díaz, Díaz Ruiz, and López Díaz 2006); and both "Slikebal Kuxlejaltik: Creación" (Creation) and "Vu'un Li'oyunkutike: Soy los que Estamos Aquí" (I am the we who are here) by Tsotsil poet Enriqueta Lunez, from her poetry collection *Yi' Beltak ch'ulelaletik: Raíces del alma* (Roots of the soul, 2007). The second section of the chapter engages with the oral deliverance of the poetry and the immediacy such an act carries in the production of the poetry by centering on four additional poems by the same poets and from the same publications: "Jun k'ak'al: Un día" (One day) and "Ta'lo xa: Basta" (Enough) by López Díaz, "K'unil lajel: Agonía" (Agony) by López Sántiz, and "Yavu: Lunario" (Lunary) by Lunez. The movement the work of these poets creates—and the reclamation of their role as orators and carriers of knowledge—recenters their presence in the world and sets forward new possibilities and new visions for the future. Such a position connects to the trajectories of the EZLN and its narratives of the insurgency, particularly regarding its vision of "a world where many worlds fit" (further developed in chapter 4), where the recognition of "different" is essential to the continuation of the collective.

I frame my analysis of the poetry in direct dialogue with the work of U.S. Native scholars of the last five decades, such as N. Scott Momaday (Kiowa), Simon J. Ortiz (Acoma), and Leslie Marmon Silko (Laguna Pueblo). This analysis highlights the relationship between the role of language, the written and oral word, the interweaving of their stories to reveal their worldviews, and the reclamation of their place in history. These relations are always rooted to place (land) and time and are in continuous dialogue with one another. My analysis also brings into conversation the work of Indigenous and Indigenous studies scholars, such as Gloria E. Chacón's (2018) concept of *kab'awil* or the double gaze, which addresses Indigenous writers' search within their worldviews to reaffirm their presence as Indigenous peoples; Paul M. Worley and Rita M. Palacios's (2019) concept of *ts'íib*, which decenters the Latin alphabet by placing other methods of recording knowledges alongside it; Elicura Chihuailaf Nahuelpan's (Mapuche from Chile) (2009) concept of *oralitor* (oraliture), which underscores the ways textual narratives are informed by millennia-old oral traditions; and Miguel Rocha Vivas's (2021) concept of "oralitegraphy," which, in line with the work of Chacón and Chihuailaf, stresses the usage of multimedia in Indigenous scholarship, and the ways that textual, oral, and visual narratives are in constant dialogue in Indigenous knowledge production. The work of these poets also brings out the concept of *caracoleando*, which speaks of the movement the poetry creates, the production of new ways of being that are drawn from the old ways and in a constant process of change. Through my readings of the poetry, I ask the following questions: What are the central themes articulated by the

EZLN and Maya writers of Chiapas? How do orality and writing, as well as the specific languages used, produce these central themes? As these poets move through the practices of orality and writing, I suggest that the central theme the poems address is this notion of presence, revealing new visions of Maya worlds that are not just about claiming a Maya identity but also about claiming a space to perform this Maya identity.

Wording Worlds into Existence

Jalbil k'opetik: Palabras tejidas (Woven words, 2005) is the poetry collection of Tseltal poet Adriana del Carmen López Sántiz, recipient of the 2003 Premio Estatal de Poesía Indígena Pat O'tan (Pat O'tan State Prize for Indigenous Poetry) from the state of Chiapas. The award is part of the state's efforts to support the work of Indigenous scholars. In the book's introduction, the poet's work is described as follows:

> La joven poeta escribe para desnudar su pensamiento y dejar como testimonio el arte de la palabra en las letras tseltales. . . . Su poemario muestra la habilidad para observar y atrapar en sus escritos la cotidianidad indígena tseltal y, a través de su creación, reivindica esta cotidianidad, cosmovisión, en fin, la vida cultural y social de los tseltales de Chiapas.

> The young poet writes to bare her thinking and leave as a testimony the art of the word in the Tseltal letters. . . . Her poetry shows the ability to observe and capture in her writings the everyday Tseltal Indigenous life and, through her creation, claims this everyday life, [this] cosmovision, well, the cultural and social life of the Tseltal peoples of Chiapas. (12)

Writing is thus an affirmation of her worldviews, identities, the values that everyday life offers, and the importance of reciprocal relations in this art of writing, as the poet's use of language demonstrates. I begin this section with the poem "Sts'ibujon: Yo escribo" (I write) (38) (see pages 26–27 for the full text).

"I write," the poet states in the opening line, bursting open the space that in her role as a poet she is to enter. "I write," she says, and with this she pushes her presence into history. The following lines in this first stanza assert the cosmocentric connections in her writing, the ways she carefully selects the words that speak of these reciprocal relations of language and environment, and the ways the world around her becomes the palette from which she gives life to her world. The fourth line lands the work in history, a crude reality of destruction (which can be environmental destruction, or the destruction of the people who have always honored the earth) that interrupts the idyllic message of the first three lines. The poet is conveying not a contradiction but only a reality of the world from where she writes, and acknowledging that by highlighting the wounded state of the world, she is also highlighting the wounded state of herself, her peoples, and her communities.

The second stanza begins with "I also paint," stating with these words an additional dimension to the production of her poetry, which places her within the ancient Maya tradition of visual text production as captured in codices, architectural structures, and various artifacts. With this "I also," the articulation of her worldviews travels in various spaces, written and visual texts, yet continues to be rooted in cosmocentric relations. The poet solidifies these relations with "I sculpt," which also recalls the millennia-old tradition of Maya sculpting as seen in the pieces (stelae, sculptures, artifacts) that have survived the course of time and continue to reveal the knowledges of Maya peoples. The poet's articulation of these relations speaks to the Maya concept of *ts'íib* that Worley and Palacios develop in *Unwriting Maya Literature* (2019, 3). Worley and Palacios write that the concept of *ts'íib* speaks to the recognition of Maya peoples as recorders and transmitters of knowledges. This recording process does not always follow the printed Latin alphabet but comes in different formats; furthermore, such an approach is not in opposition to the Latin alphabet, but rather in dialogue with and alongside "a number of other forms of recording knowledge."

The language in this second and third stanza ensures that, now that she writes and paints and sculpts, her word will leave a mark that will not be easily erased. Her Tseltal dreams will be forever captured in paint, and her language bursts into the silence of history to scream their ongoing existence. In this selection of words and language, the poet paints and voices her declaration of writing. The writing alone, then, is not enough to capture the past to give way to her present. The articulation of words alone is not enough; she must also embody these experiences and undergo these transformations as part of her emergence at the center of her history and as part of the process of wording herself into existence.

STS'IBUJON

Ka'iy ts'ibujel
ta sba xnichimal ch'uch' jaben,
ta yelaw lum k'inal
exchenajem yu'un ja'wiletik.

Ka'iy bonwanej uuk
ta k'unil bonil k'atbujem ta ti'bal
te sna'el yot'an tseltaletik
sk'unbil ta sk'u sakubel k'inal.

Ya'ka'iy joswanej
sok yaw xch'ababet k'inal
snamey kuxlejal jbats'il k'op.

Ya jwol ok'el k'opetik
ta stojol bats'il winiketik,
mach'atik xch'abajik ta stojol
  xchanebal schikin ch'ulchan
sok ya xbeenik ta xchololal namey
  kuxlejal

Sok ya jbon ajk'abal,
sakubel sok mal k'aaletik
k'alalto ta sk'ubulil lum k'inal
banti ayinem sboniletik te xaab.

Ya ka'iy ts'ibujel,
ta jtsajal k'uxul te nak'bil
ta sk'in k'opetik
ya jt'anantes snopibal ku'un
ta stojol sikil yaxinal lajel.

YO ESCRIBO

Yo escribo
sobre pétalos de lirios,
sobre el rostro de la tierra
herida por los años.

También pinto
con suave tinta encarnada
sueños tseltales
abrigados con el ropaje de la aurora.

Y esculpo
con el grito del silencio
la historia de mi lengua milenaria.

Moldeo palabras que lloran
por los hombres verdaderos,
los que oran hacia las cuatro esquinas del cielo
y caminan por el surco de la historia.

Y pinto noches,
mañanas y tardes
desde las entrañas de la tierra
donde yacen los colores del abismo.

Yo escribo
con mi dolor purpúreo escondido
con el concierto de las palabras,
desnudo mi pensamiento
ante la sombra fría de la muerte.

I WRITE

I write
on petals of lilies,
on the face of the earth
wounded by the years.

I also paint
with soft embodied ink
Tseltal dreams
wrapped up in the garb of dawn.

I sculpt
with the cry of silence
the history of my millennial language.

I mold words that cry
for the true men,
those who pray to the four corners of the sky
and walk along the furrow of history.

And I paint nights,
mornings and afternoons
from the entrails of the earth
where the colors of the abyss lie.

I write
with my purple hidden pain
with the harmony of words,
expose my thought
before the cold shadow of death.

As the poet moves to the fourth stanza, the tone and control over language read stronger, as if in the first three stanzas she is pulling the tools together that are necessary to frame the space that she is entering. "I mold words that cry," she states, expressing that through the reclamation of writing she also gains control of the words and language, and finally of the message these words are to convey, thus giving way to Maya history. In the fifth stanza, the poet recalls the painting process of history again. Her worldviews are revealed as she roots the source of this history to the entrails of the earth. This is where the source of everything is, where the tools, inspiration, and knowledge necessary for the production of work lie.

In the last stanza, the poet goes back to the statement of "I write," coming full circle, returning to the importance of writing. There is a level of rawness in these lines, the nakedness of her thoughts, as if in the writing there is no more hiding. She is screaming through the silences, the hidden pain is now revealed through the multitude of words, and she too is revealed as the journey of the poem reveals the multilayered approach that leads to the "I write" statement.

The poetry is thus a vindication of the poet's worldviews. Even as she shapes her world by writing "on the face of the earth," the history of her "millennial language" guides her work as well, breaking through the silences of time. *Caracoleando* is deployed here as the author, through the written word, spirals into the various Maya formats of producing and recording knowledges—oral, written, painted, sculpted. The layers of denouncement present in the writing trace a map to the awakening process. She writes about painting "tseltal dreams" and molding "words that cry / for the true men," noting with these written lines the voice that she gifts to the Tseltal peoples. The poet also highlights all the beautiful attributes of her relation to the world, the ways she claims access to histories and knowledges through her writing, and the ways this interaction contributes to the materialization of her being in the world. There are difficulties, pains, silences that she is breaking away from, but with the "I write" the poet claims her newfound voice through her writing, and reclaims control of her histories.

The relations of language to a person's sense of being and connection to the land and place are also addressed in the introduction to the compilation *Incantations by Mayan Women* (Past, Okotz, and Ernándes 2005, 18), where Ambar Past notes that in the Tsotsil language "*to write* and *to paint* are the same verb (*tz'ib*)." When López Sántiz, in her poem "I write," asserts the different methods she is utilizing to bring herself into being and insert herself into history, she is recognizing these relations sustained over time—these traditions—and naming the different methods that make her existence possible. However, according to the women's voices in *Incantations by Mayan Women,* one does not have to practice both painting and writing to record one's histories. Chadwick Allen, in *Trans-Indigenous* (2012, xxii), shares this position when he notes that Native writers have often had to "work in multiple media and . . . juxtapose genres and forms, such as a written poem and a drawing, painting, sculpture, carving, textile, basket, photograph, moving image, or live performance." In *Word Mingas* (2021), Rocha Vivas's concept of oralitegraphies similarly speaks to the use of multimedia in Indigenous scholarship, and the ways that textual, oral, and visual narratives are in constant dialogue in Indigenous knowledge production. And in *Unwriting Maya Literature* (2019), Worley and Palacios engage with the concept of *ts'íib* to draw attention to the nontextual production of knowledge by Maya writers of Chiapas and Guatemala. These relations, which have been in place in the Indigenous Americas for millennia, continue to inform the poet López Sántiz's relation to place as she weaves the worlds of her existence.

The position the poet takes in the poem on the relations of language (written and orally delivered) and worldviews is central to the field of Native American studies, where scholars such as N. Scott Momaday (Kiowa), Simon J. Ortiz (Acoma), and Reid Gómez (Diné [Navajo nation]) have worked with language to weave their stories, reveal their worldviews, and reclaim their place in history. These relations are always rooted to place (land) and time, and are in continuous dialogue with one another. In *Woven Stone* (1992, 153), Ortiz explains the meaning of writing: "Because Indians always tell a story. . . . The only way to continue is to tell a story and there is no other way." Ortiz further emphasizes the importance of writing for those who are present, those who will come, and those who are gone, as they are all part of the life cycle one is to take as part of the journey. Writing is thus integral to the sustainment of life, the storytelling that is part and giver of life. Mapuche scholar Elicura Chihuailaf Nahuelpan captures these relations in *Message to Chileans* (2009) through his concept of oraliture, which recognizes the oral tradition that informs the written word and reads their relations as ever interacting and in movement. Language is in this sense the continuous interaction of the written and oral delivery of the word that sustains Indigenous worldviews.

Central to the significance of telling a good story is the value of the words that give life to that story, words that "accept the risk and responsibility to account for birth, movement and continuance" of the story itself (Gómez 2003–4, 89). These carefully selected words that give life to language are what Momaday (1999b) says give way to the articulation of the idea that a person, a Native person, has of themselves. Language is, then, the essence of oneself, and as such, Native peoples must know their language in order to always remember their origins. In this argument, however, the focus is not just on the mother tongue, but on a language that carefully positions words together to speak of philosophies and cosmovisions that place peoples in relation to the world. Thus we find the power and value of oraliture, which centers language as sustainer of life, because, as Chihuailaf (2009, 35) adds, "poetry—which is the fundamental Language—and all that is touched by it, is the best expression of the permanent dialogue between the spirit and the heart." Language in this sense gives life to the poetry that speaks to the essence of being and further guides the value of the responsible word that "carries with it other words and worldview(s)," exemplifying how word exchanges are wor(l)d exchanges (Gómez 2003–4, 65). Writing is thus the space where the relations of words, language, and storytelling come into place, as Ortiz (1992, 151) notes: "Without this sharing in the intellectual, emotional, physical, and spiritual activity, nothing much happens." He highlights these relations as closely connected and necessary to ensuring peoples' continuance.

These relations of storytelling, language, and the power of the word are rooted to place and time. This interconnection reflects the constant interplay of the language with the environment, through which the meanings behind Indigenous peoples' worldviews emerge (Varese 2006). Jeannette C. Armstrong (Okanagan) (1998, 183) alludes to the idea of word/world exchanges when she highlights the interaction with her Okanagan land and landscape that makes her feel at times like the translator of the language that her land speaks. In effect, she asserts the influence of language on the environment and, conversely, of environment on the language. These relations also speak to Chacón's (2018) concept of Indigenous cosmolectics, where, through a *kab'awilian* practice, the authors engage with all that inhabits the cosmos, read all human and other-than-human relations present in the cosmos, and allow these knowledges to inform their place in the world. Leslie Marmon Silko (Laguna Pueblo) (2010) states that this dialoguing begins with the practice of oral tradition, but is carried as people travel the land, honoring and respecting the land and the life that the land sustains. The strong relation of language and words that weave worlds into existence is central to the reclamation process of presence in the world. It is a relation that Indigenous writers of Mexico also share, as their work demonstrates.

In *Del lingüicidio al plurilingüismo* (From linguicide to plurilingualism, 2011) Tsotsil scholar José Daniel Ochoa Nájera narrates his experience as part of the project of translating the San Andrés Accords into ten Maya languages.[3] The value of this experience connects to the fact that the accords are the only official document between the EZLN and the government to outline Indigenous rights to autonomy, as I discuss further in chapter 4:

> La traducción, implico promover la escritura de estas lenguas, demostrar con ello la existencia de gramáticas propias, y sobre todo dar participación activa a sus hablantes, como una premisa para el desarrollo social, cultural y lingüístico en la vida comunitaria y más allá de esta.
>
> The translation implies promoting the writing of these languages, demonstrating thereby the existence of their own grammars, and especially giving active participation to their speakers as a premise for social, cultural, and linguistic development in community life. (20)

Here, too, language is identified as central to the writing process. Ochoa highlights the importance of the translation of this historic document into the various Maya languages of Chiapas because of the acknowledgment Maya languages and speakers received. Ochoa further notes of this connection, "cuando las pienso, también me pienso" (when I think of them [the languages] I am also thinking myself) (13). With these words, he emphasizes the connection between the art of writing and the art of thinking himself, of creating himself, of elevating the value of Maya languages and in turn elevating the sense of value of Maya peoples of Chiapas. The completion of this project is thus "uno de los primeros pasos para reconocer a las lenguas y la vinculación de estas con los hablantes, es evidente que cuando ellos denominan a sus lenguas, están definiendo su identidad lingüística" (one of the first steps to recognizing the languages and the connection of these [languages] with their speakers, it is evident that when they name their languages, they are defining their linguistic identity) (15). Through the affirmation of their language, Maya speakers affirm their sense of Maya identity.

The works of Indigenous scholars and writers of Mexico also reveal nonlinear relations to language. In their practice, Indigenous peoples strategically navigate these linguistic interactions. The choice Maya writers make in the presentation of their written text (always published in their mother tongue and in Spanish) and in the articulation of the work (written or voiced) speaks to this strategic maneuvering of linguistic interactions. When asked about this ongoing process of translation and navigation between mother tongue and Spanish, Tsotsil poet Enriqueta Lunez (2012) noted that she does not apologize for having to write her work in Spanish first and then translate it to Tsotsil. When she started going to school to receive a formal education, the curriculum was in Spanish only. If she was to succeed academically, she had to learn how to read and write in Spanish. No one taught her how to read and write in Tsotsil. She admits that she has heard stories in Tsotsil from her grandparents and others in the community since she was little, and that her inspiration can come in Tsotsil as well, but when it comes to writing, she goes to Spanish first. She also notes that in order for her work to circulate, this has to happen in Spanish, as there is little audience in Tsotsil. The state-issued curriculum in schools is still in Spanish, and children continue to be told to put their mother tongue aside. She notes that the ongoing challenge in language-preservation efforts is to promote a readership in both Spanish and peoples' mother tongue (Lunez 2012).

The nonlinear relation to language and the negotiation poets undertake in relation to their mother tongue speak to an awakening process. The efforts both to reclaim these languages and to showcase the vulnerability of the languages in such linguistic exchanges emerge in the poem "A'yej: Discurso" (Speech) by Andrés López Díaz (Tsotsil) (2006a).

A'YEJ
La lo'il a'yeje
ta x-ulbatel ta yok sk'ob
avalab anich'nab,
chanojes ta mu'yuk
yojtikinel ti jlumaltike.

Jk'opojel,
la lo'iltake
ta xjoybij ta takin banomil,
ta sjipobil avo'nton chka'batel lavibele.

Mu'yuk ayanen ta melel la lo'il a'yeje,
ja'no'ox chk'ejin jutk'opale,
ti jbakilkutike xchi'uk jtakepalkutike,
apixojanan ta sjutbil lo'il maxil.

Xokolaltik ta lo'il a'yeje,
amokoj ta k'oj ti sat jkuxlejalkutike:
tspat ti ch'iel kuxlejal ta melele,
chtukanuk ya'lel satiletik ta jutbilal k'op,
tspat ti ya'lel satiletike oy k'uxul vokolil ta melel.

Jk'opojel, tanae mo'oj xaun,
mu xa spas avu'un jech,
ti k'ak'al tana li'e oy kich'ojtalel ta smuk'ul yutil jts'ijlej:
jun snopbenal jolal ti nojem ta vu'un ku'unkutike.

Jbel a'yej ti sak ts'ilanik svoke
ti mu sna' ch'ay batel ta osiltike,
ti ta xmuk'ib batel yu'un xch'ulelkutike,
jun kuxlejal ti mu xa stak' utilanele.

Tana li'e, sts'ibun bats'i vinik antsetik,
satun jvi'naletik xchi'uk tenbil vinik antsetik,
ti jk'ope ma'uk yu'un xbol ma'uk yu'un jeche'
ti jk'opojele ja'snichimal sbelel kuxlejal.

¡Aaa!
jech no'ox xtok
ja' xnich k'ok',
ja' xojobal k'ak'al yu'un ok'om cha'ej,
yu'un ti jts'ibe ta sk'i sba batel ta sjamlej vinajel
k'ucha'al x-an-un ch'ich'sbak'esobil sjol yo'onton k'ak'al.

DISCURSO

Tu lengua
se desvanece
en tus propios retoños,
al pueblo multiplicas
el desconocimiento.

Orador,
tus palabras
se vuelven tierra seca,
tu raíz se pudre en el olvido.

La verdad de tu discurso no existe,
sólo cantas mentiras,
y nuestros huesos y carnes
arropas de falacias.

Vacío tu discurso,
máscara que cubre nuestra realidad:
detrás de la verdad nacen lágrimas por la mentira,
detrás de las lágrimas
hay una verdad de dolor.

Ahora no, orador,
ya no podrás hacerlo:
traigo en el volumen de mi silencio
una consciencia llena de nosotros.

Un discurso de burbuja transparente
que no se pierde en el espacio,
que hace crecer en nuestra conciencia
una vida de rebeldía.

Soy la letra de los bats'i viniketik del presente,
rostro de los hambrientos y humillados,
mi palabra no es tosca ni blanda,
es flor de la historia.

¡Ah!
y también
es flor de fuego,
es calor y luz por su futuro,
porque mis letras se extenderán al cosmos
como sangre ardiente en los nervios del tiempo.

SPEECH

Your tongue
disappears
in your own offspring,
to the people you multiply
ignorance.

Orator,
your words
become dry soil
your root rots in oblivion.

The truth of your speech does not exist,
you only utter lies,
and bundle our skin and bones
in fallacies.

Your empty speech,
mask that covers our reality:
behind the truth tears are born for the lie,
behind the tears
there is a truth of pain.

Not now, orator,
you can no longer do it:
I bring in the volume of my silence
a consciousness full of us.

A transparent speech bubble
that is not lost in space,

that grows in our consciousness
a life of rebellion.

I am of the word of the present-day bats'i viniketik [true men and
women],
face of the hungry and humiliated,
my word is neither rough nor soft,
it is the flower of history.

Ah!
and also
it is a fire flower,
it is heat and light for their future,
because my letters will extend to the cosmos
like hot blood in the nerves of the time.

In the first four stanzas of the poem, the poet focuses on a historical sense of language loss, the ways the language fades into the landscape of place, masking a reality that can no longer be sustained, withering away in the lies the language holds. However, when the poet moves to the fifth stanza the readers realize that the language he is referencing in the first four stanzas is the dominant language (Spanish). The poet creates a shift as he moves to the fifth and sixth stanza, noting that the power of a discourse (their language, their worldviews) has not been lost but rather continues to grow in their consciousness, leading them to a life of rebellion and a new world of possibilities. The poet, through the shifts and movement he creates in the writing, brings about a new sense of awareness. "I am of the word of the present-day bats'i viniketik" (the true men and women), the poet states in the opening line of the seventh stanza; "it is the flower of history" (the word, that is), the poet continues as he closes this stanza. It is here that he articulates this transformation, the ways his language (Tsotsil) falls on fertile land, grows, and flourishes. The transformation of the poet's relation to language throughout the poem is not subtle. The level of difficulty inherent in describing this awakening into language is seen in the poet's carefully selected words in the last six lines of the poem: "Ah! / and also / it is a fire flower, / it is heat and light for their future, / because my letters will extend to the cosmos / like hot blood in the nerves of the time." Thus, in the course of this poem, the poet transforms the historical relation of his Tsotsil language to the Spanish language, elevating the sense of value of his mother tongue, and reaffirming his own sense of being in relation to the language.

What López Díaz accomplishes in this poem is what Ochoa Nájera (2011, 18) underlines as the main accomplishment of the translation of the San Andrés Accords into ten Maya languages. The Maya languages were reawakened through this project, causing an explosion of thought and an act of liberation. The connection of the word, language, and spaces the poet navigates in the process of telling the historical experience is a position shared with Native and Indigenous writers, particularly with Ortiz (1992) and his defense of writing and storytelling as vital to the continuance of Native peoples. *Discurso*, the Spanish-language title of the poem, translates into "speech" or "discourse," and it is in this process of playing with words and language that the poet captures this history of the relation of his language and Spanish. The discourse of the denial of the language and thus the denial of the people has been forced on his community for centuries, but this discourse is finding less fertile soil in the communities. The power of his true word centered in the Tsotsil worldview is the key for his community's history to flourish across all corners of the cosmos.

When writing about the trajectories of literary production in Latin America, Chacón (2018) questions, in conversation with other Latin Americanists, the violent imposition of the Latin alphabet by the colonial power, which decentered Indigenous knowledges' written, oral, and visual narratives. Victor Montejo (Jakaltek Maya) (2021, 59) adds to this conversation when he critiques the imposition of an anthropological/ethnographic approach of collecting "oral narratives" that are then translated and recorded (using the Latin alphabet) "out of context, and far removed from the places of action or Native communities" but are presented as reflections of the studied communities. In this context, both Chacón and Montejo critique the imposed binary of orality and the written word, which lessens the value of Indigenous knowledge systems. The poet, however, calls on both orality and the written word to affirm his sense of being. In this way, the empowering act is the affirmation of language captured in the poetry and, by extension, the reaffirmation of the poet's Maya identity. The poetry thus becomes about the self, the poet's sense of identity, and their place and relation to their world and worldviews. Acoma scholar Ortiz (2006a) shares this position, noting that the Indigenous writer is never too far removed from their work. Native American studies scholar Dean Rader (2012) uses the phrase "poetics of participation" to speak of the intricate relations Native poets have with their work, and the ways the work becomes an extension of their sense of self and identity. The poetry itself is reflective of the poets' identities, their lived experiences, and their relations to the world around.

The "poetics of participation" emerges in the poem "Slikebal Kuxlejaltik: Creación" (Creation) by Tsotsil poet Enriqueta Lunez (2007, 83), where the poet's own relation to dreams reflects her creative process. Lunez (2007, 2019) is a prolific writer whose work has been translated into English, Italian, French, German, and Serbian. She has traveled to the United States and Europe to present her work, always in Tsotsil and Spanish. The title of this poem presents her creative process, her intimate connection to the birth of her poetry, and the uncertainty and "hidden language" of dreams that challenge her writing process.

SLIKEBAL KUXLEJALTIK
Li jkajvaltik ja la spas vayichtik
nakbil smelolal, mu o no'ox xkaitik
li vinike xchunoj
ti ja smeltsanoj li ch'ul k'opetik.
Mu mechuk, li k'opetik ja spasojik jkuxlejaltik
oy slekilal schopolal
k'alal ta jts'imatatik k'ejimolal, nichimal k'opetik
jipojbatik ta x-ielal
oy bak'intik mu o no'ox jch'untik
li k'usi ta jtatik ta jts'imtael, uni nichimal k'op.

CREACIÓN
Dios creó la incertidumbre en los sueños,
su lenguaje oculto, inentendible
hace que el hombre
se sienta creador de la poesía.
Pero, la poesía es la que nos crea
con sus dioses buenos y malos
escribimos cada verso, cada canto
y sumergidos en el espanto
hay días en que uno no cree
en lo que escribe, su poesía.

CREATION
God created uncertainty in dreams,
its hidden, incomprehensible language
makes man
feel like the creator of poetry.
But poetry is what creates us
with its good and bad gods
we write each line, each song
and immersed in fright
there are days in which one does not believe
in that which one writes, their poetry.

In this poem, Lunez writes about her creative process as if there is a separate self that she brings in when writing. There is a feeling of fright that Lunez expresses as part of the writing process, which may very well reference the impact of bringing different parts of herself together (the creative, dreamer, writer, Tsotsil, woman). Nonetheless, through the writing, the poet weaves words of her world into existence. There is movement in this weaving, *caracoleando* in practice, as the writing process creates possibilities for her poetry to come into being and for her to become a poet. She writes of inspiration as a secret language that she peels apart through her writing. This secret language, however, is part of her creative process, part of her imagination and dreams that are connected to place and time. She does not name this, but the tone is certain, rooted in place as Lunez claims her space, noting the sources of her work, and attesting to her possibilities as a poet.

Rader's (2012) concept of "poetics of participation" captures the sense of awareness of these poets and their engagement with writing. It is in this engagement that the sense of awakening emerges. The awareness itself guides the process of the writing, which, once completed, guides the poet to newfound senses of being. When Lunez writes that "there are days in which one does not believe / in that which one writes, their poetry," she is noting the awareness that she has already achieved, the shift that has already taken place, the awakening that looks back to read the final product with a new and amazed set of eyes. This close engagement with the world around that nurtures the creative process in the act of writing is shared by Okanagan poet Jeannette C. Armstrong (1998), who writes that the beauty of her Okanagan language stems directly from a constant dialogue with all that is part of the cosmos. Similarly, the ongoing reflection of Leslie Marmon Silko (Laguna Pueblo) in *The Turquoise Ledge* (2010) captures this geophysical feature of her creative writing process. Silko's attentive relation to the animal, natural, human, and sky world continually informs her writing. Thus, she too becomes a translator of the cosmos's whispers. In Lunez's work, she speaks of writing from the heart, guided by the stories shared by her grandfathers and grandmothers and all who came before her nurturing the stories of the communities (Chacón 2018, 85).

In another poem by Lunez (2007, 68), "Vu'un Li'oyunkutike: Soy los que Estamos Aquí" (I am the we who are here), she resorts to the sounding of the written word again to reaffirm the presence of Maya peoples (see pages 42–43 for the full text). In this poem Lunez shows the ways these themes of continuance and presence emerge when the articulation of Indigenous peoples' place in history falls on deaf ears.

In the first three lines of the poem, Lunez slashes open spaces and inserts herself/themselves into present time. "We are," she continues, reclaiming the collective "we" in her peoples' history of place. This is not a community that is gone, or that can be recalled at will and then relegated to the past, but a community of peoples with a continuous presence. This notion of time continues in the ensuing stanza as Lunez writes that though thousands of moons have witnessed the ongoing internment of her peoples' presence and thousands of suns have witnessed their oblivion, these are not enough to erase "[her] memory." She creates a rhythm in her use of language as she moves from the experience of the collective to the impact this has on herself, weaving in this way the connectedness of historical experiences. She traces the passing of time with the number of moons and suns that have traced her/their demise. But even then, "no one will be able to pursue the [her] secrets," which I read as knowledges, because these, she concludes, are carried within her existence.

Caracoleando is in place here, tracing that spiraling into the self and spiraling out to the collective, shifting perspectives in relation to time and place, and between the collective and the individual subject. Through this shifting process, Lunez comes to recognize the strength of the collective in order for the self or individual to reemerge strongly. There is a sense of isolation, a theme that is also present in the poems that I address in the next section of this chapter, in the ways the literature captures the efforts and struggles of the authors to write themselves into history and to leave their work with a certain level of uncertainty regarding the impact of their actions. Will their words fall on deaf ears, leaving them to continue their work on their own? Or will their words be denied the space to resonate and grow? Though the poem denounces efforts to erase the millennia-old presence of Indigenous peoples, and even though the poet is writing herself/themselves into history through the articulation of this denouncement, the last stanza leaves this situation unsolved. The future is still unraveling, a reminder perhaps that it is in the past where the future is written.

This notion of the continuity of knowledge despite the insistence of burying Indigenous presence in "this world" is what Lawrence Gross (Anishinaabe) conveys in "Cultural Sovereignty and Native American Hermeneutics in the Interpretation of the Sacred Stories of the Anishinaabe" (2003, 127–28). In this essay Gross states that in order for Native peoples to sustain their survival, to defend their sense of sovereignty, they must defend their cultural and spiritual sovereignty as well. This is the position that I read in Lunez's poem when she writes about the insistence of the dominant culture in pushing Indigenous peoples to oblivion. This, however, she notes, does not lead to the end of their knowledges or worldviews, and this is how, through this poem, she recenters herself (and her people) within the world.

The poet's understanding of the condition of her peoples is what pushes her to speak, what places her in a separate space where she may experience a sense of isolation, but through the written articulation of her position, the engagement with the community occurs. Lunez's experience speaks to the writing process Ojibwe writer Heid E. Erdrich describes in *Cell Traffic* (2012, 161) when, in "Our Words Are Not Our Own," Erdrich pays tribute to all that the universe has to offer: ancestors, environment, and histories that feed into her creative process and that accompany her until the completion of her writing process. This experience is part of collective memory (Silko 1998) or racial memory (Momaday 1999b). Native scholars reflect through their writing, a seemingly individual act that is always in relation to the collective.

Thus far, these works have laid claim to the relations of language that words peoples' worlds into existence through the deliverance of the written word. The section that follows places the emphasis on what is said through poetry and how poets reclaim the old practice of orality to word their worlds into existence. The movement the poetry creates is a journey through *caracoleando* as they travel through time and place to bring their words forward.

VU'UN LI'OYUNKUTIKE

Mu'yuk bu chamemunkutik ta yech'emal
kuxlejal
mu yu'unuk chitajinkutik ta yak'el jbakutik
ta ilel.
Vu'unkutik,
k'ux osil k'ak'al ta spat ti yoytolal k'ak'aletike,
ta yuninal mu'yuk jamen satil ta k'u sjalil
mu'yuk ch'akbil ta ilel.

Manchuk me ech'em ta o'lol yoxbok'al jme'tik u
yiloj ti la kichkutik mukele:
Ta jaylajunbok' jtotik yiloj yich ch'ayel ya
o'nale.
Ja' no'ox yu'un,
mu baluk ta jun u.
Oy van yik'al,
me jeche,
vo'vinik xcha' bok'al jtotik to xtok
ti boch'o chil chch'ay ti jol ko'ontone
xchi'uk ta xyil t'anal chlaj ti jbektale.

K'alal me laj ti k'usi t'abal ta jol o'ntonale,
mu xa boch'o ta snuts ti k'usi te nak'al
te van bak'in, te van bu',
k'ejel ta jkuxlejal.

SOY LOS QUE ESTAMOS AQUÍ

No estamos muertos en el pasado
ni jugamos a los aparecidos en este
mundo.
Somos,
y se duele el tiempo en la espalda de
los calendarios,
en la tierna ignorancia de un tiempo
sin registro.

A pesar de miles de lunas
que han presenciado nuestro
entierro:
Mil soles presenciaron al olvido.
Pero,
no bastará una luna.
Serán,
a lo mejor,
quinientos soles más
los que vean borrar mi memoria
y morir mi cuerpo desnudo.

Cuando el recuerdo fenezca
nadie podrá perseguir los secretos
alguna vez, en algún lugar,
guardados en mi existencia.

I AM THE WE WHO ARE HERE

We are not dead in the past
nor do we pretend to be ghosts in this
world.
We are,
and the time hurts on the back of the
calendars,
in the tender ignorance of an
unrecorded time.

Despite thousands of moons
who have witnessed our interment:
A thousand suns witnessed the
oblivion.
But,
a moon will not suffice.
There will be,
at best,
five hundred more suns
who will see my memory erased
and my naked body die.

When the memory expires
no one will be able to pursue the secrets
sometime, somewhere,
guarded in my existence.

Orality and the Articulation of Maya Identities

This section centers on four additional poems by these same three poets, gathered from the same publications: "Jun k'ak'al: Un día" (One day) and "Ta'lo xa: Basta" (Enough) by Andrés López Díaz, "K'unil lajel: Agonía" (Agony) by Adriana del Carmen López Sántiz, and "Yavu: Lunario" (Lunary) by Enriqueta Lunez. The practice of orality that emerges from the poetry frames this section. The deliverance of the poets' words carries an immediate effect that adds a sense of urgency to the poets' dimension and sense of wording themselves into existence. I begin with "Jun k'ak'al: Un día," where López Díaz's (2006b) words, in their deliverance, weave him into existence, center him in the world, take on a life of their own in delivering his message, and give way to change and reflection on his reality as a Maya poet (see pages 46–47 for the full text).

With "One day I spoke" the poet bursts onto the scene and marks his presence in place. Despite the difficulty of speaking, a feeling that he captures with the image of words traveling out of his throat to a resounding "boom" in the second and third lines, his tone is defiant and firm. He speaks, and the impact of his words attracts the attention of "hundreds of pairs of eyes" that "looked at" him, noting a level of acclamation to his words. The poet states not that they are listening to him, but that they are seeing him. Language, the articulation of the power of his words, is what materializes him, what makes others see him, implying that before he chose to speak on that "one day" he was not visible, heard, or acknowledged.

The past tense that the poet chooses gives the poem a reflective tone, which he also captures in the shifts in gaze that he creates throughout the poem. The second stanza shows this shift and reflection when the poet recognizes the power of his words and the waves of movement the words create as these take on a life of their own. "My verses galloped," he writes, capturing with this line the firmness and strength of his words, which he follows with "flew and traveled from city to city," making the words themselves the deliverers of the denouncement that speak of the yoke of oppression Indigenous peoples have been living under—or, as the poet states, "the whip of centuries." Here, the poet shifts his gaze again as he moves on to the third stanza and focuses this time on the weight of history. The "bitter water of history," the poet states, touching his "tongue," which prompts the naming of the oppression that gives him "courage" to fight for change and to move beyond the oppressive relations of the past.

The fourth stanza continues with this idea of change. The true word that he has spoken has liberated him, and so he flies "by the vibrant wind." But the struggle does not end here; this struggle does not take a lineal form, and in the last stanza the poet recognizes that difficulty. Here the poet pauses to look inside his home and community, where his words have no resonance and eyes do not look at him, and where his Tsotsil and Tseltal brothers still call him the "Indian." His words have created so much movement beyond limits, but the transformative power of words is still at work at home. The same words that he uses to criticize historical forms of oppression, he uses to criticize the "blind and silent" behavior of his brothers and sisters. The poet takes a stand to confront the state of denial and the conditions of internalized oppression present at home. He recognizes with these words the ongoing challenges the communities face in the continuance of their journey.

There is an emphasis on the orality of delivering the word in this poem, on the impact of voicing a language and the way it is perceived. In the deliverance of his words, an audience is immediately referenced and called in to watch and hear. The response of these others is instantly registered, and the impact of their response is strongly articulated. The poet is voicing his awakening, out loud, in the presence of others, hoping that together they can claim their presence and gain recognition. The reflective tone of the poem, the courage in López Díaz's words, the defiant tone of his verses, and the triumph that he expresses through the liberation of his words carry a lot of hope. "One day I spoke," he writes in his opening line, and with this statement, the author travels toward the liberation his words deliver, a challenging path with various turns, but with a determination toward change.

The waves the poet creates, moving from the realization of his condition to the denouncement, from the space where he finds his voice to the growing movement the raising of his voice creates, enact the act of *caracoleando*, where the poet ventures into liminal spaces that lead to affirmations of his Maya identity. In the poem, the poet traces the journey of the change, which places him in different spaces of possibilities, where his words can blossom or fall on deaf ears. In the telling, the poet faces the challenges that fall in those in-between spaces of uncertainty that he is determined to occupy, to continue to push forward his voice and give way to change. Through the poet's denouncement, he also reclaims his history and relation to the world. He names his pain, the source of his courage, and the ways the articulation leads him to his true word. Language itself, then, is the source of his liberation.

JUN K'AK'AL

Li k'opoj jun k'ak'al
stsinanan sba sbe jch'el ta jnuk',
avan batel yech'omal ti kee,
svo'vinikal ta bej satiletik laj yilikun.

K'olkinaj batel jk'os jnichim k'op,
xanavanuk, vilanuk bal, ta jujun muk'tikil lum,
ta xalalan tsitsel nukul ta vo'neal kuxlejal.

Sts'ujulal xi'el lok'anuk tal ta jtiba
ch'ail ya'lel vo'neal kuxlejal ka'i;
slok'esan yeklalil k'ak'al o'ntonal ti jk'opejele
ko'ol xchi'uk k'ok xchik'ik'an yech'omal
kuxlejal.

Livil
Livil batel
livil ta xvik'lajan ik'
li vil xchi'uk xh'ulele k'ak'al:
saktik'an bat ti jk'opojele.

Ti kuts' kalaltake
tsotsiletik xchi'uk tseltaletik
mu'yuk yilbikun jsat,
staj o yav makal yelobik, ts'ijilik,
mu xojtikinik xch'ich'elik xchi'uk yibelik,
spasoj sbaik ta bijil kaxlan lumetik,
"indio" xi yutikun o.

UN DÍA

Un día hablé
con las venas apretadas en la garganta,
mi voz retumbó,
y cientos de pares de ojos me vieron.

Galoparon mis versos,
volaron y viajaron de ciudad en ciudad
anunciando el látigo de los siglos.

En mi frente brotaron gotas de miedo,
agua amarga de la historia;
arrojaron en mi lengua signos de
coraje,
fuego que quema sombras del pasado.

Volé,
Volé
por el viento vibrante,
con el espíritu del día:
transparente fue mi palabra.

Pero mis hermanos
tsotsiles y tseltales
nunca me vieron a mis ojos,
siguieron ciegos y callados,
ignorando su esencia y su raíz,
se visten de sabios y civilizados
y me dicen el "indio."

ONE DAY

One day I spoke
with tight veins in the throat,
my voice boomed,
and hundreds of pairs of eyes looked
at me.

My verses galloped,
flew and traveled from city to city
announcing the whip of centuries.

Drops of fear sprouted on my forehead,
bitter water of history;
threw on my tongue signs of courage,
fire burning shadows of the past.

I flew,
I flew
by the vibrant wind,
with the spirit of the day:
transparent was my word.

But my tsotsil and tseltal brothers
never looked me in my eyes,
continued blind and silent,
ignoring their essence and root,
they dress up as wise and civilized
and call me "Indian."

The criticism of the blindness and deafness of his Tsotsil and Tseltal brothers and sisters speaks of his awareness and knowledge of the ways oppression is disguised, and the ways those seeking change can be isolated.

The oppressive system López Díaz describes—the sense of isolation, the importance of the denouncement to claim his space in the world—reflects a development of the work Indigenous intellectuals of Mexico have been conducting in the last few decades. Juan Gregorio Regino (Mazatec), founding member and visionary of the Escritores en Lenguas Indígenas Asociación Civil (Civil Association of Writers in Indigenous Languages, ELIAC), has spoken of his experience navigating the school system as a university student in the 1980s, a time when Indigenous peoples continued to be perceived as relics of the past that needed to be absorbed into the dominant culture. While pursuing his degree in ethnolinguistics, Regino realized the entrapments of a system that insisted on denying his Mazatec identity or belittling his Mazatec knowledges. This caused Regino to awaken, and he "radically exchanged his role as an agent of acculturation to a promoter of his own language and culture, and he now writes and thinks in his language" (Hernández-Ávila 2003, 54–55). This change was not the product of one specific moment for Regino. Rather, a process of reflection, like López Díaz states in his poem, led Regino to the "one day" when he chose to speak and create movement toward change for himself and his community.

Connected to this notion of speaking up and using the power of words to create movement toward change is a disruption of the state's establishment of a homogenous nation. Stefano Varese (2006, 126) refers to this relation as a "dialectic denied," where the state sees any "form of ethnic affirmation" as a direct threat to the homogeneous vision the state has been pursuing "since the wars of independence." The work of the writers and artists in this section is, thus, a direct confrontation to this system, where the dominant culture has historically excluded Indigenous peoples from dialectical relations with the state. This dialectic denied, however, did not erase Indigenous peoples' knowledge systems, but rather led to a stronger protection of these knowledges. Indigenous peoples have never stopped learning and sharing their knowledges; instead, these acts just occurred in strict secrecy in the communities (Hernández-Ávila 2003). This practice dates back centuries, indicative of Indigenous peoples' resilience in the protection and continuance of their knowledges (Arias 2017–18, vol. 2). Thus, the time that precedes the opening line of López Díaz's poem may very well connect to this period of learning and sharing, when people listened attentively, awaiting a time to share openly.

Language, nonetheless, what is said and what is written, continues to be central to the claiming of Native and Indigenous identity. Language is the vehicle through which Native and Indigenous writers claim presence, and it is the facilitator of their denouncement. Language here refers to both the writer's native tongue and the dominant language as carrier of Indigenous peoples' worldviews. In the case of scholar Victor Montejo (Jakaltek) (2005, 67–68), he explains that language is central to his Maya identity, and says that this relation is reaffirmed through ceremonial practices in the sacred spaces of his land, carried in his native tongue: "this is to belong to a tradition with roots still strong and deeply embedded in the land, its sacred places, and geography." Montejo's Maya language connects him to the land, and this relation reaffirms his sense of being in the world as a Jakaltek Maya from Guatemala. Kiowa scholar N. Scott Momaday, in his essay "The Man Made of Words" (1999b, 646), speaks of language as "the repository of . . . knowledge and experience," establishing the close relation of language and identity. Though very much connected to his Kiowa language, Momaday speaks of the power of the honest and responsible word that gives life to language, including English, and affirms peoples' sense of being. In this poem, López Díaz puts his honest and responsible word forward to speak for survival, to bring himself into being, and to reclaim in this way his place in history.

The poem "K'unil lajel: Agonía" (Agony) by the poet Adriana del Carmen López Sántiz (2005, 21) also lays an emphasis on claiming presence (see pages 50–51 for the full text). The poet relates the ongoing intellectual violence that slaughters Indigenous knowledges and deprives communities of hope for a future. The five stanzas of the poem speak to different spaces that the word and the voice of peoples occupy, as well as the ways these are repressed, leaving peoples faceless, which could also mean voiceless or silenced.

In the first stanza the poet writes that "the hidden language of the word cries," a condition that has left people mute. In the second stanza, the poet moves beyond the person and on to the community to write that "the voice of a people has been wounded," and with a hint of hope adds that through the whispers of the earth, "the people live." In the following two stanzas the tone is gloomy, just like the day she describes, and leaves them (her community) "prisoners in the torment of the deception," a people who have "lost their face." The poem moves from the individual to the collective, not-

K'UNIL LAJEL

TA K'UNK'UN LAJEL x-awun jun
sik'ot'anil.
Te nak'bil ya'yejal k'op ya x-ok'
jich bit'il ja'al ta yolil tajetik:
k'atbujemikix ta uma' te winiketik.

Yejchentesojikix sk'op lum . . .
Te muk'ul ot'anil ya xk'atbuj ta
sejk'arakub,
k'unk'un ya xk'opoj te sk'u' lum k'inal,
kuxul te lume.

Xmal k'aal yu'un te makbil k'inal.
Yak'ta na'el muk'ul kuxulil te k'ubul
xuxub
jich te jo'otike,
chukulotik ta wokolajel yu'un lo'loyel.

La xch'ay yelaw te lume,
la spojbey te winiketik
bayal yelawik ya yak'ik ta ilel.
Sok ya sna'ik bayal k'opetik.

Kojtesayikix te at'ejibale,
spasemal ot'an te ya yutsi'in xch'ulel
balumilal;
kojtesayikix te tujk'e,
te maba sna'el smilbey sk'op namey
kuxlejal.

AGONÍA

DE MUERTE LENTA grita un suspiro.
El lenguaje oculto de la palabra llora
como lluvia entre los pinos,
los hombres han enmudecido.

Han herido la voz de un pueblo . . .
Mas la esperanza se vuelve arco iris,
susurra el vestido de la tierra,
el pueblo vive.

Atardece el día nublado,
Un silbido distante predice dolor profundo
y nosotros,
presos en el tormento del engaño.

El pueblo perdió su rostro,
le arrebataron los hombres
que muestran muchas caras.
y hablan muchas lenguas.

Bajen ya el arma,
osadía corrompe el espíritu del mundo
bajen ya el fusil,
ignorancia asesina el lenguaje de la historia.

AGONY

OF SLOW DEATH a sigh screams out.
The hidden language of the word cries
like rain among the pines,
men have gone mute.

The voice of a people has been wounded . . .
Yet hope turns into a rainbow,
whispers the dress of the earth
the people live.

The cloudy day turns to dusk
A distant whistle predicts deep grief
and we,
prisoners in the torment of deception.

The people lost their face,
they snatched the men
that show many faces.
and speak many languages.

Lower the arms already,
audacity corrupts the spirit of the world
lower the rifle already,
ignorance murders the language of history.

ing the tragedies of a denied language. The final stanza takes a universal tone, where the poet writes, "ignorance murders the language of history," denouncing the detrimental act of oppression of languages that captures peoples' histories.

Here too, the poet identifies language—carrier of the community's knowledges, histories, identities—as central to the writing process. This connection is reflective in Ortiz's (2006b, 256) work when he writes that oral tradition "includes prayer, song, drama-ritual, narrative or story-telling, much of it within ceremony—some of it outside ceremony—which is religious and social." Such relation resonates with Montejo's (2021, 100) reference to his Jakaltec Maya language as something "sacred," a gift to name, connect, and interact with the world, though for Ortiz, that sacred relation can be in Spanish, French, or English, but always on Native peoples' own terms. That sacredness and power language holds are also raised by Micaela Morales López (2004, 17), who writes about the weaponization of language as central to the colonial project, explaining that "conocer para destruir" (to know is to destroy) was the church's approach to Indigenous languages, as part of its missionary project to decenter Indigenous knowledges.

Consequently, the agony the poet expresses speaks to the historical violence against Indigenous languages that led communities to turn to murmurs and secrecy to protect the knowledges that language carries. She speaks of a hope the people hold on to, as bright as a rainbow to reveal the faces of the men who speak many languages, which can be read as richness of thought. The poet does not present a solution; like many Maya writers, she does not reveal what the other side of change looks like in her poetry. She and other writers use a language that speaks of change and an ongoing journey to come; they write themselves into that change, as if that is all readers need to know. She does plead, however, at the end of the poem, for a cessation to the violence that only spreads ignorance and leaves communities silenced. What happens thereafter is yet to be written. The movement the poetry creates guides the gaze through a process of *caracoleando* that spirals out to the denouncement of imposed cycles of silence just to recoil; and with the call to "lower the rifle already, / ignorance murders the language of history," the affirmation of existing knowledge unfolds. This approach is also reflective of the EZLN's actions, to be further addressed in chapter 4. The EZLN's direction is nonlinear; each step taken by the insurgency during its trajectories leaves room for error, allowing for reflection and new directions. The EZLN's reliance on diplomacy, the power of the word, nonetheless guides the directions of the movement.

In "Ta'lo xa: Basta" (Enough), the Tsotsil poet Andrés López Díaz (2006c) reclaims his place in the world and, in the process, calls on the various relations he has with the elements of the universe, transcends barriers of place and time, and occupies multiple spaces at once to make room for the reemergence of the self (see pages 54–55 for the full text). The movement in this piece is captured through the physical shifts the poet creates in the poem.

The first stanza paints an awakening of his consciousness. The silence that the poet connects to the moon carries a reflective tone, which he transforms in the following stanza by referring to his spirit as a warrior, though not yet brave enough. In the third stanza, the awakening culminates as "I'm tired," marking this shift, which then concludes with the "Enough" that opens the fourth stanza. "Enough of bewitching nightmares," the poet writes, cutting through time with this statement and stopping momentarily the passing of time with the denouncement of the injustices that have always haunted him.

The poet opens the fifth stanza with "It is time to enter to know the night." The fear is gone, and he is ready to confront his nightmare. No more lies, he writes in the sixth stanza, no more freezing him in time, no more suspending his presence to a past. The culminating shift comes at the end: "I want," he writes, and with language his song will be heard and he will move once again with the rhythm of the universe.

In the poem, López Díaz denounces the silences and oppression that led to a reawakening of his consciousness, which speaks directly to the path the EZLN has stated in its communiqués since 1994. On January 1, 1994, as the EZLN declared war on the Mexican Army and used armed force to take over seven cities in the state of Chiapas, they released the First Declaration of the Lacandon Jungle. In this first declaration to the world, they denounced the system of abuse and oppression that insists on marginalizing, denying, and silencing Indigenous peoples. They also listed the endless experiences of injustice Indigenous peoples of Mexico have suffered for over five hundred years. The EZLN (1996a, 1996b) refers to this period of oppression as "the long night of 500 years." When Zapatistas decided to rise up to defend their ways of life, the long night gave way to the light of day. "But today we say ENOUGH IS ENOUGH!" were the words the EZLN (1994a, 1994b) stated in this first declaration, and with these words, the paradigm shifted, and the relations of Indigenous peoples of Mexico and the government have never

TA'LO XA

Ta staun ti jch'ulme'tike,
ta xu'niun ti sts'ijleje,
sjob k'analetik
oy ta sbijilal jol.

Li jchu'ulel ta pask'opale,
ja'ta ilolal, ta moy, ta pom xchi'uk kantilaetik:
chba xa jmilan ti jvayel xchi'uk yatel ko'ntone,
mu xa jk'an ti ak'obal xi'el tanae, ti ak'obal o'notne.

Yu'un lubemun xa,
lubemun xchi'uk ti vu'une,
lubemun xchi'uk jsak pak'an sat,
xchi'uk xk'uxul ko'nton, yelanil kelob.

Ta'lo xa ti ilbajinel vaechile
ti tsts'unan sba ta jbek'tale,
ti ich'el ta muk' joybijem ta mu'yuk ich'el ta muk'e,
ti lekil kuxlejal joybijem ta letoe.

Ja'xa sk'ak'alil yochebal yojtikinel ti ak'obale,
ti xkil xch'ich'elinuk sin'jk obtake
ti x-uk'umajuk bal ti snophenal jol
ta sjunlej spat xokon banomile.

Mu xa xkak'oyijuk ti me'onal ch'ajetele,
ti chi s-alpostaun ti jvaeche,
ti chi sjoyobtaun ti utilanele
¡Ta'lo xa chka'i ti snopbenal jolal
yijuneb ta vo'neal kuxlejale.

Ta jk'an
ti jkee yu'un xmuyubajuk ta k'ejimol,
ti jsate oyuk ta xojobal,
ti jchikine oyuk ta vob;
jxanbilukun, jbak'elukun
ta junlej osil vinajel.

BASTA

Me alcanza la luna,
me adueña su silencio,
rocío de estrellas
es mi conciencia.

Mi espíritu guerrero contiene
rezos, pilico, inciensos y velas:
iré a matar mis sueños y mis penas,
no quiero esta noche de miedo.

Estoy cansado,
cansado de mí mismo,
cansado de mi rostro pálido,
de mis gestos y mi corazón herido.

Basta de pesadillas hechiceras
que se siembran en mi carne,
de la justicia a la injusticia,
de la paz a la guerra.

Es tiempo de entrar a conocer la noche,
de ver sangrar mis dedos
y mi pensamiento que corra
en todas direcciones.

No permito más vaguedad alucinante,
mis sueños me anestesian,
las pesadillas giran en mi,
¡basta de los pensamientos
congelados de la historia!

Quiero
mi idioma elevar en canto,
mis ojos en la luz,
mis oídos en la música;
ser en el movimiento
del universo.

ENOUGH

The moon reaches me
her silence seizes me,
dew of stars
my conscience is.

My warrior spirit contains
prayers, *pilico*, incense and candles:
I'm going to kill my dreams and sorrows,
I do not want this night of fear.

I'm tired,
tired of myself,
tired of my pale face,
of my wounded gestures and heart.

Enough of bewitching nightmares
that are sown into my flesh,
of justice to injustice,
of peace to war.

It is time to enter to know the night,
to watch my fingers bleed
and my thoughts that run
in all directions.

I do not allow more mind-bending
vagueness,
my dreams anesthetize me,
my nightmares swirl within me,
Enough of the thoughts
frozen in history!

I want my language to be elevated in song,
my eyes in the light,
my ears in the music;
to be in the motion of
the universe.

been the same. The "Enough" in the title of the poem connects to this trajectory of the EZLN, when Zapatistas made the jungles of Chiapas tremble with their presence, let their word fly, and reclaimed Indigenous peoples' places in the world. The poet too is a warrior, a spiritual warrior that blazes forward to elevate his Indigenousness and dance in tune with the universe.

From the awakening the poet experiences as stated in the line "I do not want this night of fear," the poet pushes to be free from this nightmare. This line reads like an internal monologue, a mental preparation for the battle the poet is about to face, and a pivotal moment in the transformation of the poet's spirit that unfolds in this poem: "It is time to enter to know the night" the poet continues, and with this line, he takes the risks required to break away from the oppressing past that haunts him. The poet is awakening from a long night of fear and becoming in this process the person whose "language . . . [is] elevated in song," someone free of fear. Part of the breaking away and naming of the silences and denials is connected to memory rooted in time and place and a denouncement that leads to new spaces that connect him to a "universe" in motion, away from the voices in history that insist on locking him still in time. All the poet wants is for the source of his Maya knowledges to be elevated and for his voice to be heard as alive and in motion.

I conclude this section with another poem by Tsotsil poet Enriqueta Lunez (2007, 17), "Yavu: Lunario" (Lunary), where the poet expresses a sense of freedom in the releasing of her words to move and wander as they please, creating a language of possibilities.

The journey the poet describes here invokes a sense of curiosity, a search for knowledges that are not easily available. "It suffices to believe," she notes in the third line, so simple it seems, but as the literature at the beginning of this section shows, silences and denials, oppression and marginalization, have been the experience of Indigenous peoples. The discovery thus may

YAVU
Yo' k'uchal xich' na'el bu nak'al
ti vo'nejal t'ule.
Ja'no'ox me xich'ch'unel,
ti yu'un oy t'ut'ti tae
te une, stak'ilel ti jaychop epal lo'il maxil
ta xcha'kuxanan ti'eile.

be an arduous task, and the path to reach this point of belief a difficult one. But I go back to "it suffices to believe," and the power of this statement, as if in her stating and embracing it the spell is broken and truths are revealed. The knowledges have always been within a hand's reach, the poet seems to be saying, but with the belief comes recognition, acknowledgment, and a sense of vision to accept all that the knowledge can provide, if the people are willing to embrace it.

When describing her work, Lunez (2017) notes that in her Tsotsil community of San Juan Chamula in Chiapas, poetry is more closely defined as *palabra florida* (flowery word). She adds that the deliverance of the flowery word tends to occur during ceremonies by elders and leaders in the community. Yet, this is not always an exclusive act, since the flowery word is also present in various ceremonial exchanges in the community, such as weddings and other celebrations. In this relation, then, the flowery word is carried in the oral practices of the community, delivered in sacred spaces and on sacred occasions. The search for knowledge the poet thus addresses in this poem is a process of *caracoleando* into the community's histories, traditions, and beauty of language to bring to life the flowery word.

The themes Lunez expresses in her poem speak to the importance of Maya women's presence. The sense of freedom in the release of dreams—the moving and wandering of the dreams as they please—creates possibilities to materialize them. This language of dreaming new possibilities also speaks to the EZLN's (2005a, 2005b) position of building a "world where many worlds fit," where new horizons can be explored and women's dreams and aspirations can be materialized. The lines read reflectively of this new vision Maya poets are addressing in their work. The message the poem contains, again, is not a spelling out of the vision, but a sharing of the sense of freedom the articulation toward this change creates.

LUNARIO	*LUNARY*
Para descubrir la lejana guarida	To discover the distant lair
del conejo milenario.	of the millennial rabbit.
Baste con creer,	It suffices to believe,
la existencia de un lunar en la luna	the existence of a mole on the moon
y en ella, ver las mil leyendas	and in her, see the thousand legends
resucitadas en los labios.	resurrected on the lips.

Conclusion

The relation to language all these writers demonstrate reveals another element at play: the sense of the individual and the collective. In the poetry analyzed in this chapter, the articulation of words that give way to language weaves worlds and worldviews into existence. The poets in the chapter demonstrate the various ways that this language is articulated through their narratives. As they navigate liminal spaces as creators and performers, language becomes the bridge between the self and the collective. And as these poets demonstrate, this languaging into existence can occur through what is said or what is written to share the vision that they have of their worlds. This is what these poets are doing with their work: forging open new spaces, raising awareness, awakening their communities so together they can reclaim and reaffirm their Maya identity.

When Adriana del Carmen López Sántiz and Andrés López Díaz make their claim to presence using these two approaches (voicing and writing) in their poems, they reveal not just the outcome of the impact of the word or voice once it is delivered, but the process of getting there. In other words, they are not just conveying the message of the poem of reclaiming and denouncing oppressive systems, or languaging themselves into existence; instead, they are naming (showing) the steps taken that lead to this denouncement. There is a collective effort in this process. What the "I write" in the poem by López Sántiz reveals is a layer of aloneness (individually) that takes place in the process of writing: not isolation per se, but rather a solitude in the moment that the poet is pinning the ideas together, writing, painting, sculpting, and shaping, alone in her reflection and practice. The poet presumes an audience and can anticipate the response, although this is not immediately facing her. There is a delay before the moment when the poem will be read and become part of the collective. In "One day I spoke," though López Díaz also experiences a sense of aloneness, there is the presence of the collective throughout his deliverance, as what is said is immediately echoed to an audience. The poet can see the direct response in the faces of those who see him, as well as in the absence of those who refuse to see and hear him.

The power of the "flowery word" that guides the poets' gaze toward knowledges housed in the community and toward the rebuilding of their Maya identities speaks of the language of possibilities carried in the writing and deliverance of the poetry. The waves this poetry creates, moving from the realization of their condition to the denouncement, from the space where the poets find their voice to the growing movement the raising of their voices creates, is reflective of *caracoleando*. The poets are calling for the continuity of their Maya identity and its performance over time, reading the past in order to stitch their paths ahead. In the poems, the poets trace the journey of the change, which places them in different spaces of possibilities, where their words can blossom or fall on deaf ears. In the telling, the poets face the challenges that fall in those in-between spaces of uncertainty that they are determined to enter in order to push forward their voice, give way to change, and reclaim their presence. The reclaiming of presence the poets articulate in their poetry is not just about claiming a Maya identity but about claiming a space to perform their Maya identities. This relation, as the poetry shows, does not happen in isolation, but is always in dialogue with the community and the world around.

CHAPTER 2

Other Knowledges

Rescuing, Reclaiming, and Rebuilding to Restore Relations with the World

> Cada autor es un ladrón de sus propias palabras o de palabras ajenas: esa es la tarea del escritor: robarle la palabra a las cosas, a los elementos y a las personas y enfrentar la vida sabiendo qué dicen y escribiendo esa sabiduría para que otros sepan del lenguaje oculto de la propia palabra.
>
> Each author is a thief of his own words or words of others: that is the writer's task: steal the word from things, elements, and people and face life knowing what they say and writing that wisdom so that others can learn about the hidden language of the word itself.
>
> —JOSÉ ANTONIO REYES MATAMOROS, FOREWORD TO *PALABRA CONJURADA* (CONJURED WORD)

In this chapter, I examine selected literature of Maya writers of Chiapas that represents Maya worldviews rooted in the Tsotsil, Tseltal, Tojolabal, Ch'ol, and Mam traditions. The literature consists of visual and written narratives and includes poetry, short stories, a novel, and a compilation. The shared themes that emerge in the analysis of the literature in relation to Maya worldviews (and that subsequently frame this chapter) are: spiritual beliefs, cycles of life, sources of knowledge, knowledge production, and legacies as recorders of histories. Furthermore, the different literary genres highlighted in this chapter reflect Native American and Indigenous traditions on the use of multimedia in Indigenous scholarship, and the ways textual, oral, and visual narratives are in constant dialogue within Indigenous knowledge production (C. Allen 2012; Chacón 2018; Rocha Vivas 2021; Worley and Palacios 2019). The selected literature has been published in books and anthologies by different institutions at the Mexican national and state levels, including the Comisión Nacional para el Desarrollo de los Pueblos Indígenas (National

Commission for the Development of Indigenous Communities), Unidad de Escritores Mayas-Zoques (Union of Maya-Zoque Writers), and Centro Estatal de Lenguas, Arte y Literatura Indígenas (State Center for Indigenous Languages, Art, and Literature, CELALI). All the authors, however, have participated in the language and art workshops as well as the credential programs that CELALI offers. The sense of collective experience generated through their shared participation is captured in the close collaboration of writers and artists in the literature.

But as the contemporary literary movement has flourished, and as literary productions grow, what are the building blocks central to this restoration process? And what worlds are rebuilt and revealed as a result? Through the gaze of *caracoleando*, I examine the selected visual and written narratives and the process of rescuing, reclaiming, and rebuilding that writers and artists undertake in their works to restore relations with their Maya worldviews. What I suggest is that in the process of rebuilding and reconstructing this new vision of their Maya worlds, writers and artists rescue fragments of their Maya epistemologies that are essential to restoring their relations with Maya worlds. This practice is part of recentering themselves within their Maya worldviews as carriers of knowledges and millennia-old traditions.

Spiritual Beliefs: The Power of Prayer in the Sustainment of Worldviews

This first section engages with the theme of spiritual beliefs that emerges in the literature through the power of prayer, as present in the poem "J-ilol: Rezador" (The one who prays) from the poetry collection *Yi' Beltak ch'ulelaletik: Raíces del alma* (Roots of the soul, 2007) by Tsotsil poet Enriqueta Lunez, whose poetry is also examined in chapter 1. The themes are further examined in the novel *Te'eltik ants: Mujer de la montaña* (Woman of the mountain, 2011) by Josías López Gómez (Tseltal), who previously used the name Josías López K'ana (López K'ana et al. [1999] 2012). The novel is considered the first of its genre in Maya literatures of Chiapas (Arias 2017–18, 2:277). Alongside this literature, I consider the visual narrative of internationally known visual artist Antun Kojtom Lam (Tseltal) (2007a) titled "j-ilol" (the one who prays). With art exhibits in various parts of the Americas and Europe, Kojtom Lam continues to teach younger generations of artists and collaborate with Maya writers of Chiapas. For the purpose of this chapter, I am only using the visual narrative included in Lunez's poetry collection *Yi' Beltak ch'ulelaletik.*

I begin with the poem "J-ilol: Rezador" by Lunez (2007, 47–48), whose work encapsulates themes central to Maya worldviews, specifically the relations of life and death rooted in a spiritual belief system that sees life as a continuum.

J-ILOL	*REZADOR*	*THE ONE WHO PRAYS*
Jvulvunel ta sa'el skoltael	Clamor insoslayable	Unstoppable clamor
nijil patalot ta yolon yok.	te remite ante sus pies.	prostrates you at its feet.
Ti ak'ope ta xich' a'yel	Oída tu voz	Heard your voice
ti ch'ulelale cha sutesbe,	al alma sin rumbo,	you return to the aimless soul,
ti sbek'tal mu skan xch'aye.	le devuelves el cuerpo	the body
	que no quiere perder.	it does not want to lose.

In "The one who prays," Lunez shows how the one beholding the gift of healing through prayer navigates the liminal space of the dead and the living. Through the verbalization of "Unstoppable clamor," the one who prays cuts through the boundaries of space and creates a bridge for the body and spirit. Language, the way the words shape and give meaning to prayer in this context, becomes the cure that heals and brings the body and spirit together. The language in the offering of the prayer creates movement and becomes central to the translation between the two spaces. "Heard your voice," the poet states, pointing to the moment the language acts as a course of healing for the body and spirit toward the rebuilding of the fractured relation. The poem itself is a creation of movement—*caracoleando* among dimensions of time and place—and of life and death. The words that give way to language set the space in motion, as captured in the meanings of "clamor" and "Heard your voice" (hearing), as well as in the notion of "aimless soul" (wandering soul). Language thus enters this space to ground the movement, brings together the fragments, and restores the relation of the body and spirit, which are out of line with each other.

The themes that emerge from Lunez's poem are grounded in Maya belief systems of renewal of the spirit, and the building and restoring of relations within their Maya worldview. These relations can also be understood in the context of the human-*nawal* relations Nathan C. Henne meticulously analyzes in *Reading Popol Wuj* (2020, 166), where he writes that the *nawal* (or *nahual*, as others write it) "is determined by the alignment of realms at the specific place and moment in time a person is born." Furthermore, he notes, "generally speaking, the *nawal* . . . links a specific person and some related, but nonhuman, co-essence together in a bond that mutually defines their collective being" (141). This human-*nawal* relation—or co-essence, as the term Henne prefers to use in this context—is interactive, two complementary parts of one whole. Henne's extensive analysis of the various translations and editions of the *Popol Vuh*, the sacred book of the Maya, supports these relations to affirm that this co-essence exists for life and is nurtured through prayer and other spiritual practices.[1]

In *Mayan Tales from Zinacantán: Dreams and Stories from the People of the Bat* (1997), U.S. anthropologist Robert M. Laughlin transcribes the stories Zinacantecs have shared with him over decades, during his long trajectory working with this Tsotsil community.[2] The stories capture the worldview of the Zinacantecs, their relation to the dream world, cycles of life, human and other-than-human relations, and the power of prayer and ceremony. One theme in his collection of stories is the impact on the communities when ceremonial practices are interrupted. The reasons for the interruption are not stated, but the impact of the absence of offerings (food, flowers, candles, drinks) and prayer central to the ceremonies is clearly manifested in physical illnesses in the communities, hopelessness, and broken social relations. The moral of the stories is the value of ceremony and power of prayer in the sustainment of their worldviews.

Victor Montejo (Jakaltek) (2001, 177–78) similarly contributes to this discourse, stating that Maya cosmology comprises "a three-dimensional relationship—humans, environment, and the supernatural or spiritual world." The ongoing dialogue of this relationship takes place through prayer and is rooted in the teachings of the *Popol Vuh*. Montejo (2004, 2005) agrees with Henne (2020) on the human and other-than-human relation that is established at birth. Montejo connects this relation to an animal spirit that resides in the sacred mountains associated with the community; throughout their life, a person honors the spirit of the animal through offerings and prayer. This offering and prayer takes place at the individual and collective level. When the animal spirit becomes ill, the person manifests this illness physically, and the co-essence also suffers. Ceremony and prayer become essential to the healing of these relations.

The *Popol Vuh* captures this relation in the way the forefathers (first mothers and first fathers) of the Maya peoples create humans out of maize. According to the narrative (*Popol Vuh* 1950, 2009; Henne 2020), the decision to create humans was reached during a council meeting of the first mothers and fathers, which was witnessed by the moon, sun, and stars. The decision was reached at the moment when darkness was fading and sunlight was rising. Animals such as the crow and coyote contributed to this creation by bringing ears of corn to the forefathers to create the dough to make humans and the food to nourish them. In this way, all these elements came together to form the world, and, as demanded by the forefathers, this is a symbiotic relationship that must be honored with offerings and prayers. An understanding of these horizontal and inclusive relationships with all that inhabits the cosmos infuses the works of Maya writers and artists I present in this chapter. Their work highlights the notion that survival, and importantly the survival of their worldviews, depends on the respect and honoring of these relations.

The themes that emerge in Lunez's poem of the various parts of the self that make the self whole express shared Indigenous belief practices. Such is the case of the work of Paula Gunn Allen (Laguna Pueblo/Sioux) in *The Sacred Hoop* (1986, 60), where she writes that "the natural state of existence is whole" and emphasizes the power of ceremony and "healing chants" to re-create the "harmony of the whole." The "whole" that Allen writes about includes human and other-than-human relations, all of them part of the circle of life, which is in continuous movement. *Caracoleando* encompasses these relations and practices of the Tsotsil worldviews, which are in conversation with Indigenous belief systems that ground people to place. These practices also connect Maya peoples' values and relations, which are nourished as they are essential for survival. Language is used to articulate these relations and to reveal the "truths that give to humanity its greatest significance and dignity" (P. G. Allen 1986, 55). Thus, according to Allen's statement, the ceremonial practices that Maya peoples nurture as articulated through the language of written and visual narratives speak of maintaining these relations in balance, inclusively and completely.

The themes of spiritual beliefs that emerge in the literature through the power of prayer continue in the novel *Te'eltik ants: Mujer de la montaña* (Woman of the mountain, 2011) by Tseltal writer Josías López Gómez. The novel centers on the daily life of Petrona and her activities as a daughter, wife, mother, and community member. When Petrona marries Martín, they follow tradition by settling in his community. Shortly after the move, they are invited to participate in the planning committee for the annual celebration of the water well, where they learn just how this celebration came to be central to the welfare of the community.

The community's story begins in a timeless period, when the people of Jolbaetik, the land of Martín's family, suffered a terrible drought:

> Cuentan los abuelos de los Jolbaetik que hace años el Dios del agua no envió lluvia, el sol quemó tanto que dejó sin agua al pozo. Nadie recordaba algo así, ni los más viejos del linaje de esa época, nunca padecieron una tragedia semejante.
>
> The grandfathers of the Jolbaetik recount that many years ago the God of Water did not send rain, the sun burnt so much that it left the well with no water. No one remembered anything like this, not even the oldest of the lineage of that time, never did they suffer such tragedy. (213)

In dreams, one of the eldest elders of the lineage of that time saw himself before the guardians of the true men and women (Tatil me'iletik) of Oxchuc and begged them for water. The guardians listened and agreed to provide the water he requested to end the community's suffering. In exchange, the community was to honor the guardians once a year with a ceremony. From this time on, the people of Jolbaetik have honored the true men and women of Oxchuc with an annual celebration that lasts all day and all night. The celebration takes places near the water well, where members of the community engage in prayer, place offerings of incense and candles to the owners of the water, and partake of food, music, and dance. This is how the Tseltal men and women of the land of Jolbaetik restored their relation with their creators, the true men and women of Oxchuc. The practice and continuance of this ceremony, as the story tells, are essential to their sustainment as a people as it roots them within their Tseltal worldviews.

The three-dimensional relationship of humans, environment, and spiritual world that is central to Maya cosmology is captured in the artwork of Tseltal artist Antun Kojtom Lam (2007a), in his piece titled "j-ilol" (the one who prays). The art piece, as the title indicates, centers on the one who prays, as he appears kneeling, holding his hands tightly together and arms close to his body, and staring attentively ahead. Several speech scrolls emerge out of his mouth, capturing in this way the ceremonial act of praying that is taking place and the offering of the prayer. The passage of time is depicted through the lit candles in various sizes lined up before him, along with a smoking incense burner. The ceremony takes place in an open field, surrounded by mountains as if to frame the sacredness of the place. One big cloud is positioned on top of one set of mountains, and a second cloud hangs at the head level of the one who prays. A person is standing on top of this cloud; their upper body is not revealed, but the bottom half wears a long gown, showing bare feet. Two small heads emerge from the bottom of this cloud, facing the direction of the one who prays and staring ahead as if looking straight at the mountains. In this piece, the artist unveils the liminal space created by "the one who prays," a space where the spirit and physical world meet through prayer. The open field where the ceremony takes place shows the importance of nature and the environment and brings together Maya notions of sacredness. Though this image is fixed in this moment of prayer, the smoke emerging from the incense burner, the flame of the candles, and the speech scrolls that reach the cloud create a sacred interaction that brings life and movement to this art piece. The prayer connects to the spirit world and bridges this present (time and space) to a practice that travels back millennia.

Spiritual Beliefs: The Rebalancing of Natural and Animal Worlds

The themes of spiritual beliefs, cultural practices, and Maya cosmology are woven further into the novel *Te'eltik ants: Mujer de la montaña*, as this section explores. The analysis of the novel that frames this section is placed alongside another visual narrative of Kojtom Lam's (2007d), this one titled "ta ba mukinal" (about the burial). In the novel, the discussion of Petrona's experiences highlights the importance of the renewal of spirit that accompanies Maya cycles of life. When Petrona first moves into her husband's community, they face several hardships. On this occasion, the heavy rains have destroyed the family's cornfield, its primary source of sustenance for the year. After struggling for months, Martín, Petrona's husband, decides to take on the difficult task of clearing a new space in the jungle and preparing the soil for a new cornfield. They are successful in their effort, but the harvest does not come in time to ease the hunger the family is experiencing. In a moment of desperation, Petrona goes to the field and picks the fresh corn. She knows that this will affect their harvest, but she is determined to do something for her starving children. While out in the cornfield lamenting her situation, she is visited by Jch'ulme'tik (Madre Luna or Mother Moon), the feminine goddess from whom all proceeds, who provides light to all living beings, and who embraces all people inside her own being when their days are over (López Gómez 2011, 270).

While contemplating the cornfield, Petrona hears a female voice tell her not to worry, and to take as much corn as she needs because her days of suffering are nearing an end. Mother Moon addresses her by saying:

> Escúchame, hija mía. Vengo de muy lejos, donde surge la mujer Venus, la estrella de la mañana, la mujer de la luz que barre todos los días el camino del padre sol. Escuché tu nombre, vine a hablarte, vine a conocerte. Tu humildad, tu paciencia ha llegado hasta los misteriosos lugares de los seres *ch'ul jme'il jtatiletik*. No entristezcas tu corazón, te ayudaré.
>
> Listen, my daughter. I come from far away, from where the woman Venus rises, the morning star, the woman of light that sweeps the road every day for father sun. I heard your name, I came to talk to you, I came to meet you. Your humbleness, your patience has reached the mysterious places of the *ch'ul jme'il jtatiletik* beings. Do not make your heart sad, I will help you. (271)

The two women engage in dialogue, leading Petrona to take as many ears of corn as she needs to feed her family. Petrona fills her net as full as possible, but when her husband, enraged by Petrona's actions, visits the cornfield the following day to examine the loss, he finds the cornfield intact. Petrona's heart is full of gratitude, as the visit of Madre Luna confirms her faith in always honoring Mother Earth and reciprocal relations with the land. When recounting the story, Petrona explains that she was in a dreamlike state during the encounter. Her description hints at a shifting state of mind as she entered new spaces, navigating the physical and spiritual world through prayer while pleading for viable solutions. Though the world around may seem to stand still for Petrona, the encounter creates much movement.

This encounter also occurs while Petrona is in the cornfield, out in nature, amid the milpa and the sounds of the jungle, under the sky and the bright sun. Petrona is reflecting on her situation and possible actions, and the offering of one final prayer is recognized by the presence of Madre Luna. The book presents Petrona as a woman of great faith, someone responsible and hardworking. The encounter assures her of the importance of continuing these relations with all (family, community, cosmos). The corn is a gift in recognition of Petrona's good relations with the world. When Petrona wants to hug Madre Luna to thank her, the latter reminds Petrona that she is an intangible being, leaving no misunderstanding as to the collapsing of the spirit and nonspirit world that is taking place at this moment. The ceremonial and sacred act of this encounter is made possible because of Petrona's ongoing efforts to honor her traditions and make offerings in gratitude of the creators.

These connections are also captured in Kojtom Lam's (2007d) visual narrative "ta ba mukinal" (about the burial), where the artist portrays a ceremonial gathering of the community in a cemetery. The ceremonial act is indicated through the flowers and candles placed throughout the burial sites, as well as through the kneeling figures and bowed heads, indicating offered prayers. The ongoing movement in this image is captured through the different stages entailed in setting up the altars, and the passage of time is shown through the dripping candles of different sizes. The women in the art piece wear the traditional *traje* of San Juan Chamula. Suspended in space, above all the men and women who are in prayer, is a woman who is also wearing her traditional Chamula *traje*. From her waist down, however, she is wrapped in flowers, and with her right hand she waves a piece of printed paper. The position of this arm and the way the flowers travel down her body suggest motion. Elevated at the same level as the woman, a set of hands emerge from the side of the art piece, with speech scrolls coming out of the hands. This action adds to the idea that someone is receiving the offering of prayer, creating a sense of movement. The ceremonial practice of prayer facilitates an occupation of in-between spaces.

The literary and visual narratives presented in this chapter thus far engage with a process of *caracoleando* that speaks of Maya peoples' human and other-than-human relations, the movement created while navigating liminal spaces, and the ways Indigenous peoples choose to look inside their own knowledges and traditions in moments of stress. Allen (1986, 55) adds to the power of these practices when she writes, "The tribes seek—through song, ceremony, legend, sacred stories (myths), and tales—to embody, articulate, and share reality, to bring the isolated, private self into harmony and balance with this reality, to verbalize the sense of the majesty and reverent mystery of all things, and to actualize, in language, those truths that give to humanity its greatest significance and dignity." Thus, Allen reaffirms the power of the narratives that capture Indigenous worldviews. Through the articulation of these relations, Indigenous peoples shape their lives and emphasize all that is important to them in the world.

Cycles of Life: Healing and the Renewal of Spirit

Cycles of life, as well as notions of the different spaces the body and spirit occupy, are central to Maya worldviews, as is shown in the poems "Vobil Vayich: Delirio" (Delirium) by Enriqueta Lunez (Tsotsil) (2007, 26) and "Xch'ulel jmam: Espíritu del abuelo" (Spirit of Grandfather) by Adriana del Carmen López Sántiz (Tseltal) from her poetry collection *Jalbil k'opetik: Palabras tejidas* (Woven words, 2005). The poems are analyzed in this section alongside a visual narrative from Kojtom Lam (2007e) titled "vo'ne xatal" (long ago). I begin with Lunez's poem "Delirium."

VOBIL VAYICH	*DELIRIO*	*DELIRIUM*
Te xi niknun	Temblaba	Trembling
ja no'ox jna	solo recuerdo	I just remember
ti te xi niknun	que temblaba	trembling
k'alal li julab	al despertar	on awaking
la kil mu chamen vinik	vi aquel cuerpo	I saw that body
li bucho'o chamem	el muerto	the dead one
vu'un la jvektal kil.	era yo.	was me.

The poet captures in this poem the meanings of a body in constant movement. With the opening line, "Trembling," the poet sets this relation of in-between spaces in motion. The subject of the poem experiences the shaking of the body, but remembers nothing else. A shift occurs when the poet writes "on awaking," noting the coming into awareness of the subject, who sees at this moment a prone body, dead and motionless. "[It] was me," the poet writes as a concluding line, playing with the subject and emphasizing the multiple spaces the subject occupies in these seven lines. The person is dead, and in the articulation of the transition the poet bridges the physical and spiritual worlds the spirit navigates. The movement that Lunez creates is not just in the overall meaning of the poem, but in the words that she also chooses—"trembling," "remember[ing]," "saw" (seeing)—all words that capture the actions of a subject who seems to be giving testimony on the experience of death. The movement the poem creates illustrates renewal processes, transformative actions, and ceremonial practices that sustain life cycles.

These themes continue in López Sántiz's (2005, 69) poem "Spirit of Grandfather" (see pages 72–73 for the full text). In this poem, López Sántiz takes the reader on the journey of a ceremony for the grandfather, who has transitioned into the spirit world. Throughout the poem, the poet navigates the in-between space of the spirit and physical world, revealing the complexities of these relationships and the importance of sustaining them. The poem is a conversation with the grandfather, as the poet opens with a question—"how do you find yourself?"—followed by another, asking whether the grandfather has been able to protect himself from "the angel of ill." Through the exchanges, the poet emphasizes the protection afforded by the ceremony and identifies the offerings that will help her grandfather transition into the spirit world and protect him on his journey. There are candles to light the grandfather's path, hard liquor to cease his thirst along the way, and marigolds to keep away the *pukuj* (bad spirits). The poet finishes by stating that she will offer final prayers to keep her grandfather from the *k'atimbak* (underworld, glossed in a note appended to the Spanish-language version as *inframundo*).

The articulation of prayers central to the ceremony collapses the physical and spirit world and creates a timeless space where the poet can reach out to her grandfather and present him with offerings for his protection. The offering of prayers is to help her grandfather move away from chaos and unbalanced relations. Another theme that emerges is the idea that even after the person transitions to the spirit world, their work continues. The poet demonstrates that to maintain all good relations in balance, an ongoing dialogue with the cosmos and all that is part of it must continue. The ceremony thus becomes "the ritual enactment of a specialized perception of a cosmic relationship" (P. G. Allen 1986, 61). Through this ceremony, the poet reestablishes her relationship with her grandfather and, in turn, their relationship with the cosmos.

The importance of a renewal of spirit is central to the poems presented in this section. In this relation, death is part of the cycle of life, of one's passing to the spirit world and to another life-form; death is not an end. The honoring of this relation takes place through ceremony and the offering of prayers, which, as the poems show, is an interactive spiritual practice.

These themes are captured in Kojtom Lam's (2007e) visual narrative "vo'ne xatal" (long ago). The artist brings into this piece Maya beliefs of death and cyclical relations to time central to the continuance of these communities. In the art piece, a woman sits on a small hill, facing the sky, which is covered by seventeen small suns and twenty-three small moons. They are all different sizes. Some suns have faces looking in different directions, some are small circles with radiant lights encircling them, and others contain a face with no radiant light. The moons are different sizes and shapes as well, depicting the different lunar phases and thus the passage of time. The woman looks in the direction of the sky, yet only a partial side of her face is revealed, though it also seems that the suns and moons are looking at her, each with a different expression on its face. She wears her traditional *traje* of San Juan Chamula and is barefoot, sitting with her hands on her lap. She sits there, timeless, at the center of the piece. Next to her, at the foot of the small hill, a naked body sticks out, the head of the body seemingly half buried, just below

XCH'ULEL JMAM

JMAM, ¿BIN AWILEL?
¿akananteyoj aba yu'un te yabat
pukuje?
Talemon k'alal le'to yu'un tal japbat
kantelaetik yu'un ya xojobtes ach'enal
xnich trawo yu'un ya ach'abtes atakin
ti'il.

Sok kich'oj batel
xnichimal tusus,
te ya xiwtes pukuj ta sbonil.
Yo'tik ini xch'abajonix ta atojol
yu'un ayuk awu'un slamal k'inal
sok yu'u manchuk sbaat ta k'atinbak.

a simple cross. The body lies in an angle toward the foot of the hill, hands on the side, hair loose, and a facial expression of calmness, showing a partial smile. The hair is loose, falling and hugging the neck, and at the base of the left hand lies a small new moon. The body appears to have the anatomy of a woman, but the long facial hair deceives the reader of the painting. Perhaps the artist is marking with this the passage of time, as hair is believed to continue growing after death. Life and death lie next to each other, as the two bodies occupy different spaces, as if existing in parallel universes. There is a sense of stillness in the position of the bodies, but the images of the moons and suns convey a sense of motion as well. The bodies exist in relation to the whole that surrounds them; they come into being in relation to the cosmos that is watching and, perhaps, listening too.

Sources of Knowledge: Other Ways of Knowing

The theme of sources of knowledge, as well as knowledge production, is captured in another poem from López Sántiz, "Te binti ijkitabil: Herencia" (Heritage), published in the poetry collection *Jalbil k'opetik: Palabras tejidas* (2005), as well as in the poem "Sejk'arak'ub: El arcoíris" (The rainbow) by

ESPÍRITU DEL ABUELO

ABUELO, ¿CÓMO TE ENCUENTRAS?
¿te has cuidado del ángel del mal?
He venido hasta aquí para ofrecerte
velas que alumbren tu sepultura,
aguardiente para calmar tu sed.

También traigo
flores de cempasúchil
cuyo color ahuyenta el *pukuj*.
Ahora rezaré por ti
para que tengas paz
y evites el *k'atimbak*.

SPIRIT OF GRANDFATHER

GRANDFATHER, HOW DO YOU FIND YOURSELF?
have you protected yourself from the angel of ill?
I have come all the way here to offer you
candles to light up your grave,
hard liquor to quench your thirst.

I also bring
marigolds
whose color banishes the *pukuj*.
Now I will pray for you
so you can have peace
and you can avoid the *k'atimbak*.

TE BINTI IJKITABIL

T'ANAL OK MAM

koltayawon ta beel ta sba tonetik,
ta xch'ixal kuxlejal;
ak'bon jnop ya'yejal te sk'ayoj
amayetik sok arpaetike.

Ya jk'an kil te binti maba ya kil,
kich'bey yik' te bin maba kich'bey yik',
ta stael te melelil be
yu'un sbeentesel nopibaletik te bayal sbonil.

Jal ch'ajan mam
albon bit'il ya jtiles k'opetik,
bit'iil ya jch'al ta te'eltik mut te beetike;

ak'bon jnop xcholel te wayichetick,
ta stsalel te nak'bil xiwele.
¡Maba ya jk'an meba ya xjilon!
Mam,
¡ak'bon jilel snabete'ul ap'ijil!

HERENCIA

ABUELO DE PIES DESCALZOS
ayúdame a caminar sobre las piedras,
por los espinales de la vida;
enséñame a entender el cántico
de las flautas y las arpas.

Quiero mirar lo que no veo,
respirar lo que no respiro,
encontrar el camino verdadero
para transitar los pensamientos coloridos.

Abuelo tejedor
dime cómo resplandecer palabras,
cómo adornar con pájaros los senderos;

enséñame a descifrar sueños,
a enfrentar ocultos temores.
¡No quiero quedarme huérfana!
Abuelo,
¡déjame el bastón de tu sabiduría!

HERITAGE

GRANDFATHER OF BARE FEET
help me to walk on the stones,
by the spinals of life;
teach me to understand the song
of the flutes and harps.

I want to see what I do not see,
to breathe what I do not breathe,
to find the true path
to travel the colorful thoughts.

Grandfather weaver
tell me how to make words bloom,
how to decorate the paths with birds;

teach me how to decipher dreams
to face hidden fears
I do not want to stay an orphan!
grandfather,
leave me the baton of your wisdom.

José Osbaldo García Muñoz (Mam), published in the poetry collection *Snojk'ental beel ta Yaxinal u Nichimal k'op: Versos y huellas bajo la luna* (Verses and footprints under the moon), edited by Armando Sánchez Gómez and Carlos Córdova Solís (2011). The poems are analyzed alongside two visual narratives: one from Marlene Rodríguez Gómez (Tseltal) titled "La luna centellea" (The moon twinkles), published in the poetry collection *Sab xojob: Vapor de luz* (Vapors of light, 2007), edited by Armando Sánchez Gómez and José Antonio Reyes Matamoros, and one from Kojtom Lam (2007b) titled "l'amtabanejetik: llamador" (Caller). A return to López Gómez's novel *Te'eltik ants: Mujer de la montaña* closes this section on other ways of knowing. I begin with the poem by López Sántiz (see pages 74–75 for the full text).

In this poem, López Sántiz once again, like in "Spirit of Grandfather," calls on her grandfather, but in this case she is not offering protection through prayer but rather pleading for teachings that encapsulate their worldview. The poet wants to learn to walk through the difficulties of life, to listen to the sounds of the world around, to see the offerings the world provides, and to speak truths and beauty. Simple teachings she is requesting, but teachings that make sense of her world rooted in Maya cosmology, where the natural world and animal world are carriers of knowledges—and her grandfather holds the wisdom to decipher them. There is another element to these teachings and worldview that the poet highlights, which is that wisdom comes with living and age, and thus the importance of relations with elders.

The poet conveys a tone of longing, a feeling of anguish, as if she is working against time to learn from her grandfather before it is too late. The poet recognizes that without this knowledge she will continue to feel fractured, and that all the pieces can only come together with teachings from her grandfather so as to lead her to the path of truth. The movement the poem creates centers on the actions the poet seeks in every piece of knowledge passed on to her. That is, the poet does not just seek to become the recipient of knowledge, but desires to embody this knowledge as well, as the last two stanzas demonstrate. The pleading tone reads as a prayer to her grandfather. She continues this tone to the end of the poem as she expresses fears of becoming an orphan without her grandfather's knowledge. This theme of rescuing pieces of histories that are essential to the continuity of Indigenous peoples is carried through the poem.

The relations of longing, learning, and teaching that López Sántiz conveys are captured in an acrylic by Tseltal artist Marlene Rodríguez Gómez (2007) titled "La luna centellea" (The moon twinkles). The background of the piece is a dark blue sky full of stars, with a full moon to the right of the frame. A light, scattered fog covers the sky and touches on the green mountains. A small hut sits to the left of the mountains, and an old man who sits on a small bench and smokes a cigar takes center stage to the right of the hut. The ground is green, covered with little plants, and a big blooming tobacco plant stands to the right of the old man. He sits calmly, holding his cigar, staring straight ahead. His head is full of white hair, and the expression of his face is not clear; only his dark round eyes under a set of white eyebrows are visible. He sits with legs stretched out, arms folded, under the light of the moon and stars. The man looks like he could be the grandfather López Sántiz writes about, calm and quiet, sitting in the center of his world, full of wisdom, full of calmness—a world that the poet López Sántiz yearns for and attempts to piece together through the language of her poem.

There is a reclamation of the familiar in both the poem by López Sántiz and the art piece by Rodríguez Gómez. The knowledge that López Sántiz desires entails the everyday activities of her grandfather, and the image that Rodríguez Gómez captures in her art piece reads like an everyday occurrence. It is in these relations that we can read the concept of *caracoleando*, as the artist and poet circle on the simplicity of everyday life and the intricacies of their world, where knowledges are carried by elders and grandfathers: thus the importance of maintaining relations to restore their balance in the world. These themes also emerge in the poem "Sejk'arak'ub: El arcoíris" (The rainbow) by Mam poet José Osbaldo García Muñoz (2011) (see pages 78–79 for the full text).

García Muñoz writes about witnessing the birth of a rainbow out of a drop of rain that falls on the leaf of a tree. This is no ordinary rainbow, as the poet describes its precious characteristics as those of a newborn baby. So precious it is that the poet decides to take the rainbow home to look after and feed with "chunks of soil with drops of rain." They become each other's companions, spending the days wandering around the fields of corn and the nights chasing stars. The analogy that the poet develops captures the notion of the rainbow as an awakening or origin of a sense of consciousness. The poet further develops this idea when writing at the end of the poem that during moonless nights, "when the fear of the family awakens / I will take it between my open hands / so that the light of the house is turned on again." Through this action the poet highlights the importance of an emerging awareness of the need to protect himself and those around him, and in a way his most precious weapon of defense is this newly gained knowledge and perspective on the world. The poet articulates this awakening of consciousness as a rainbow

SEJK'ARAK'UB

Ta wel ya'benalte' xnik' xt'ula soel
te ja'
xch'abana ye' yilel ta sit te sejk'arak'ub
sjach' sk'ab, stij ya' jich bit'il tok'el
alal.

sak' t'ujbilnax te sbonile
ya xbo'on sok
ya kanantay ta sepsepbil ixtabil ta
wayib
ta jujun sakubel kínal bakel lum yilel
t'ulujt'ulja'ya kabey swe'

ta yolil ixmaltik, nichimetik ya
xbenotik
lom joybatik xbenotik ka'aytik
ta yanil xojobil ejk'etik

ta tsaj, ta sak
jich ay stael te kuxineltik

ta ajk'abal k'alal mayuk xojobil u
k'alal xiw ta st'unel te me'tatile
ya mukbe'el ta k'u' jpak'
yu'un jich ya xch' xojoba ta yutil na.

EL ARCOÍRIS

De la gota que bota en la hoja de un
árbol temblón
un arcoíris de ojos y boca halagüeña
estira los brazos y piernas imitando
un bebé.

qué colores más limpios tiene
he de llevarlo conmigo,
lo guardaré en una esfera junto a mi
cama
y cada mañana trozos de tierra
con gotas de lluvia le daré de comer

en los maizales y flores del campo
andaremos
como buenos amigos echaremos a andar
tras las estrellas nocturnas

¡rojas y blancas!
Todos los días la vida nos hallará

y en las noches sin luna
cuando el miedo a la familia despierte
lo llevaré entre mis manos abiertas
para que la luz de la casa se vuelva a
encender.

THE RAINBOW

Of the drop that bounces on the leaf
of a trembling tree
a rainbow of eyes and flattering mouth
stretches its arms and legs imitating
a baby.

what clear colors it has
I must take him with me,
I'll keep it in a sphere next to
my bed
and every morning I will feed him
chunks of soil with drops of rain

among the cornfields and wildflowers
we will walk
as good friends we will walk
after the night stars

red and white!
Everyday life will find us

and on moonless nights
when the fear of the family awakens
I will take it between my open hands
so that the light of the house is turned
on again.

that on a given day was born, fragile as a baby, but that with proper care becomes his strongest form of protection. New relations are thus established, with the rainbow as an analogy for the importance of restoring relations that have perhaps been lost and recaptured, and that are fragile yet strong enough to nurture his continuance. The human environment and spirit world are thus brought together in this poem as well, with its recognition of the interconnectedness of all that is part of the cosmos.

Subcomandante Marcos, spokesperson of the Zapatista Army of National Liberation (EZLN), demonstrates these relations of interconnectedness in "The Story of Questions" (2001), where he places the importance of dialoguing to create movement as central to the formation of Maya worldviews.[3] In "The Story of Questions," Marcos narrates a short story on how the very first gods, Ik'al and Votán, set the world in motion through the practice of asking. According to the story, Ik'al and Votán were opposites. "One was light, like a May morning in the river. The other was dark and cold like night in a cave. They were the same. The two were one, because the one made the other." They are two entities from one source, a relation rooted in Maya worldviews, where complementary forces and relations are at the center of the world. At the beginning of time Ik'al and Votán were motionless, standing still, pulling in opposite directions and bored with nowhere to go. "'Let's walk,' said the one, who was two. 'How?' asked the other. 'Where?' asked the first," and with this exchange, they took a step in the same direction. They liked the sort of dance this movement created and begin to move forward: "the Gods walk with questions and never stop" (93–94).

Tsotsil artist Kojtom Lam (2007b) also captures this relation of dialogue and movement rooted in Maya worldviews in his piece titled "I'amtabanejetik: llamador" (caller). In this piece, the artist depicts the world with five coyotes lying around a small road, a bird flying above them, and an owl sitting on the branch of the only tree in the frame. Speech scrolls emerge from all the animals' mouths and from the opening on the top of the only house present. The small road that cuts through the image has prints of bare human feet going in both directions, showing in this way transit over the road. This movement brings the image to life and acts as a reminder of the fluidity and vividness of all that inhabits the world and cosmos. There is a sense of calmness in this scene, a visible balance, as if in all the movement captured through the speech scrolls that emerge from the animal and natural world, the world reaches equilibrium.

Beth Brant (Mohawk) writes about these horizontal relations in the natural world in her book of short stories *Food and Spirits* (1991). Central to the creation of the world, as her story "This Is History" shows, is the importance of close interactions among the natural, animal, spiritual, and human worlds. In "This Is History," Brant narrates the story of Sky Woman, who, following her curiosity, falls from the sky on top of Turtle's back, which soon comes to be the earth. The animals guide her toward food for survival, and Mother Earth herself nurtures her through life, always reminding her to honor the earth through care and respect. When Sky Woman dies, she asks her daughter, First Woman, to bury her heart and to cut the rest of her into little pieces and "fling them into the sky" (25). This is how Sky Woman also gives birth to the moon and stars. Sky Woman left her sky people, the world that she knew, to embark on a new adventure, one that gives birth to life on earth. She had great curiosity, always asking questions about all that there was around her. When she fell from the sky, her inquiring mind led to her survival. In order to survive, she recognized the value of reciprocal relations, of respect and honor for all that surrounded her, and together they gave birth to the human world.

Rigoberta Menchú (K'iche'), human rights activist and the first Indigenous woman to receive the Nobel Peace Prize (in 1992), shares this perspective of the world in *I, Rigoberta Menchú* (1984), stating that K'iche' children begin learning in the womb. Pregnant women walk around the fields and mountains, talking to their unborn children. The mother-to-be points out different animals and plants found near home, so that the child can begin to recognize and learn to name the world around them (27–28). The dialogue that takes place between the world of the unborn child and the world of the mother-to-be creates a solid relation between the two. As Menchú notes, when the baby is born, the child enters a world that is already part of their memory, where the mother has already established a bridge of understanding for their survival. In this tradition, the mother has already given what López Sántiz is still pleading to gain from her grandfather in the poem opening this section.

What Brant and Menchú highlight in their works is that relations with the world do not exist in isolation; rather, there is an ongoing conversation essential for the continuance of life, an active dialoguing that is part of survival, as López Gómez's novel *Te'eltik ants: Mujer de la montaña* (2011) also demonstrates. In this novel, the theme of dialogues of understanding rooted in Indigenous knowledge systems is seen through the establishment of the school in Petrona's community and the arrival of the first teacher. Daniel Mena is a formally educated Tsotsil man who decides to return home to teach the children in the communities. When Mena first arrives, he is not well received, especially because his presence obliges parents to send their sons to school or receive a fine for the violation. The parents have no money to pay a fine, and they need their sons to help them work the cornfields. Tensions thus arise, and the community turns against the teacher. He responds to these tensions by calling a meeting with the elders of the community. The teacher asks the elders for permission to join their community and to consult with them on matters related to school and the education of the children. Though the school is out of the purview of the elders, the teacher invites them in since what happens in school has great impact in the community. The elders agree to welcome him as long as he abides by the community's rules and participates in all cultural and spiritual activities. As he begins to participate, relations shift and he is no longer seen as an outsider.

The move to ask to join the community reflects the understanding the teacher gains after he spends time in the community, works with the students, and gets into a few arguments with the parents. The teacher learns the new space that he is navigating, recognizes the contributions of all members in the community, and works toward the building of those relations. Just like Ik'al and Votán, as long as they pulled in opposite directions, the community and the teacher were at odds with each other. In order for this relation to work, these two forces had to work together and establish a dialogue of understanding, raising questions and agreeing on a direction to follow. And these relations are just what the works of these poets, writers, and artists in this section show. As artists, poets, and writers of Chiapas reclaim their Maya identity, they bring to the fore the complexities of their stories and

TEPNAX LA JNOP

La jkil buch mamal k'antulante'
balenta ch'in nichim ch'iem ta sk'ab
—ja'kati te jmame—
ch'ay beel ta k'inal sok sbijil
tebnax la jnop.

the ongoing negotiations they engage in to survive. They emphasize in the process that all these efforts do not take place in isolation, but are part of an ongoing understanding with all the cosmos.

Knowledge Production: Fragments and the Rebuilding of a Worldview

The theme of carriers and producers of knowledge continues in the poem "Tepnax la jnop: Poco aprendí" (Little I learned) by Tseltal writer Armando Sánchez Gómez (2011), which is gathered in the same collection as García Muñoz's poem "The rainbow." The poem is analyzed alongside a visual narrative by Kojtom Lam (2007c) titled "nichimetik" (flowers). At the heart of these narratives is the importance of recognizing and rescuing knowledges housed in the communities, and the power of piecing them together. I begin with the poem from Sánchez Gómez (see pages 82–83 for the full text).

In the poem "Little I learned," Sánchez Gómez (2011) finds himself longing for knowledge his grandfather has taken with him to the spirit world. The poet talks about the broken branches of an old tree blooming despite its age. The small flowers represent for Sánchez Gómez the growing knowledge his grandfather carried. With this metaphor, Sánchez Gómez emphasizes the importance of recognizing the value of elders in the community as keepers and carriers of knowledge. His grandfather is gone, and with sadness the poet notes that he has learned very little. He is both acknowledging his shortcoming in learning from his grandfather and becoming aware of the knowledge he has yet to learn. The shift in gaze captured in the poem creates movement that speaks of the poet's effort to re-create his relation to the world through the fragments of knowledge available to him.

The messages that Sánchez Gómez reads in the fallen tree, and the ways he portrays this encounter as a message from a grandfather who has tran-

POCO APRENDÍ	*LITTLE I LEARNED*
Vi caer un árbol de k'antulante'	I saw a k'antulante tree fall
Lleno de flores pequeñas sobre sus ramas	Filled with small flowers on its branches
—era mi abuelo—	—it was my grandfather—
se fue con su sabiduría	he went with his wisdom
poco aprendí.	little I learned.

sitioned, connect to the essay "Land Speaking" by Okanagan author Jeannette C. Armstrong (1998). When writing about the importance of language and the interconnectedness of humans, land, and nature, Armstrong observes that the land is a carrier of knowledges and memories. As she walks the land, it whispers messages to her, and this in turn makes her a carrier of the language the land speaks. In this way, language is maintained through interaction with the environment, through a reciprocal relation with the world (Varese 2006). Both Armstrong and Sánchez Gómez read the messages of the land, deciphering what the land whispers. For Sánchez Gómez, the whispers take place through the blooming of flowers, and for Armstrong language is revealed in the palette of the landscape. Mapuche scholar Elicura Chihuailaf Nahuelpan, in his *Message to Chileans* (2009), speaks about the power of silence to facilitate learning from the world, and the power of knowledge that grows through silent exchanges. What these interactions also reveal is the ceremonial act of listening to the messages of the land, the attentiveness required, and the certitude of the understanding of language that is created as part of this interaction.

These relations of the land speaking are captured in Kojtom Lam's (2007c) visual narrative titled "nichimetik" (flowers). In the piece, a cornstalk sits in the middle of the frame. Two small plants (possibly bean plants) sit on either side of the cornstalk, at the base of the frame, and two larger ones (possibly coffee plants) frame the background. Two additional cornstalks hang from the top of the frame, facing down, altering with their presence the center of the frame. All the plants, however, appear to be in full bloom, alive and breathing. As the artist places the cornstalk, the maize, at the center of the frame, he is also recentering maize in his world and highlighting that this is the source and sustenance of life. There are no dialogue expressions, just an image that screams the centrality of maize in Maya cultures, and Kojtom Lam's desire to honor it in this art piece so that others can also remember that maize is the source of life.

Legacies as Recorders of Histories

The theme of Maya peoples as recorders of histories (a theme I explore further in chapter 3), writing about the world they know and sharing their knowledges and histories, emerges in the compilation *Memoria indígena de la revolución en Chiapas* (Indigenous memory of the revolution in Chiapas, 2010), edited by Enrique Pérez López (Tsotsil). During a presentation of the book in San Cristóbal de las Casas, Chiapas, in summer 2012, Pérez López noted that according to official history, the revolutionary wars did not reach the state of Chiapas. Thus, this publication is critical in bringing Indigenous voices to the centennial anniversary of the Mexican Revolution. In the stories collected, Pérez López addresses the complexities of this historical period in Chiapas, specifically the ways that various factions faced one another: "social factions (political proprietors), regional (confrontations between the cities of Tuxtla Gutierrez and San Cristóbal de las Casas), and state level (the reaction of farmers and proprietors in response to the intrusion of Carrancistas and Zapatistas to the state)" (9).[4]

This collection brings together Tseltal, Tsotsil, Ch'ol, Tojolabal, and Zoque stories about their experiences during the Mexican Revolution. Here, I focus on a single poem from the collection, "Conclusión" (Conclusion) by Jacinto Arias Pérez (Tsotsil) (2010). As I present in the introduction, Arias Pérez was the first Maya to leave his community in pursuit of postgraduate studies, and he is also a leading force in the Maya intellectual movement of Chiapas. In the poem, Arias Pérez addresses the main figures of the Mexican Revolution (Porfirio Díaz, Venustiano Carranza, Francisco I. Madero, Francisco Villa, and Emiliano Zapata) and denounces their actions during this historical period.[5] The title references the conclusion of the section in the collection, but also the conclusion of a historical period in Mexico and the impact that this had for Indigenous peoples of Chiapas.

In "Conclusion," Arias Pérez reflects on the power that Porfirio Díaz held for over thirty years; the initial bravery of Madero, father of the revolution, in taking Díaz out of office; and Madero's subsequent actions, which steered him away from the goals of the revolution (79). He notes the power of Carranza, who abolished the system of servitude that so affected Chiapas, but also recalls that Carranza's hunger for power led him to assassinate Madero, Zapata, and Villa. Arias Pérez stresses the role of Zapata and his greater desire for change than for power, and observes that though Carranza might have eliminated Zapata physically, he could not eradicate the leader from the minds and hearts of peoples. The poet concludes this poem by recognizing the work of President Lázaro Cárdenas, who ensured that land reform was implemented in Chiapas.[6] Arias Pérez's long denouncement reads like a litany, as if in the naming of all the wrongdoing in history against Indigenous peoples of Chiapas, new air is inhaled into their lives.

In Arias Pérez's process of remembering this anniversary, he brings these characters to life, lines them up before himself, and confronts them all with their brutal actions. He highlights the good deeds of those who kept the needs of the poor and the campesinos (corn and coffee planters) in mind because, as he says, "there are good / and bad governments." Time and space collapse, and through the words that Arias Pérez presents, language is formed by the raising of the voice of those who were silenced during this period of time, which moves beyond barriers of geohistories. In-between spaces are created, as Arias Pérez navigates present and past, questioning and denouncing the actions of these historical figures.

This exercise reflects the millennia-old practice among Maya peoples of recording their histories. Writing about Mesoamerican cultures, Mexican scholar Miguel León-Portilla (1996, 12) observes that the Maya developed a written system that captured "fully the sequence of thought and the expression of the word." In *Uk'u'x kaj, uk'u'x ulew: Antología de poesía maya guatemalteca contemporánea* (Anthology of contemporary Guatemalan Maya poetry, 2010) Emilio del Valle Escalante (K'iche') continues this conversation, emphasizing that the production of Maya poetry in Guatemala is consistent with the legacy of the written word central to Maya cultures. The resurgence of Maya writers of Guatemala in the last few decades, he adds, is the continuance of this legacy. Victor Montejo (Jakaltek) (2004) and Feliciano Sánchez Chan (Maya/Yucatec) (in Hernández-Ávila 2003) add to this conversation, noting that when the practice of writing has been interrupted, Maya peoples have always found ways to share their knowledges. At times, these acts of transmission have just been conducted in secrecy and enveloped in the practice of oral tradition. Gloria E. Chacón in *Indigenous Cosmolectics* (2018) describes the violent decentering of Indigenous knowledges that occurs through the imposition of the Latin alphabet, which favors the printed word over oral tradition, and observes the use of multimedia in Indigenous scholarship. When we move beyond the written text, Indigenous peoples' legacies as recorders of histories across millennia emerge. Paul M. Worley and Rita M. Palacios in *Unwriting Maya Literature* (2019) engage with this notion when they conceptualize *ts'íib* as a way to move beyond the written text in both the study and the production of Maya epistemologies. Herein lies the importance of the compilation *Memoria indígena de la revolución en Chiapas*: not only does the content bring to Indigenous communities a sense of dignity historically denied, but the work itself disrupts the official narrative that "la Revolución no llegó a Chiapas" (the revolution never reached Chiapas). Such is the power of Arias Pérez's poem, and the story the poem tells, to understand these relations to place, which Maya peoples continue to fiercely defend.

Conclusion: Restoring Relations to the World

On the eve of December 22, 2012, hundreds of Indigenous Maya members of the EZLN descended onto the city of San Cristóbal de las Casas to take part in what they called the Silent March of the Zapatistas. They gathered on the outskirts of the city and slowly and in a highly organized manner marched to the center of San Cristóbal. They were wearing their characteristically black ski masks and, on that rainy day, small ponchos to protect themselves from the light rain. A small platform was placed in front of the Cathedral of San Cristóbal, where a large group of observers watched as all the marchers walked across the platform raising their left fists, then continued their march to the outskirts of the city and back to their communities. The Zapatistas did not utter a single word during the course of the march; their presence, however, screamed through centuries of silences. "The ominous silence of the Zapatistas" was the headline of the coverage of the march the following day (EZLN 2012). After centuries of ongoing efforts to eliminate Indigenous peoples, pushing them to oblivion, Zapatistas chose this date (the last day of the cycle of the Maya calendar, 13 baktun) and place (the same place where on New Year's Eve 1994 they read to the world the First Declaration of the Lacandon Jungle [EZLN 1994a, 1994b]) to remind people of Chiapas, Mexico, and the world that the Maya presence continues. Such an act of *caracoleando* is depicted in this action, where the EZLN spiraled into the heart of Maya worldviews to affirm their continuous presence.

The Maya writers and artists in this chapter engage in a similar act through their literary and artistic productions, engaging *caracoleando* to reclaim their place within the long legacy of Maya writers and artists. They pick up their pen or brush to connect with their traditions, and embark on a journey guided by the knowledges of worldviews that they are rescuing. Their works reveal that in order to ensure the continuance of Maya peoples, the journey must be inward, into the histories and knowledges they have been so carefully guarding for generations. The images captured in the art and the central themes of the poems speak to the essential elements or building blocks necessary to restore this worldview: practices of everyday life, spiritual beliefs, cultural practices, and Maya cosmology. They write about the ways they honor their elders and recognize the wisdom and knowledges that they carry; the ways they respect the natural and animal world, which are alive and continue to offer them teachings; and the central role of spiritual traditions in their lives, whether through the honoring of those who have passed on to the spirit world, or through ceremonies to maintain a balanced relation with the world. They write about their histories, and pivotal moments in their lives that have undone imposed colonial silences. Their work speaks of the long trajectory of Maya traditions that capture in written text or glyphs their daily lives and other major occurrences.

The creations of these artists and writers also reveal that it is in the pieces and fragments of memories that histories are rebuilt, relations with their communities are restored, and traditions are reawakened. Their productions speak of disruptions, interruptions, and challenges, but most importantly, their work validates the importance and the process of rescuing and rebuilding these practices. Their actions reveal that it is in the process itself, in the practice of rescuing pieces of their past, that balance with the world is restored and a recentering within their Maya worldviews unfolds.

CHAPTER 3

"The Interminable Wound"

Historicizing Maya Experiences

> These wars and uprisings tell the story of the failure of conquest, of rebellion, and of the historical affirmation of Indian peoples and their will to survive.
>
> —GUILLERMO BONFIL BATALLA, *MÉXICO PROFUNDO*

Early publications situating the 1994 Zapatista Army of National Liberation (EZLN) uprising within long histories of Indigenous rebellions in Chiapas focused on the legacies of the 1712 Tseltal Revolt in San Juan Cancuc and the 1867 Tsotsil Rebellion in San Juan Chamula (Collier and Quaratiello 1994; Harvey 1998; Womack 1999). Scholars' long-history approach explained the actions of Indigenous communities in Chiapas against a context of Spanish colonial projects: encroachment on their lands, labor exploitation, and ongoing subjugation to church and state powers. This chapter expands on these narratives by bringing to the historiography of Indigenous insurgencies in Chiapas the Tseltal and Tsotsil voices of these two rebellions.

Poets Diego Torres Sánchez (Tseltal) and Luis López Díaz (Tsotsil) intervene in these narratives with the first published Tseltal and Tsotsil accounts of these two historical events. Torres Sánchez's "Yokinel Ch'ich'elil 1712: Sangriento 1712" (Bloody 1712) from his book *Ma'yuk slajibal te ejchenil: La herida interminable* (The interminable wound, 2006a) is a four-part narrative poem that traces the inception of the uprising, its wins and losses, and its historical impact on the communities. López Díaz's "Oxlajuneb k'ejimol sventa Tsajaljemel: Trece cantos por Tsajaljemel" (Thirteen songs for Tsajaljemel) from the anthology *Sbel sjol yo'nton ik': Memoria del viento* (Memory of the wind, López Díaz, Díaz Ruiz, and López Díaz 2006) moves through a preamble on the violent encounter with the colonial power, to a thirteen-part poem, to a final reflection and future outlook in the epilogue. Both poems disrupt official histories, decentering the rebellions as efforts to eliminate ladinos (non-Indian mestizo people) and the colonial power and instead focus them as struggles to affirm Maya presence and worldviews. Through their poetic narratives, Torres Sánchez and López Díaz rewrite into history the Maya leaders of these rebellions, and demonstrate the reemergence of Maya worldviews as sustaining the rebels and rebellions. Lastly, the historical poetic narratives present new directions for the contemporary Maya literary movement and new approaches to Maya literary production.

Ahead of the analysis of the poems, I present a brief account of these two rebellions in chronological order. The 1712 Tseltal Revolt was the culmination of years of tension due to the brutal exploitation of the Spanish colonial power (Bricker 1981; De Vos 2011; Gosner 1992; Stephen 2002; Womack 1999). Several areas in Chiapas had been experiencing bad harvest cycles and were unable to meet the increasing tributary demands of the church. Moreover, these drastic changes altered the relations that peoples had with their land, and the cultural and spiritual practices connected to tending and harvesting the land. In the middle of this crisis, news circulated that in San Juan Cancuc a young Tseltal woman, María López, who later adopted the name of María de la Candelaria, had witnessed the apparition of the Virgin. The Virgin's message was a request to build a hermitage for her adoration in the community. The shrine was built, and in a matter of days followers of the Virgin began arriving with offerings. Once news of this newfound faith reached the church, its leaders ordered the destruction of the shrine, but their order was ignored. At this time, María de la Candelaria delivered yet another message from the Virgin: "to start the rebellion against the Spanish rule." She added, "believe me and follow me, because there is no more tribute, or king, or bishop, or district magistrate, and do no more than follow me and believe this Virgin." The message spread throughout the communities, reaching the church and all ecclesiastical figures, that "the end has come and the prophecy was fulfilled of throwing off the yoke and restoring their lands and liberty"; it was purportedly "God's will that [the Virgin of Cancuc] had come for her sons the Indians to liberate them from the captivity of the Spaniards and the ministers of the Church" (Womack 1999, 85). Over thirty-two communities revolted, and Indigenous people took over some towns by force in their stance against the Spanish. The leaders were persecuted and violent confrontations continued for months, until the better-armed Spanish were finally able to put this insurgency to rest (Bricker 1981; Gosner 1992).

The beginning of the 1867 Tsotsil Rebellion in San Juan Chamula can be traced to the moment when a young Tsotsil woman, Agustina Gómez Chechev, declared that "three sacred stones had fallen from the sky and communicated with her" (Bricker 1981, 119; Stephen 2002, 93–94). Following the stones' messages, a hermitage was erected, and, as in the case of Cancuc over a century before, the people of Chamula and nearby communities began delivering offerings to the sacred stones. The church and ladinos, alarmed about this newfound faith, mobilized and openly attacked the communities adoring the stones. "Angered at the attempts to stop their activities, and fearful of ladino reprisals, Indigenous people in a few towns took up arms and directed their wrath at a handful of landowners, a school teacher, and a priest." The ladinos responded with a brutal attack that left several hundred Indigenous people dead. According to U.S. anthropologist Jan Rus, what the Indigenous peoples wanted "was to be left alone to farm their fields, conduct their markets, and worship their saints as they themselves chose" (cited in Stephen 2002, 94). Any act of rebellion against the interest of the church and the ladinos, however, was viewed as a threat to their economic status, thus, the need to repress the movement.

Retelling of Histories

The narrative poems by Torres Sánchez and López Díaz contribute to the trajectory of the literary movement of Chiapas because of the way that they do not simply denounce the colonial project but also add to the understanding of the histories of these rebellions. Mexican writer José Antonio Reyes Matamoros (2006) celebrates these poems' contributions to Tseltal and Tsotsil histories by likening the work of these two poets to that of Mexican anthropologist Miguel León-Portilla in *Visión de los vencidos: Crónicas Indígenas* (1989, translated as *The Broken Spears: The Aztec Account of the Conquest of Mexico*, 1990b). Reyes Matamoros (2006, iv) writes: "*Trece cantos* . . . es el primer poema histórico y de largo aliento en poesía maya" (*Thirteen songs* . . . is the first historical and long-winded poem in Maya poetry). He adds:

> Si *Visión de los vencidos* es el resultado de la derrota producto de la invasión europea; con *Oxlajuneb k'ejimol sventa Tsajaljemel, Trece cantos por Tsajaljemel*, (y de *1712*, del tseltal Diego Torres, poema refiere

> a la rebelión de Cancuc de 1712) los poetas mayas deberán remitirse a esta lectura para su apreciación y crítica.
>
> If *The Broken Spears* presents the Aztec account of the European invasion, *Thirteen songs for Tsajaljemel* (and *1712*, a poem by the Tseltal poet Diego Torres that centers on the Cancuc rebellion of 1712) presents Maya poets with much material to appreciate and assess. (iv)

León-Portilla's text disrupts official narratives of colonization by describing the encounter of the Spanish and Indigenous communities of central Mexico through the lens of the Nahua communities. He uses his acute research skills and attention to detail to focus attention on the complex histories, philosophical differences, violence of the colonial projects, and fierce determination of Indigenous communities. Reyes Matamoros's likening of the poems to León-Portilla's work is a great testament to the poets' efforts and influence of their work on the histories of Indigenous rebellions in Chiapas.

In framing my analysis of the narrative poems, I engage with Haitian American anthropologist Michel-Rolph Trouillot (1995, 14–15, 25), whose scholarship on "memory-history" argues that history is not fixed and that historical facts are not sitting and waiting to be found. History (what happened) exists only in relation to the present because we can only know and understand the past from the position we currently stand in. Trouillot writes: "For what history is changes with time and place, or better said, history reveals itself only through the production of specific narratives. What matters most are the process and conditions of production of such narratives." U.S. anthropologist Jonathan W. Warren (2001, 19) adds to this argument with his research in northern Brazil into the way that fragments of traditions, language, and cultural and spiritual practices that have barely survived over time have been rescued to reconstruct worldviews of Afro-Indigenous communities. Māori scholar Linda Tuhiwai Smith (2005, 159) shares this approach when she recognizes the importance of decolonizing research by rooting research to place and peoples in the communities because "communities are the ones who know the answers to their own problems." She further emphasizes the value of reconstructing memories housed in the communities to give shape to Indigenous hi/stories.

Demonstrating such values, Jakaltek Maya Victor Montejo (2005) reconstructed his community's ceremonial practice of the "Year Bearer's celebration," which was disrupted by the colonial project during the first half of the twentieth century. Montejo consulted the ethnographic work of U.S. anthropologist Oliver La Farge from the early 1900s, collected testimonies from elders, and rescued collective memories sheltered in his community to piece together this dormant practice (La Farge and Byers 1997). Montejo thus tapped into a nonstatic past and memories of the elders to re-create the sacred ceremony, which was celebrated for the first time again in 1997, in the town of Jacaltenango in western Guatemala. A similar approach—piecing together fragments of traditions to reconstruct histories—can be found among the Yurok and Karuk communities in Northern California, where women have brought back the 111 chin tattoo practice. L. Frank Manriquez (Tongva/Ajachmem) shares that the revival of this practice entailed following patterns from old photographs and reading historical records to understand the processes of the practice. "My tribe has been deemed extinct by the federal government. . . . This is a way to hold hands with my sisters through time. I just wanted that connection" (quoted in Hostler 2013). This tradition was reawakened in the community because its members treated the archive as alive, with fragments of knowledges ready to be stitched together.

I frame the central role of women in these rebellions within the legacies of equilibrium and duality in Maya worldviews and through the deployment of *kab'awil* (double gaze) or *kab'awilian* practice, which recenters gender roles within Maya cosmovisions (Chacón 2018; Hernández Castillo 2002, 2006). Stories of origin as told in the *Popol Vuh* show male and female energies present from the very beginning, when the first fathers and first mothers created and gave life to both men and women on an equal plane. The Women's Revolutionary Law, announced by the EZLN in 1994, elevates the contribution of women in the communities and the insurgency, but mostly realigns gender relations with millennia-old Mesoamerican belief systems (EZLN 2006). The significant contribution of women leaders in retellings of these historical rebellions is about rebalancing the duality of relations, realigning sacred knowledges, and recuperating time and long memory grounded in Indigenous cosmology.

In my analysis of the poetry, I also engage with the work of U.S. anthropologist Jan Rus (1989) and Belgian historian Jan de Vos (2011), who have both undertaken extensive ethnographic work in Chiapas and research on Indigenous rebellions. Mapuche scholar Elicura Chihuailaf Nahuelpan's (2009,

65–66) concept of *itrofil mogen* is also part of this meditative analysis. *Itrofil mogen* avows a unified and inclusive living world, reciprocal relations with all that is life-sustaining in the cosmos, and balanced relations among human and other-than-human kin. The deployment of *itrofil mogen* guides my analysis of these relations in both poems, particularly in the way that the natural world enters as a vital character in their histories.

Last, the concept of *caracoleando*, as in the previous chapters, adds to my analysis of the nonlinear narrative of the poems, which anchor their narratives within Maya cosmologies to inform the direction of the rebellions. The language that gives life to these historical accounts, the power of naming figures that have been silenced in official histories, and the rage that permeates the words that fill the gaps of these official histories are all central to this process of unearthing the buried knowledges of Maya Indigenous consciousness.

"The Interminable Wound"

Diego Torres Sánchez's (2006b) narrative poem "Yokinel Ch'ich'elil 1712: Sangriento 1712" (Bloody 1712) has at its center the voice of María de la Candelaria, the young woman who claimed to have direct communication with the Virgin and led to an organized mobilization of thirty-two Maya (Tseltal, Tsotsil, Ch'ol) communities in the Zendales region of Chiapas.[1] The four-part poem presents a nonlinear approach to the history of this rebellion. In the narrative, Torres Sánchez engages in a *kab'awilian* practice by elevating the story of the fourteen-year-old María de la Candelaria and reclaiming her role in the history of this rebellion. The omnipotent force of her messages and actions carries the rebels through the struggles of the rebellion. Such an act is a process of *caracoleando* as the successes of the rebellion are guided by realigning the struggle within the heart of the communities and cosmocentric relations nurtured over millennia. The first part of the poem introduces María de la Candelaria and affirms the oppressive conditions under colonial rule that lead the communities to mobilize. María's voice emerges to inspire resistance and action in the communities. The second part focuses on the message of the Virgin to María that encourages the communities to rebel against the mandates of the church but also, significantly, affirms their worldviews to lead their path forward. The third part engages with the violent attacks on the communities and the valiant role of rebel leaders, and it connects their actions to the rhythm of the cosmos. The last part is a calling, an affirmation of the reasons for the uprising to defend Maya worldviews. There is an order to the poetic narrative, but time is altered in the details of the actions of the rebels and the response of the colonial authorities.

"SPETON AJKUBAL TA JWAYICH, spotsbon jbak'etal / yijk'al xch'ailel sibak, jo'on María de la Candelaria"—"YO, MARÍA DE LA CANDELARIA SUEÑO: la noche me abraza, / cubre mi cuerpo la oscuridad de la pólvora" (I, MARÍA DE LA CANDELARIA DREAM: the night embraces me, / the darkness of gunpowder covers my body), opens the first part of the poem, centering María's voice in the development of this historical rebellion. These opening lines also present María in a liminal state of mind, lying down under the dark sky, engulfed in a torturous nightmare that is captured with words of violence: "Sk'u'inteson snojk'etal lajel . . . / Xnijk yu'un k'uxulil te jbak'etal . . . / jkuchojbey te swokol jlumal"—"La sombra de la muerte me viste . . . / Mi cuerpo tiembla de dolor . . . / y cargo el sufrimiento de mi pueblo" (The shadow of death covers me . . . / My body trembles with pain . . . / and I carry the suffering of my people). Her echoing message places an emphasis on the power of the word and the richness of the language to describe the conditions of her community and the threat of the colonial power. But also emphasized is the strength of the peoples, nurtured through reciprocal relations with their environment, relations that are reflected in the act of slowly waking up and feeling the vibrations of the cosmos: "Sna'liyon te k'aale, / tsajnax sit yelaw, / xbeenon ta lum"—"El Sol me mira, / rojo su rostro / camino la tierra" (The sun looks at me / red his face / I walk the land). This call for a realignment with the cosmos will be a constant plea in María's role in the rebellion as she searches for those cosmic relations to sustain her path forward. The awakening realization is the responsibility to her community and the weight this bears. "I walk the land," she states, as if this act alleviates the weight of her responsibilities (Torres Sánchez 2006b, 21).

The theme of language encompassing Maya belief systems and the realignment of María with the cosmos, which reflects Chihuailaf's concept of *itrofil mogen*, continue in the poem. The use of the first person in this case affirms the active subject, which engages with literary traditions in Chiapas, as Micaela Morales López (2004, 16) writes: "En cualquiera de los dos constructos de la voz: el oral o escrito, el sujeto se proyecta como conciencia, ser pensante, presencia activa" (In any of the two constructs of voice: oral or written, the subject is projected as a conscious, thinking being and active presence). The following lines from the poem further reflect these language and subject relations:

> Ta stojol Jch'ultatik ch'abajon, jo'on María de la Candelaria,
> tey la yilon-a, tey la kil-ek-a.
> Kejelon ta sk'anel sok kantela, pom
> ta skoltayelotik ta milel.
>
> Yo, María de la Candelaria, le rece al Padre Sol,
> ahí me miró y mire a él.
> Seguí hincada, pedí con velas e incienso
> nos protegiera de la guerra.
>
> I, María de la Candelaria, prayed to Father Sun,
> there he looked at me and I looked at him.
> I continued kneeling, I asked with candles and incense
> we be protected from the war. (29)

This moment of prayer is not to the Virgin who speaks to her, but to the creator. María offers candles and incense, along with a prayer to bless the space and open the dialogue. She pleads not just for her own life, but for that of all her peoples. The recognition of Father Sun, Morales López (2004, 160–61) also notes in her work, reflects Maya cosmovisions that speak of stories of origin with a strong presence of the sun as father and protector of life. In this exchange María speaks of these relations and, even more, flattens hierarchies as the young woman and Father Sun are on the same plane in mutual acknowledgment. Such an exchange also reflects the work of Maya poets like those analyzed in chapters 1 and 2, who raise their poetic voice to balance their relations with the creators. In this reciprocal exchange the narrative further notes that it is through these sacred relations that María engages with the cosmos and her peoples. Like this, in the poem, María assumes her earned place in history. Her role, however, always unfolds in relation to her communities.

The emphasis on the voice of María de la Candelaria elevates a reliance on the power of the word that gives life to language to transform life, fight back, and offer protection. The word gives way to prayer that offers security to the rebels; it gives way to dialogue between María and the Virgin; and, last, it gives way to the messages to all followers.

Xchajpan jkoltaywanej jchol k'op a'yejetik,
jchol k'opetik skoltay te jlumtik.
Xk'atbuj te k'ope,
xchajpan yach'il lumetik bit'ilnx k'opetik.

La tierra fabrica frases revolucionarias,
frases que habrán de salvar nuestro universo.
La palabra se transforma,
construye mundos nuevos con la palabra misma.

The earth fabricates revolutionary phrases,
phrases that will save our universe.
The word is transformed,
builds new worlds with the word itself. (29)

The words in these lines spring from the land, contributing to the collective and unifying force of the cosmos. María's message needs no interlocutor; she walks and listens to the whispers of the land to construct the language to save her communities (Morales Lopéz 2004). This position also echoes that of Okanagan writer Jeannette Armstrong (1998, 174), as mentioned in chapter 2. For Armstrong, language emanates from the land and makes her feel at times as the translator of the language that her land speaks. History shows that violence ensues during the 1712 rebellion, but the defense strategies are rooted in Maya worldviews captured through the deployment of the word. In her messaging, María reminds her followers of these relations as the only way to survive in the lands of the "tseltal, tsotsil, ch'ol" (Torres Sánchez 2006b, 25).

Toward the end of this first part of the poem, and as part of its work of naming the perpetrators of the violence, the poet brings in the voice of Fray Simon de Lara. He is the religious figure who applies all the force at his disposal against the communities who have dared to defy the church's authority in its call for Indigenous peoples to denounce the falsehood of the apparition of the Virgin and repent of this evildoing. Such a position highlights the authorities' failure to understand the condition of peoples' lives and their reasons for mobilizing. The poet also eloquently paints the violence exerted against the rebels, the violation of the women, and the blood spilled in the communities. When María and relatives are forced to leave their homes to escape the violence, the mountains protect them and watch after them. These are the relations the authorities and soldiers cannot see or comprehend.

Sbon sbaik ta xch'ich'el lekil o'tanetik te jmilawaletik,
slejbeyik soltaro María de la Candelaria,
sjojk'obeyik te witsetik,
ma sujtesik te bin ya yich'ik jojk'obeyel te witsetik.

Los asesinos se manchan de sangre humilde,
buscan a los militares de María de la Candelaria,
les preguntan a los cerros,
los cerros no responden pregunta.

The murderers are stained with the blood of the humble,
they look for the soldiers of María de la Candelaria,
they ask the hills,
the hills do not answer a single question. (35)

The natural world extends its embrace, responding to the call of the communities, sharing their pain, and understanding the severity of the threat. María's source of strength is established as knowledges rooted in place, relations sustained with her peoples, her natural environment, and the higher powers: the creator, mother-father, of all that constitutes Maya worldviews. In this first section, the Virgin has spoken, María has carried her message, the communities have followed, and the church has violently responded.

The second part focuses on the message of the Virgin, the organizing of the communities behind the Virgin's messages, the violent response of the church backed by the state, and the communities' affirmation of their worldviews as they resist the church mandates. In the narrative of the poetry, María always emerges in the natural world, and this setting extends to her encounters with the Virgin. In their exchanges, an affirmation of place, the importance of shared messaging, and blurred hierarchies are discernable.

"María, ja' kantsil alat, la', noptsajan tel,
ya xk'ajinotik li' ta slum bats'il pak' sok tsekel . . ."

"María, tú eres mi hija, ven, acércate,
ahora cantarás conmigo en esta tierra de huipiles y enaguas . . ."

"María, you are my daughter, come, come closer,
now you will sing with me in this land of huipiles and underskirts . . ." (39)

Just like in the first part, when María speaks face-to-face with the holy father, here too, both women are on the same plane when the Virgin delivers her message. María responds: "Melel, me'el señora, ja'me jme'at, yame joyinat / sok yame jmuktik te jajchem k'op sok te uts'inel"—"Sí, señora, tú eres mi madre, y estaré contigo / y enterraremos la guerra y el odio" (Yes, ma'am, you are my mother, and I will be with you / and we will bury war and hate) (41). The affirmation of these relations in the exchanges and setting further reveals that the Indigenous communities were never alone. In this rebellion, they were always under the protection of all human and other-than-human kin.

The Virgin is similarly not acting alone in her call to organize the communities to erect a hermitage in her honor. "Slekil yo'tan jtat"—"Es voluntad de mi padre" (It's my father's wishes) (39). The collective "we" is part of her messaging for the communities to mobilize. The language in this part of the poem resonates with the research of historian Jan de Vos (2011), who argues that the altar where the Virgin was adored in 1712 included various sacred figures, in particular the image of a sacred jaguar. These figures, including that of the Virgin, were never visible to followers but were rather kept behind a screen. De Vos argues that central to this rebellion, which shook the Spanish Crown to its core, was not the Virgin's message alone, but a direct return to precolonial Indigenous practices. This position is in line with other colonial accounts reflective of the polyculture of Maya peoples: even when the Virgin appears and delivers a message, she does not take over religious practices. The Virgin, too, is embraced as one of the sacred beings that constitute their beliefs. The Virgin does not hold omnipotent power; this power is nurtured in her relation with the communities of followers, the mandates of her father, and the shared sacredness with Maya deities.

The sharing of pain and sorrow is ever present in this part of the poem too. The narrative names the historical figure of Toribio de Cosío, then president of Guatemala, as a lover of death.

Sjoyinejik ta beenel cha'oxtul chopol tsotsiletik te espanyoletik,
xbeenik sok machit, punyal, sts'ijlajan yu'un sbolil o'tanil.
Sk'ambeyik yo'tan al nich'anil yo'tik sok pajel cha'wej.

Los españoles caminan con algunos indignos tsotsiles,
andan con machete y puñal, chillan de odio.
Quieren el corazón de los hijos de hoy y de mañana.

The Spaniards walk with some unworthy Tsotsiles,
they walk with machete and dagger, and screech of hate.
They want the heart of the children of today and tomorrow. (49)

These lines capture the colonial hunger for the extermination of Indigenous peoples and any possibilities for a future. The legacies of genocidal actions are also spoken in these lines. The audacity of the communities to claim what De Vos (2011, 20–26) refers to as a "falso milagro" (false miracle) and demand that the devotion to the Virgin be recognized fuels the hunger for destruction among the Spanish and their insatiable thirst to destroy all Indigenous ways of life.

The mountains become a character in this part of the poem, as the narrative describes the rebels seeking refuge, and the mountains embracing the Virgin's soldiers to protect them from the eyes of the Spanish militia. María de la Candelaria finds refuge in the mountains as well, carrying the pain and sorrow of the community of followers, those who have fallen and those who continue to resist. From this space, with the soldiers following closely, she delivers one more message from the Virgin.

"Ma xba ayinuk ajwalil sok tojomalil
li' ta sk'inal spakel te kerae,
ja'nax majtantestik te pasero, ajawetik
sok Ch'ul Lum."

"No habrá más rey ni tributo
en esta tierra de lucha,

sólo adoraremos el copal, los cerros sagrados
y a la Madre Tierra."

"There will be no more king or tribute
in this land of struggle,
we will only adore the copal, the sacred hills
and Mother Earth." (55)

The impact of these words increases the rage of the colonial power against the rebels. The statement aligns the poem with scholarship on the social, economic, and religious aspects of this rebellion (De Vos 2011; Gosner 1992). As the rebellion unfolded, contributions to the church such as "daily domestic service, including furnishing firewood, fodder, and mail service whenever demanded," ceased (Bricker 1981, 119). Furthermore, the actions of the rebels meant that the communities were carrying on their activities away from the grip of the church and "escaping their [church] control administratively" (Rus 1989, 1038). Mexican historian Juan González Esponda's research adds to the growth of these tensions when stating that some people claimed at the time of the persecution of the rebels that the Virgin's proclamation had been "there is no longer tribute, nor King, nor God," which led to a stronger wave of violence in response to what Spanish authorities considered a great blasphemy (González Esponda 2013). The poem thus aligns with existing research that the rebellion was part of Indigenous struggles to practice religion and life on their own terms, and mostly to affirm their autonomy and self-determination.

The language the poet uses to describe the role assumed by men in the leadership also contributes to more precise readings of the rebellion. Once the hermitage was erected, the men led Mass and participated in other roles that the church reserves for ordained priests. As such, the church unleashed its wrath on them not just for blasphemy in believing María's messages, but for their daring to undertake roles that the church considers sacred. The gravity of this action can be seen in the aftermath of the 1994 EZLN uprising, when Bishop Samuel Ruíz of the Diocese of San Cristóbal de las Casas was targeted for removal due to his alleged involvement with the rebellion. The primary concern was that Ruíz had appointed Indigenous deacons and granted them all the responsibilities of priests to practice the Christian faith in the most desolate of communities.

The poet uses the word *kapitanetik/capitanes* (captain) (39) to describe the participatory role of the men who accompanied María de la Candelaria, protected her with their own lives, and assumed leadership positions within the rebellion. In doing so, Torres Sánchez engages with other narratives such as that of Kevin Gosner (1992, 131), who draws a connection between those who were appointed as *capitanes* in this rebellion to their *nahual*, or nonhuman co-essence. Gosner argues that the stronger the *nahual*, the stronger the role the person had in support of this rebellion.

According to Nathan C. Henne in *Reading Popol Wuj* (2020, 166), as addressed in chapter 2, the *nawal* (Henne's spelling of *nahual*) "is determined by the alignment of realms at the specific place and moment in time a person is born." He writes that "the *nawal* . . . links a specific person and some related, but nonhuman, co-essence together in a bond that mutually defines their collective being" (141). With the use of the term *capitanes*—and not priests or bishops, the terms that the literature tends to use to identify these leaders—the poet recognizes their leadership position beyond their affiliation with the Catholic Church. In a similar move, other scholars have turned to the Tseltal term *tuhunel* (Le Bot 1997, 183), *tu'hunel* (Harvey 1998, 74), or *tu'uneles* (Stephen 2002, 124–25) to identify those who were at the head of the traditional cargo system in the communities, local authorities outside the dictates of the church. This choice affirms the communities' own terminology for the leadership positions, outside colonial structures of power.

Torres Sánchez's narrative also gives continuity to María's life. Whereas most narratives of the rebellion talk about the uncertainty of her final days, the poet carries the history of her life to the end. His narrative reads in line with the work of De Vos (2011), who writes that María de la Candelaria escaped the wrath of the Spanish with her father and husband and remained protected in a neighboring community. A villager, however, denounced them to the authorities, and, just before they were recaptured, María died while delivering her stillborn baby. The poet touches on this historical version when he writes, "Kajal beel ta buro te María de la Candelaria bajt ta Lacandón, / sujtel ta yoxwinik xchanbajk' k'aal"—"María de la Candelaria en un burro caminó a El Lacandón, / volvería dentro de mil doscientos sesenta días" (María de la Candelaria traveled on a donkey to El Lacandón, / she would return within one thousand two hundred and sixty days) (45). Though hers is a tragic end, bringing María's story to closure breaks the historical silences around her fate and that of the rebellion.

In the third part of the poem, a nonlinear telling of events unfolds. The narrative follows the "soldiers of the Virgin," their actions and commitment to the rebellion. Stories of women are also central here, particularly that of one of the leaders, Nicolasa Gómez, and her untimely death. The mountains emerge as yet another strong character in this part of the poem, providing shelter and soothing the pain of the rebels. The narrative presents the magnitude and inspiration of the rebellion as follows:

> Jaito ja'me ya'tel te María de la Candelaria,
> pujkem ta lajcheb xcha'winik jpam lum tseltal, tsotsil sok ch'ol,
> banti ya xch'ij sakil sok k'anal ixim.
> Xch'ich'el lumetik te ya stsak sba sok skontroik
> ta skoltayel sk'inal yal xnich'anik,
> bats'il pak', tsekel, ch'ul we'el uch'elil.
>
> Ésta es parte de la obra de María de la Candelaria
> extendida en treinta y dos pueblos tseltales, tsotsiles y ch'oles
> donde nacen el maíz amarillo y blanco.
> Sangre de los pueblos que luchan por defender
> la tierra de sus hijos,
> el huipil, la enagua, el alimento nutriente.
>
> This is part of the work of María de la Candelaria
> extended to thirty-two Tseltal, Tsotsil, and Ch'ol villages
> where yellow and white maize are born.
> Blood of the peoples who fight to defend
> the land of their children,
> the huipil, the underskirt, the nutrient food. (67)

The role of María is reaffirmed in the naming and making of the rebellion. With these lines, the poet also affirms the essence of the soldiers: they are members of the three named Maya groups, children of the corn, and inheritors of millennia-old languages and cultural practices, who have been deployed to defend their lands and communities and are faced with bloody violence. As the violent Spanish forces hunt them, the basic elements of their worldviews are articulated, an act of *caracoleando*, a journey inward and into the source of their essence.

But histories are complex, and just like the Spanish found Indigenous allies to destroy the city of Tenochtitlan and the Aztec Empire two centuries prior, the Spanish found Chamula allies to help them in the destruction of the rebellion. Even so, the lines in the poem carry a forgiving tone, suggesting that just as the rebels are being hunted by the Spanish, the allied Chamulas are being hunted too, and forced to attack the rebels. This tension speaks, too, of nonbinary relations, of an ongoing search for equilibrium in the forces of the cosmos.

> Xbeen sok jo'winik ta jtul jtujk'awanejetik jchamo'etik
> te fray José Monroy,
> stek'ik ajch'al sok st'omik yijk'al ajk'abal,
> tembilik ta smilel te mach'a pajal sk'opik sok
> soknix slajinel stajal namey kuxlejal.
>
> Fray José Monroy
> camina con cien chamulas armados,
> baten lodo y rompen la oscuridad de la noche,
> obligados a matar a sus hermanos de idioma,
> y al color de la historia.
>
> Fray José Monroy
> walk with a hundred armed Chamula,
> hit the mud and break the darkness of the night
> forced to kill their language brothers,
> and the color of history. (57)

The "hundred armed Chamula" are identified as carriers of the violence against the rebels, but that they are "forced to kill their language brothers" speaks of a blind alliance. The lines almost identify them as "brothers" not awakened into the message of liberation María delivers. But the rebels remain strong, navigating their known lands in search of Spanish soldiers to pulverize.

> Xbeenik ta jujun jwol wits te soltaro jalal me'il,
> ta jujun asento; x-atin ta ch'ich' te Chilón,
> sk'atp'untesik ta tan kaxlanetik.
> Snoptsajik ta Ocosingo, tey smilik alal espanyoletik-a
> ta sit yelaw sme'ik
> ja'ikito la sbonik ta ch'ich' te namey talelil.

Los ejércitos de la Virgen marchan de cerro en cerro,
de hacienda en hacienda; Chilón se baña de sangre,
convirtieron en polvo a los kaxlanes.
Avanzaron a Ocosingo, ahí ejecutaron a niños españoles
frente a sus madres
y éstos pintaron con su cuerpo la historia.

The armies of the Virgin march from hill to hill,
from farm to farm; Chilón bathes in blood,
they turned the kaxlanes into dust.
They advanced to Ocosingo, there they executed Spanish children
in front of their mothers
and they painted history with their bodies. (61)

The detailed descriptions highlight the gravity of the fight and severity of violence on both sides of the conflict. Also highlighted are the rage that results after centuries under the excruciatingly tight yoke of colonial power and the commitment of the rebels to defend Indigenous ways of life. These relations De Vos (2011, 25–26) identifies as expected, as the actions of civil and religious authorities only give way to resentment among Maya communities.

María de la Candelaria and her immediate family are forced to find refuge in the mountains to escape the rage of the authorities. The Spanish soldiers, riding high on their horses, search through the dense foliage of the jungle for signs of María and her family, yelling racist insults. But the mountainous jungle protects them from the brutality of the Spanish forces: "sleik María de la Candelaria, ma staik ta toyem k'inal, / ja'nax te st'ujbilal ska'yoje"—"persiguen a María de la Candelaria, no hallaron en los bosques, / solo belleza de su canto" (they chase María de la Candelaria, they did not find anything in the woods, / only beauty of her song) (71). The human and other-than-human relations are further elaborated in lines that suggest that an attack on María is an attack on Mother Earth: "xchol k'ajk' te sibak, sbik' xch'ailel beneno te ch'ulchan"—"la pólvora forma llamas, el cielo traga humo de veneno" (gunpowder forms flames, the sky swallows smoke of poison) (59).

In this part of the poem, the leader Nicolasa Gómez takes center stage in the narrative of fallen ones. She is taken prisoner by the Spanish authorities, and she suffers as she waits for her death, grieving for her family and children and imagining their fate. Her silence is the strength of her character. "Kol awa'ay lo'loywanej sok aman tojel / ta xojbil pukuj Nicolasa"—"Nicolasa, quisiste engañar con tu suerte / Iluminada por el diablo" (Nicolasa, you wanted to cheat with your luck / Enlightened by the devil), the authorities scream at her, to which she is only able to respond with silent motions: "La stoy sk'aal sit yelaw te Nicolasa Gómez, / k'an k'opojuk, ma'bin la yal"—"Nicolasa Gómez levantó la cara enojada, / Quiso hablar, no dijo nada" (Nicolasa Gómez raised her angry face, / She wanted to speak, she said nothing). She is tortured and forced to denounce María as possessed by evil, but Nicolasa will not talk: "Mukem ya xlok' ta ye te k'ope / limilik jilel ta ik'"—"Las palabras que salen silenciosamente de su boca / Quedaron suspendidas en el aire" (The words that quietly come out of her mouth / were suspended in the air) (63–65). The narrative shows Nicolasa's paralyzing pain in captivity. The detail in the exchange with her captors lifts her voice, brings her to life, and shows her true nature. The exchange also shows that beyond the grief of imminent loss, her children and family are her companions until the end, as she embraces their memory in the solitude of her cell.

The end finds Nicolasa contemplating recent events and mourning the fate of her children, who will be lost without her. Nicolasa is beheaded as if to inflict ongoing suffering in the afterlife. Her final words in the narrative exalt her role in the rebellion, and her life.

Cha'xojt' metsel te antse
stselet sjol, te sbak'etale ya x-awun,
ma'yuk mach'a x-a'aybot stojol yu'un.
Ta snuk' lok' te k'ope moj ta ch'ulchan.
Tsajub te balumilal, smel yo'tan, ilinem, la xh'ay te antse
ja'xanix ma la xch'ay te namey talaelil.

Ella, tirada en dos pedazos,
su cabeza rueda y su cuerpo grita
sin que nadie la escuche.
De su garganta un sonido sube al cielo.
El universo rojo, triste, enojado, pierde a la mujer
no la historia.

She, lying in two pieces,
her head rolls and her body screams

without anyone listening to her.
From her throat a sound rises to the sky.
The universe red, sad, angry, loses the woman
not the history. (67–69)

The beheading is reminiscent of actions during the colonial-era revitalization movements among the Quechua and Aymara peoples in the Andean region. Indigenous leader Túpac Amaru was captured and his body quartered and separately buried, but these actions only increased the faith among members of the communities that he would return and rebuild their Indigenous worldviews (Varese 2006, 110–13). The revolutionary Ghost Dance movement that spread in the western United States in the late 1800s also captures these shared Indigenous beliefs. Settler colonial attacks on the Native populations could not disrupt the essence of American Indians, the Piute, Sioux, Lakota, Dakota, and all those who joined in the ceremonial dance. They were killed too, but the spirit will live forever and inspire future generations (Estes 2019). The attention in Torres Sánchez's narrative to Nicolasa's transition also brings her to infinite life. She might have been killed, but her voice resonates through the echoes of history. Her spirit joins the lineage of sacred beings, increasing the protection of the rebels.

In the fourth and last part of the poem, the emphasis is on the sounds: the wind that carries the music, the voices that announce death and life, and the prayer that echoes through the earth to elevate the followers of the Virgin. The name of María de la Candelaria is uttered several times in recognition of her place at the center of the rebellion, affirmation of the ways her prayer, which is always in tune with the cosmos, elevates the spirit of the rebels, and in announcement that her death brings the world to a silent state. The attacks and violence continue, and for María, these attacks continue after her imminent death.

The deadly attacks carry sounds of hope, announcing a rebirth. "K'atbuj ta cha'oxt'ul ja' te xch'ailel sibak / t'ulaj koel ta yo'tan jmilbenetik / k'otix ta pasel sk'op te ik'e"—"El humo de pólvora se transforma en gotas de agua / y cae el corazón de los muertos, / la palabra del viento se ha cumplido" (Gunpowder smoke transforms into drops of water / and the heart of the dead falls, / the word of the wind has been fulfilled). The gunpowder kills, but the wind carries powerful messages that transform death, emphasizing the alignment of life and the cosmos. This attunement with the wind is also part of the sounds that emerge from this last part of the poem. The opening lines note the presence of music in the call to fight: "Xcholetik ta beenel jpas k'opetik ta slametel k'ayob, / te yamayik ya yik' lumetik ta spasel k'op"—"Los sublevados marchan al ritmo de tambores, / flautas llaman a los pueblos a luchar" (The rebels march to the beat of drums, / flutes call the people to fight). But mostly, the sounds acknowledge the continuity of life and its cycles (75).

The followers of the Virgin continue on the defense, affirming their strength and leadership despite their disadvantaged position in the battle. The narrative of the fight denotes their battle position always in relation to place.

Ta slok'ib k'aal wokolil sok chamel,
ta smalib k'aal kermanotak tsotsiletik,
ta ye'tal balumilal tujk' sok sibak,
ta sjol balumilal lumetik te ch'ayem ta o'tanil.

Al oriente dolor y enfermedad,
al poniente hermanos tsotsiles,
al sur mosquete y pólvora,
al norte comarca en el olvido.

To the east pain and disease,
to the west Tsotsil brothers,
to the south musket and gunpowder,
to the north region in oblivion. (79–81)

The soldiers of the Virgin are presented not only in relation to their struggles, but also in relation to life and death, and in relation to the cosmos. Where is there to go when all directions seem to lead to a demise and the fight reaches an end point?

Lamaj ta ts'o'etel te sibak,
xlaj yipik mach'atik ayik ta pas k'op
k'alal te xwix María de la Candelaria
stsakoj ta tilel te taje.

La pólvora dejó de silbar,
los combatientes agonizan

cuando la hermana de María de la Candelaria
sostiene la llama del Ocote.

Gunpowder stopped whistling,
the fighters agonize
when the sister of María de la Candelaria
holds the flame of Ocote. (81)

The end of the fight, the end of the battle, is called with the *llama del ocote*, that part of the pine tree that sparks with ease and burns strongly. The fight has ended, but the fire will not be put out permanently, as it is always ready to spark again.

The theme of cosmocentrism, or recognition of interconnectedness with all that inhabits the cosmos—which also reflects *itrofil mogen* and its all-inclusive, reciprocal, and balanced living world—is emphasized in relation to the ultimate fate of María. This part of the narrative is very much in line with the work of De Vos (2011) and the archival records of this rebellion. While hiding in another community, María delivers a stillborn baby and dies shortly thereafter. The narrative gently moves through this untimely fate.

Xnoj ta mel o'tan te wamaletik sok nichimetik,
x-ok' kantela, laj ta yutil yawil ya'lel kuxinel te pulil,
nojel ta ch'ich' yawil kuxinel, chik'inem sbak'etal sok ma xk'opoj.
Sjik' ik', sikub sbak'etal sok ma'yukix xch'ulel te spule
sman tojel li' tan lum k'inal.

Plantas y flores se llenan de llanto,
velas llorando, el retoño ha muerto en la fuente,
su vientre empapado de sangre, su cuerpo sudoroso y callado.
Respira ligeramente, su cuerpo se hiela y su retoño sin vida
es su destino en esta tierra.

Plants and flowers are filled with tears,
crying candles, the offspring has died at the source,
her belly soaked with blood, her body sweaty and quiet.
She breathes lightly, her body freezes and her lifeless offspring
it is her fate on this earth. (85)

The language used to describe the death of María is kind and caring and reflective of her impact on the communities. The reciprocal relation with humans and other-than-human kin again is reflective of the concept of *itrofil mogen*. This relation can also be grasped through the descriptive language of the ways the cosmos feels and mourns Maria's death.

> Stejk'an sba te k'aal,
> ta yak'el k'axel te slajibal ajk'ubal unin u ta sk'aalel sik.
> Tup' bael te sjietel toyem k'inale,
> te ch'ulchan noj ta ek'etik, spots sba ta mel o'tan yajwal te lume.
>
> El sol se ha puesto
> para dar paso a la última luna nueva del invierno.
> Los ruidos del bosque se fueron,
> el cielo se cubrió de estrellas y la multitud viste de tristeza.
>
> The sun has set
> to make way for the last new moon of winter.
> The sounds of the forest left,
> the sky was covered with stars and the crowd wears sadness. (87)

The death of Maria and her baby resonates across all corners of the universe; it weeps along with all those who witnessed her life and are now hearing of her death. There is an almost palpable movement in the language, as if tracing that cycle of life that is now going to sleep, to rest for a while. And though that cycle is not gone forever, the weight of its end is demonstrable in the language of the poem.

Official narratives of this rebellion leave the final fate of María de la Candelaria as an enigma. In his extensive research on Indigenous rebellions in Chiapas, De Vos (2011) writes that days after María's death, the Spanish soldiers arrived to the community where she had found shelter for a number of years with her husband and father. By the time they arrived, María was dead and buried. Her death, however, would not impede her castigation. The soldiers forced her father, not her husband, to unbury her body and to carry her to Ciudad Real, present-day San Cristóbal de las Casas and then capital of the state, to present her dead body to the authorities. Due to the heaviness of the body, María was beheaded and her father was forced to carry her head all the way to the authorities. The narrative of the poem captures this end as follows:

> K'ax k'aal yich' lok'esel ta smukenal te María de la Candelaria,
> ta Yajalón yich'beyik bael te sjole,
> yaxal k'inal, k'ulej k'inal sok k'unil lum.
> K'alal k'ot sjol te animail awun te yajwal lume, ma bin la yal te yantik.
>
> Días después María de la Candelaria fue desenterrada y
> llevada su cabeza a Yajalón,
> tierra húmeda, rica y suave.
> Al llegar el cadáver la gente gritó, otros en silencio.
>
> Days later María de la Candelaria was unearthed and
> her head taken to Yajalón,
> moist, rich, and soft soil.
> When the body arrived the people cried, others in silence. (87)

The narrative notes the violent action, but the reference to place reads of care and reassurance. The posthumous beheading places María and her story alongside Indigenous leaders of the Americas, and returns us to the ever-present theme that María de la Candelaria is one with the universe. She is dead, but not gone, and she will forever be in the minds of peoples waiting for her return.

> Yalbey slajel slum k'op a'yej te kerae.
> Maba kechel ta ch'iel te k'opetik tseltal, tsotsil sok ch'ol,
> xbeenik sok sk'op lum k'inal sok namey talelil.
> Nopol jun ja'wil
> ko yipik mach'atik skoltay sbaik ta milel,
> ya xjil xnichimtes kuxlejal te k'ope
> sok ta sk'atp'unel xch'ulel te lume.
>
> La guerra sentenció el mundo del habla.
> La lengua tseltal, tsotsil y ch'ol siguen su curso,
> caminan con verbos de tierra y de su historia.
> Al transcurrir un año

la potencia de los sublevados ha disminuido,
la palabra se queda para florecer la vida
y transformar el alma del pueblo.

War sentenced the world of dialogue.
The Tseltal, Tsotsil, and Ch'ol languages continue their course,
they walk with earth's vitality and their history.
After a year
the power of the rebels has decreased,
the word stays to germinate life
and transform the soul of the people. (89)

Death has been stalking the communities; they have buried their loved ones, silencing their lives forever, and a little bit of those who survived too. The stars shine a little less, their voices sound dimmer, but the seeds have been planted and will flourish once again—this seems to be the final message. The *palabra florida* (flowery word) will rise and resound in all corners of the Indigenous world.

The recentering of María de la Candelaria in the telling of the 1712 Tseltal Revolt in San Juan Cancuc by Torres Sánchez is in itself a *kab'awilian* act. The poet applies the double gaze of looking back into history to rescue María's role in the revolt and realign her in the revolt's history. The language, style, and tone of the poem are themselves *caracoleando* in practice. The language creates constant movement, following a nonlinear route and giving room in the process to bring into the historical account the role of other women in the revolt. Such an approach exposes the ongoing aim of a more gender-balanced account of histories, recognizing, as Morales López (2004, 160–62) notes when writing about literary trajectories of Chiapas, that many of the stories reconnect with stories of the universe's origin. "Una veta de riqueza mítica la constituye los relatos que dan cuentan del origen del universo" (A vein of mythical richness is constituted by the stories that give an account of the origin of the universe). Morales López is quick to note that "myth" is not just attributed to fiction, but is part of something very real and at times overwhelming, given its ideological weight. Official narratives might have obfuscated María de la Candelaria's central role in the revolt, but Torres Sánchez's *kab'awilian* approach not only recenters her role but reactivates her participation in all layers of the defense of the communities' ways of life. Recentering María de la Candelaria in the account of the Tseltal Revolt thus reactivates these histories and breeds news ways of seeing and being with more balanced worlds.

Thirteen Songs

"Oxlajuneb k'ejimol sventa Tsajaljemel: Trece cantos por Tsajaljemel" (Thirteen songs for Tsajaljemel), a narrative poem by Luis López Díaz (Tsotsil) (2006), moves forward in history to the time of the 1867 Tsotsil Rebellion. The "songs" referenced in the title is part of the legacies of "flower-and-song" that are central to the intellectual trajectory of Indigenous peoples of Mesoamerica, particularly in the Nahua tradition (León-Portilla 1990a). The narrative of the poem is anchored in the history of the rebellion, which spread through the municipality of San Juan Chamula in 1868–70 and centered in the hamlet of Tsajaljemel.[2] Through the song, the poet brings to life the actions of the rebels, naming the leaders and attesting to the rage that grows in the rebel communities out of years of oppression and exploitation. Whereas Torres Sánchez grants María de la Candelaria omnipotent presence, López Díaz brings a multitude of voices to his narrative. The voice of Agustina Gómez Chechev is introduced early in the narrative, alongside those of her allies and enemies, and always in relation to place.

Historically, the rebellion broke out after the 1810 War of Independence against Spain and the 1859 enactment of the Leyes de Reforma (Reform Laws) on the separation of church and state, during the 1857–72 presidency of Benito Juárez (the first Indigenous president of Mexico) and amid the annexation of the state of Chiapas.[3] The narrative moves linearly through a preamble on the violent encounter with the colonial power, the thirteen songs, and a final reflection and future outlook in the epilogue. The narrative's repetitive tone gives the songs a rhythm both sorrowful and joyful and indicates a strong reflection on the unfolding historical events.

The preamble and the first two songs present the historical context of the Spanish disruption of the Tsotsil communities' ways of life. The narrative situates the origins of the rebellion in relation to over three hundred years of Spanish imposition and the communities' resilience and survival. The titles of each of these songs—"Yochebeal. Skapemal sjol ojovetik" / "Preámbulo. Enojo de los Dioses" (Preamble. The wrath of the Gods), "I. Snak'obal epal vo'vinik ja'vil" / "I. Sombra de los siglos" (I. Shadow of centuries), and

"II. Snenal k'ak'al" / "II. Espejo del tiempo" (II. Mirror of time)—carry an introspective tone on the violence lurking in the communities. The Spanish settlement is referenced as a tempest that leaves the environment opaque (25). Such language contrasts with the description of the communities, which, despite the colonial order, have remained strong. "Vo'tik svok'emal jtotik / ti chtal jxojobaltike / ja' te slikeb kayanebtik"—"Somos una vertiente del sol / que ilumina la música de la montaña / de allí surge nuestro origen" (We are a slope of the sun / that illuminates the music of the mountain / from there our origin arises) (31). Despite the inflicted Spanish violence, the communities have adapted to change and their traditions have endured.

Ti chamulae la scha' kuxesik
yich'el ta muk' ch'ul banomil,
la scha' kuxesik sk'ejimol
ch'ul vinajel,
la xcha' meltsanik stoyel
xch'ul lekilal vo',
ta kajal ch'ul lo'il la sk'oponik xojobal kajvaltik.

Los Chamulas volvieron a rendir cultos
a su amada tierra,
mezclaron sus cantos
para reverencial al cielo,
recrearon sus danzas
para la imprescindible lluvia,
en voz alta rezaron al resplandeciente sol.

The Chamula returned to worship
their beloved land,
mixed their songs
to reverence the heavens,
re-created their dances
for the essential rain,
loudly prayed to the shining sun. (31)

The narrative can be very direct, but the details—people living collectively, harvesting the land offerings, and constantly interacting with the world around—bring to life the communities, with their peoples and belief systems (27).

The linear narrative moves to the third song, "III. Jk'opojel ton" / "III. Piedras parlantes" (III. Talking stones), where the young woman Agustina Gómez Chechev is introduced. The narrative presents the figure of Chechev as one in tune with the cosmos, "ja'jun ants xch'ulelinoj xik"—"mujer con ch'ulel de águila" (woman with eagle ch'ulel), who moves through the open fields until she feels, not hears, but feels a voice calling her to build a shrine in honor of the three stones (32). *Ch'ulel* refers to the essence of a person, encompassing the person's worldviews, ontology, and all that constitutes their past, present, and future. Manuel Bolom Pale (2010, 127) speaks of *ch'ulel* as something that "tiene que ver con el desarrollo de las capacidades del ser; es decir, está relacionado con la conciencia, porque el Ch'ulel no nace con el individuo, sino que madura junto con él" (has to do with the development of the capabilities of the person; that is, it is related to consciousness, because Ch'ulel is not born with the individual, but rather matures alongside the person). Granting Chechev such a trait places her as one with the cosmos and in movement with the conditions of her communities.

Chechev's spiritual character is vivid when she first identifies the stones: "La tsak batel, ja' xchi'il yiluk kucha'al / sjamlej yo'nton ti sk'obe"—"Las tomó como si sus manos / fueran extensión de su corazón" (She took them as if her hands / were an extension of her heart) (34). The encounter is described as a sacred exchange and acknowledged as a gift from the creator.

Ja' ta melel k'opoj ti totilme'iletike,
ajvaliletik yu'un vinajel
xchi'uk ch'ul vitsetik.
Ja'xch'ulel mayaetik,
Pakal xchi'uk jtotik Ojov
ti ta xal sbaik ta ik'xchi'uk ta sleb k'ak'al.

Fue la verdad proclamada por los totilme'íles,
ajvaliles del cielo y de los cerros sagrados.
Fue el ch'ulel de los mayas:
el rey Pakal y el Dios Ojov,
clamando su presencia
en vientos y fulgores.

It was the truth proclaimed by the totilme'íles,
ajvaliles of heaven and of the sacred hills.
It was the ch'ulel of the Mayas:
King Pakal and God Ojov,
claiming their presence
in winds and glares. (33)

As with the 1712 rebellion, the act of embracing the message indicates a desire for a return or reaffirmation of the communities' spiritual practices. The naming of their sacred beings connects to lines in the previous song, which states that despite the imposition of Spanish religion and ways of life, the Chamulas do not forget the sacredness of their traditions. And here too, we see unfolding that reconnection to stories of origin and the sacred (Morales López 2004, 160–62). What is also in place here, in this realignment with Maya worldviews, is the reaffirmation or reclamation of their sense of Indigenous autonomy. Anishinabee scholar Lawrence Gross refers to this process as the maintenance of "cultural sovereignty." In his article "Cultural Sovereignty and Native American Hermeneutics in the Interpretation of the Sacred Stories of the Anishinaabe" (2003), he notes that American Indians have seen the end of their worlds, but not their worldviews. This is visible, according to Gross, in the ongoing practices of spiritual and cultural traditions such as song and dance. López Díaz's characterization of this encounter manifests this view too of Indigenous autonomy and Maya spiritual practices.[4]

Chechev accepts the stones as a transformative gift affirming the resilience and sustainment of Maya ways of life: "¡Ja'k'opoj ti k'ak'al o'ntonil / ta skoj li skuxul yayijemal ta tsatsal utilanele!"—"¡Es el coraje que habla / por las heridas vivas del sometimiento!" (It is the courage that speaks / for the living wounds of submission!); "Ta stonaltak yilel sjamalil ch'ul vinajel / vul ti yaj-almantal bats'i vinik antsetik"—"En apariencia de piedras de universo / llegó el mensajero de los batsi vinik antsetik" (In appearance of stones of the universe / arrived the messenger of the Batsi Vinik Antsetik). Furthermore, the communities' embrace of the gift, "sventa ti jk'opojel tonetike"—"esas piedras con voz" (those stones with voice), leads to the flourishing of devotion at the shrine in Tsajaljemel; the abandonment of "la yiktaik komel ti ch'ulnae, / ti santoetik xchi'uk ti paleetike"—"el tabernáculo / de santos y sacerdotes" (the tabernacle / of saints and priests); and a refusal to comply with the church's demands, voiced as "mi ja'uk lajuneb pexu / stojel spojel schulelik ta alel"—"no solventaron más tributos de bautismos / ni diezmos de salvación" (we will no longer pay more baptism taxes / tithes of salvation) (35–36). There is no denying the schism between church and tributaries at work in this rebellion, but in the naming of sacred beings and sacred relationships, the rebellion moves beyond a direct attack on the church and ladinos and into a quest for the reaffirmation of Maya worldviews. Such a position engages with Robert Allen Warrior's concept of "intellectual sovereignty" as developed in *Tribal Secrets* (1995, 123–24). In the context of Chiapas Maya histories, the discourse is centered on autonomy, not sovereignty, but the ideas are shared just the same. Intellectual sovereignty has to do with "a decision—a decision we make in our minds, in our hearts, and in our bodies—to be sovereign and to find out what that means in the process." Warrior writes that "sovereignty is not a struggle to be free from the influence of anything outside ourselves, but a process of asserting the power we possess as communities and individuals to make decisions that affect our lives." The embrace of the miracle stones and simultaneous distancing from the church are a reclamation of that "power . . . to make decisions that affect [their] lives," and to build something new in the process.

The historical narrative tells that the initial response of the authorities to the establishment of the shrine and adoration of the talking stones was to arrest Chechev and Pedro Díaz Cuscat, her strongest ally, but they were shortly liberated. Jan Rus's (1989) research indicates that the immediate release was due to the fact that the newly established Leyes de Reforma prevented the state from engaging in matters of the church. And thus, Chechev and Cuscat returned home to spread the message of the Virgin through the adoration of the talking stones.

The message the stones carry and the value the community places in them connect to Elicura Chihuailaf Nahuelpan's (2009) concept of *itrofil mogen*. Mapuche communities recognize the contribution of the cosmos to people's understanding of the world and the value that attunement with the universe carries in knowledge production. This exchange is reciprocal and integral to human and other-than-human relations. In line with this recognition is the way that Indigenous communities understand sources of knowledge in various mediums and appreciate the offerings and teachings of the cosmos. Native American and Indigenous scholars as well as scholars in Indigenous studies have highlighted the use of non-Latin alphabets in the recording of

Indigenous knowledges such as baskets, carved stones, weavings, paintings, and other artifacts (C. Allen 2012; Chacón 2018; Rocha Vivas 2021; Worley and Palacios 2019). The communities' embrace of the stones and the message they carry are part of an understanding of the universe as a source of knowledges. Such an offering affirms the value of active listening and the power of communities to search within their knowledge systems to decipher their world in a time of despair.

The fourth and fifth songs—"IV. Sleb jut k'opal" / "IV. Lumbre de mentiras" (IV. Light of lies) and "V. Sat snopbenal jolal" / "V. Frutos del pensamiento" (V. Fruits of thought)—emphasize the power of naming, another valuable contribution of the poem. The narrative names not only enemies but also allies, who believe in the three stones and support the stones' followers. The authorities Flavio Antonio Paniagua and José María Robles are presented as deceivers who raise their web of lies out of fear at the unification and strength of the stones' communities. They only see a growing threat to their power that must be destroyed, and a fight between savage and civilized humans (38). With this dichotomous mindset, the authorities dismiss the complexities of the stones' growing following and the rising power of the communities' leaders. Hannah Burdette's concept of "insurgent poetics" as developed in *Revealing Rebellion in Abiayala* (2019, 21) is seen in practice here. Burdette advances this concept in her close analysis of Indigenous literatures of the Americas emerging from periods of social unrest, political instability, and civil wars. Through the literary analysis, Burdette "argue[s] that insurgent poetics functions not simply as an escape from an oppressive reality but rather as a vehicle for creating collective consciousness and for acting in and upon the world." In the case of the Tsotsil Rebellion, the authorities failed to see that the communities were not just mobilizing against church authorities, but also affirming their agency in relation to their Maya belief systems socially, culturally, and spiritually.

The rebels, however, find an ally in Ignacio Fernández de Galindo, professor of philosophy, who comes to understand the conditions of the Indigenous communities that sustain the rebellion. Drawing on his philosophical stance, Fernández de Galindo questions the two-sided view of the rebellion (Indigenous communities versus Spanish authorities) and leans toward a focus on the condition of Maya communities under the grip of an authoritative power: "la sna'ti ch'abal smul ti tsotsil maya vinik-antsetike / ti jeche' xyuk'et sk'oplalik, / ti naka oyik ta tsatsal mosovinel / yu'un li yajval muk'tikil pinkae . . . /sva'anel ch'ulnaetik / xchi'uk muk'tikil naetike"—"supo que los tsotsiles no tenían culpa / de esa amenaza que agitaban en contra suya; / esos mayas vivían esclavizados / en las fértiles fincas . . . forzados a construir / capillas y mansiones" (he knew that the Tsotsiles were not to blame / for that threat that they waved against them; / those Maya lived enslaved / in the fertile farms . . . forced to build / chapels and mansions) (40). Fernández de Galindo's role in the rebellion almost predates the role of mestizo revolutionaries in the foundation of the EZLN over a century later. In the case of the EZLN, leftist revolutionaries escaping political persecution traveled to the southernmost state in Mexico, Chiapas, to grow their leftist revolutionary wars in the late 1970s (I develop this history more in chapter 4). Their encounters with the Maya communities in the Highlands of Chiapas instead transformed their thinking, leading them to focus on the reality of Indigenous communities and the foundations of the Maya Indigenous insurgency, which would become the EZLN. In his extensive work on the founding of the EZLN, Nicholas P. Higgins (2004) speaks of a decolonial encounter where non-Maya revolutionaries learned to carefully listen to and accompany Maya communities in their struggles, working shoulder to shoulder for change.

The song carries a series of questions on the condition of Indigenous peoples and the imposed label of savage. The introspective tone of the narrative is in direct response to Galindo's philosophical stance.

¿Vu'um con bolomunkutik . . .
ti skoj chich' k'oponel ch'ul banomil
k'al sk'anto xich' ak'el ti jts'unobale
xchi'uk skoj k'alal ta jk'oponkutik li vitsetik
ti yu'un ja' yajval ch'ul voe'?

¿Somos salvajes . . .
por pedir permiso a la adorada Tierra
antes de cultivarla
y al rezar a los cerros
porque son nuestros dueños de la lluvia?

Are we savages . . .
for asking permission to the beloved Earth
before cultivating it

and when praying to the hills
because they are our owners of the rain? (40)

The narrative draws attention to the polarized views of the time, including the false accusations made against the communities and the dehumanizing perception of Indigenous peoples. The song ends by naming two individuals—Galindo's wife, Luisa de Quevedo, and his pupil Benigno Trejo—as allies of the communities in rebellion, labeled traitors by those in power. The decision to ally with the rebels ultimately costs all three their lives.

The line of questioning in this part of the poem resonates with an early question voiced by the EZLN: "Who should ask for pardon, and who can grant it?" This question was made in response to the government's offer to "pardon" EZLN insurgents if they gave up the armed struggle. The EZLN continued its denouncement: "Why do we need to be pardoned? What are they going to pardon us for? For not dying of hunger? For not accepting our misery in silence?" (EZLN communiqué, January 18, 1994; EZLN 2001e). Both the poem and this communiqué of the EZLN respond to a failure by authorities to understand the significant reasons driving insurgents to rise up in defense of a dignified life.

A turning point for the followers of the three stones is at the center of the sixth song, "VI. Schopolil sjol pale" / "VI. La maldición del cura" (VI. The curse of the priest). The main priest of San Juan Chamula, Miguel Martínez, enraged by the stones' growing following, visits the shrine, destroys it, and attempts to take the stones with him. Members of the community become incensed with his behavior, stop him, and kill him. "Li palee la slikesbe sk'ak'al sjol ch'ulelaletik . . . / jech yich' lilinel va pale Miguel Martines, / chopol jch'unulajel skuyoj sba ta Ojov / te lilij xchi'uk chanvo' xchi'iltak"—"El cura despertó la ira de los nahuales . . . / así aniquilaron a Miguel Martínez, / católico ángel venenoso, / junto con sus cuatro verdugos" (The priest awoke the wrath of the nahuales . . . / thus they annihilated Miguel Martínez, / Catholic poisonous angel, / along with his four executioners) (43). According to Rus (1989) this historical action resonated across the state and neighboring ones, leading to outpourings of violence against the communities.

The killing of the priest is well documented, but the voice of the followers of the stone is new in this narrative. The clash between the priest and the followers of the stones is magnified through the poetic tone in this song. "Laj xa'ox yik'ubtasbe slekil snopbenal sjol ti tsotsiletik, / la slilinbekomel slok'tomba ti k'usi sch'unojike / la yal komel ti ja' yabtel pukuje, / yo'jech tsokes slekil yech'omali li tsobob baile"—"Trató de oscurecer la conciencia iluminada, / despedazando los símbolos sagrados, / acusando que eran obras del demonio, / y así menguar ese eco de unidad" (He tried to obscure the enlightened conscience, / tearing apart the sacred symbols, / claiming that they were works of the devil, / and thus diminishing that echo of unity) (42). For the priest and other authorities, the followers of the stone are engaged in mere idolatry and blatant blasphemy. But for the communities, the act of killing the priest is not just a violent response to the priest's attack; it is the defense of their integrity as members of the community and their dignity as peoples. Stefano Varese, Guillermo Delgado (Aymara), and Rodolfo Meyer (2008, 388), drawing on extensive work in the Andes, write about the importance of recognizing different relationships of humans to the land and to beliefs that are grounded in nature and that fall outside the frame of "Euro-American notions of time, space, and the *subject*." The actions of the stones' followers echo this call for the recognition of Indigenous values that Varese, Delgado, and Meyer describe in their work.

Violence, bloodshed, and the complexities of history are at the center of the next six songs. What is distinctive about this narrative is its emphasis on naming both the perpetuators of the attacks and the allies, and on recognizing the losses to accentuate the enormity of this rebellion. Also, as the violence spreads, and as the rebels fight for their lives, the natural world emerges as a character in this history, offering refuge for those in need.

On the violence that ensues, the poet draws direct connections between the communities' actions and the authorities' response. Historical narratives of the rebellion, however, are not always as direct. Rus's (1989, 1040–43) extensive research on this rebellion, which includes accounts from communities involved in the rebellion and from descendants of participants, addresses one aspect of the mobilization of violence. In his attempt to credit the memories of Indigenous peoples directly affected by this rebellion, he denounces false readings of this rebellion, including the notion that the crucifixion of a young Tsotsil boy on Holy Friday incited the violence against the communities. Based on his archival research, Rus learned that this version of history only seems to exist among ladinos, fabricated perhaps in their interest to further dehumanize Indigenous peoples and justify their violent actions. Rus also notes that this rebellion is never identified by Indigenous communities as a "caste war" or a war against ladinos, as scholars in Maya studies have characterized it in the past; rather, it is known as the Cuscat War, after one of the Indigenous leaders of the rebellion. Rus's findings are in direct response to the work of Victoria Reifler Bricker, a member of Harvard Chiapas Project and student of its founder, Evon Z. Vogt. Writing in *The Indian Christ, the Indian King* (1981), Bricker elaborates on the narrative of the crucified Tsotsil boy that Rus's research dismisses. Arturo Arias (2017–18, 2:184) also engages in a reading of this rebellion, including López Díaz's work, presenting a critique of Bricker's findings on this story of the crucified boy. At the core of Arias's critique is the way that racist ladinos disempower Chamulas in their telling of the rebellion, reducing them to an anecdote that is driven by ladinos' "highly biased [position] against Chamulas." Thus, we find the valuable contribution of the multiplicity of voices López Díaz brings to this narrative to untangle the knots of history, as well as the role of Chechev in these histories.

In line with the work of Rus (1989), the seventh song, "VII. Slikeb lajebal" / "VII. Preludio de la muerte" (VII. Prelude to death) focuses on the role of Fernández de Galindo, professor of philosophy, as an ally. Accompanied by a group of supporters, Galindo turns himself in to the authorities in exchange for the liberty of Cuscat and Chechev, who have been detained again. "Ta yabtelanel k'anbail / ta lekil abtelal, spasel vinikal sventa sa'el lekilal, / Galindo xchi'uk Trejo laj yak' sbaik / ta k'exolil yo'xlok' ti jchukeletike"—"Es un acto de amor por la paz, / por el honor, en un acto de hombría, / Galindo y Trejo se entregaron / a cambio de la libertad de los cautivos" (It is an act of love for peace, / for honor, in an act of manhood, / Galindo and Trejo surrendered / in exchange for the freedom of the captives) (44–45). Galindo's valiant act is met with an untimely death at the hands of the authorities Pantaleón Domínguez and José María Robles. The voice of Galindo affirming his faith as death nears pierces the lines of the narrative in the ninth song, "IX. ¿Ja' Jtotiketik?" / "IX. ¿Son Dios?" (IX. Are they God?): "*Li ta xnichimal jch'ich'ele / ja'te slikebal jtoyobail*"—"*Las flores de mi sangre / son causa de mi orgullo*" (The flowers of my blood / are the cause of my pride) (50). Galindo dies in pursuit of his beliefs and place in the world. He is a strong defender of justice who is executed by a system founded on prejudices, racism, and inequalities.

Once free, Cuscat and Chechev return to their communities, where they are impatiently awaited. On their way home, Cuscat and Chechev traverse the mountain range of Moxbikil, "ti ja' yav to'ox ak'ot xchi'uk lekil k'opojel ta vo'ne / tukibil ta sk'ak'alil tsaltel"—"ruina de rituales y de ceremonias antiguas, / devastada durante la conquista" (ruins of ancient rituals and ceremonies, / devastated during the conquest) (45). Their return to their communities is a return to their peoples, the shrine, the new rebellion, and the knowledges housed in spaces that have been destroyed but that maintain the spirits of living peoples. The violent disruption of the rebellion, the arrest of the leaders, and their release is a cycle reflective of colonization projects, where the colonial power relies on violence to exterminate Indigenous worlds, only to lead Indigenous peoples to be more protective of their worldviews. Chapters 1 and 2 engage with this discourse of protection of knowledges (such as stories of origin for the communities) and ceremonial practices (which at times took place in the secrecy of caves) in the face of colonial expansion, and the ways Maya poets tap into these protected knowledges through their poetry to realign their worldviews. In this part of López Díaz's poem, the arrest of the leaders does not bring the adoration of the stones to a halt. Rather, the ceremonies continue, always awaiting the leaders' return.

The next five songs center on the violent attacks leading to the end of the rebellion. The vivid language is gruesome, but it is through the telling of the story that healing unfolds. As Simon J. Ortiz (1992, 153) has stated, and as I reference in chapter 1, "Indians always tell a story. . . . The only way to continue is to tell a story and there is no other way." Ortiz also notes in this context of telling of a story that this is a reminder of where peoples come from, where they are now, and where they are going. In this way, the reclamation of these events, reframing the stories of the violent attacks, restores the communities' relations to these histories, giving way to their agency and to healing. Such actions are also in direct engagement with the decolonizing methodologies that Linda Tuhiwai Smith (2005) advocates for in the recentering of Indigenous knowledges systems.

The eighth and tenth songs, "VIII. Slikeb yak'obalil lajebal" / "VIII. Primera noche de la muerte" (VIII. The first night of death) and "X. Sk'inal milbail" / "X. Celebrada matanza" (X. Celebrated killings), focus on the violent attack led by Pantaleón Domínguez against the poorly armed Tsotsiles. The emphasis on the number of fallen Tsotsiles references the unevenness of the fight, and the precise dates of the attack punctuate its mark on history. The language is crude and the description is raw, but there is no going back but to face the wrath of the attack.

Ma'uk leto,
ja'jun k'uxul milbail,
oxib sien, oxib sien,

oxib sien milbil ilaj ti tsotsiletike
ta jun no'ox smalel k'ak'al, ta jun no'ox ak'obal,
tu mu xpaj y'alel sat yayijemal:
ta mu'yuk albil
k'usi chk'ot ta pasel,
ta chamen bek'talil
ta t'ilemik takopalil,
ta xvokoletik xkejeletik
slajesel o'ntonal,
li mu'yuk xchikintaik li soltaroetike
li sk'ak'al yo'ntoninojik ti totil me'il mayaetik ta vo'nee
li sti'emal sjolik ts'inil ta yo'ntonike,
li ja'no'ox yiloj stuk ch'ul vinajel
xchi'uk li buch'u ko'ol sbaik mu xalike.

No fue una guerra,
fue una matanza despiadada:
trescientos, trescientos,
trescientos tsotsiles masacrados
en una sola tarde y en una sola noche,
un llanto inagotable de heridas
por la inaudita sorpresa,
por los cuerpos muertos,
por los miembros desprendidos,
por las suplicas de perdón
que imploraron postrados de rodillas
que no escucharon los soldados,
por el coraje contra esos mayas,
por el odio sembrado en esos corazones,
ante los únicos testigos:
el firmamento y la complicidad
de quienes guardaron silencio.

It was not a war,
it was a ruthless killing:
three hundred, three hundred,
three hundred Tsotsiles slaughtered
in one afternoon and in one night,

an inexhaustible cry of wounds
for the unprecedented surprise,
for the dead bodies,
for the detached members,
for the pleas of forgiveness
for those who implored on their knees
that the soldiers did not hear,
for the courage against those Maya,
for the hatred planted in those hearts,
before the only witnesses:
the firmament and complicity
of those who kept silent. (46–47)

The rhythm of the verses denouncing the actions on that dreadful evening of June 21, 1868, reads like a constant state of violent climax. The repetition of *trescientos* (three hundred) also reads like an offering prayer for all the fallen ones. The reference to the numbered, nameless bodies seems to invoke their spirits, and honors their death if just for a moment. Adding to the weight of the history of this massacre is the vivid count of the lost Tsotsil lives. This was not a war; the unjust imbalance between poorly armed Tsotsiles and heavily armed soldiers turned this battle into a massacre. The courage of the poet is visible in these lines as he reclaims and reframes these histories. The names of all those fallen may have been lost in time, but the grief of the loss remains in people's memories, and in the act of reclamation, the healing process may begin.

A massacre of the peoples is a massacre on the land itself: this is the sentiment captured in Domínguez and Paniagua's continuation of violence.

Ta 1869, ya'vilal milob bail xchi'uk nach'satiel ibajinel,
ti kaxlanetike la sjoybinik jlumaltik cha'mo
ta yosilal banomilal k'uxul vokolil,
ch'abal xojobal xa ti chobtike,
pas ta ton yu'unik ti banomile,
takij yu'un ti ch'ichetike,
le'ne ja'xa jech syaxalinoj ti kiximtike.

1869, año de masacres y acechanzas,
la caxlanada racista convirtió Chamula

en geografía del dolor,
en milpa sin crepúsculos,
petrificó la tierra
con coágulos de sangre,
nuestro maíz tiene esos nutrientes.

1869, year of massacres and stalks,
the racist caxlanada turned Chamula
in a geography of pain,
in a cornfield without twilight,
petrified the earth
with blood clots,
our corn has those nutrients. (55–56)

Pain seeps through these lines, emphasizing the intervention of the narrative in this historical rebellion. The violence against Tsotsil communities is an attack on the environment, and on the foundation of the land that gives life to these communities. The land becomes carrier of memories as it witnesses and senses the violence.

Xi'el, xi'el, banomilal xi'el, muk'ul xi'el,
ep, mu albajuk la sts'unik xi'el
li pukuj abtel patane, jpuchvanejetik ta tek'el,
li jlo'lavanej abtel patan la stsakik ta k'op tsotsiletik

Terror, terror, terror, terror,
más, más y más terror cultivaron
los autoritarios, los poderosos,
los corruptos gobernantes contra los tsotsiles

Terror, terror, terror, terror,
more, more, and more terror they cultivated
the authoritarian, the powerful,
the corrupt rulers against Tsotsiles (56)

The repetitions in these verses are like weeping sounds evoking the sorrow of the massacre. "Yan sba j-ok'el ti ta yaxal banomile, / japemik sts'akalul takopalil ta yut chobtik, / joybijem ta uk'um ti ya'lel satiletike"—"Gemidos abundaron en las tierras fértiles, / miembros desprendidos en la milpa, / llantos convertidos en arrollo" (Moans abounded in the fertile lands, / members detached in the cornfield, / cries turned into a creek) (56). The bloodshed and pain do not stop, and the retelling of such atrocities is done so that these cannot be forgotten, again.

The theme of the geography of pain and complexities of the rebellion continues in the eleventh and twelfth songs, "XI. Satak lo'lael" / "XI. Los ojos de la traición" (XI. The eyes of betrayal) and "XII. Slajebal milbail" / "XII. La última matanza" (XII. The last killing). Here, traitors within the Tsotsil communities, Salvador Gómez Tuch'ni and Antonio Gómez, who tracked and informed on the leaders of the rebellion, are loudly named. They escaped to the mountains seeking refuge and protection. They have betrayed their community, but still find comfort in the sacredness of the mountains. The refuge the mountains provide acknowledges the love the land carries and its willingness to forgive when it is invoked for assistance and protection.

Crecencio Rosas's authoritative presence is named as his reinforcement of 360 soldiers unleashes another wave of violence in the community. The sense of resistance rooted in the community's faith is continuously present in the narrative. "Li 'jbel xal' jbajvanejetike yalojik xa mi te ta xtoy / smuk'ulik k'alal ta smilvanike, / pe li ta jtekelaltik mayaotike ja'kich'ojbetik / sbak'esobil li sjamalil ch'ul vinajele"—"Los 'valientes' racistas creen que / con la muerte realzan su poder, / pero los mayas todos somos / nervios del universo" (The "valiant" racists believe that / with death they enhance their power, / but the Maya are all / vitality of the universe) (59–60). These lines affirm that all the force exerted on the communities cannot erase the Tsotsil peoples, that they are one with the land and as such will continue to exist. Such a stance resonates with the work of Stefano Varese in *Witness to Sovereignty* (2006, 111). When writing about histories of Indigenous resistance in the Americas, Varese recalls the words, "you can kill me, but I will return, and I will be millions," which he attributes to the "18th century Aymara rebel Julián Apasa Túpac Katari" at his untimely death. Varese expands on this statement by noting that various Indigenous rebellions—such as those of the Quechua of Peru (with Inkarrí as a leader) in 1742, the Totonac of Papantla in southeast Mexico in 1778, and the Chinantec of Oaxaca in 1973—all have stories of Indigenous leaders' untimely deaths (56–57). Part of these communities' worldviews is the position that these heroes are hiding underground, waiting to reappear when the time comes. The sustainment of ceremonial practices and reciprocal relations to land and place becomes essential for communities to keep the path open for the leaders' return. The words of the poet here speak to this Indigenous cosmovision and the affirmation of Indigenous continuities that the authoritative figures of Crecencio Rosas and Pantaleón Domínguez cannot understand.

And so, the violence continues with another dreadful day of bloodshed, July 26, 1870, when thirty-six people are robbed of their lives: "sbek'tal vinik antsetik, / joybijem kom ta uk'umal ch'ich ti banomile"—"treintaiséis hombres, mujeres y niños, / convertidos riachuelos de sangre" (thirty-six men, women, and children, / turned streams of blood). The pain inflicted on the communities is also experienced by Mother Earth, who is witness to it all: "¿K'u s-elan cha'i x ana li ch'ul banomil / K'alal t'uxul sat yelob ta xchi'ch'el epal vinik antsetike? . . . / ¿K'usi chal xa na' li vinajel ti yiloj yepal / sjamlej ti lajem vinik antsetike?"—"¿Qué sentirá la Madre Tierra / al ver su rostro empapado de víctimas? . . . / ¿Qué dirá el Cielo que abarca su mirada / en todos los espacios de la masacre?" (What will Mother Earth feel / seeing her face drenched in victims? . . . / What will Sky say that encompasses her gaze / in all the spaces of the massacre?) (65). The earth and the sky are witness to the violence and recipients of the pain and bloodshed, connecting to Indigenous cosmovision of the land as witness of the violence but also giver of life.

The last song narrates the fate of the young woman Agustina Gómez Chechev and her strongest ally, Pedro Díaz Cuscat. Galindo is dead, and hundreds of peoples have been massacred, but not Cuscat. "Kuskat kuch yu'un snak'el sba / ta kachajtik vinajel / ta ch'ench'en xojobal jmeme'tik / ta o'lol Nujulbin"—"Cuscat logró esconderse / en las rendijas del universo, / en la cóncava luz de la luna, / en medio del cántaro en bruces" (Cuscat managed to hide / in the slits of the universe, / in the concave light of the moon, / in the middle of the pitcher's face). When his time came, "xchi'uk ta sbatlej osil / chvay li sbek'tal ta pukuke / xchi'uk ta xbak'li xch'ulel ta tulane"—"hoy y para siempre / duerme su cuerpo en polvo / y agita su espíritu en roble" (today and forever / his body sleeps in dust / and his spirit agitates the oak), the cosmos embraced him forever (66). A similar fate follows Chechev:

Kustina Komes Chechev
t'ujbil ants ta yu'un jch'ultotiketike,
ch'ay ta te bu junukal xokolal vinajel ch'ay,

te mi ta xanvil li k'usi k'ot ta pasele,
te mi ta o'lol be,
ta o'lol xemuna;
mu'yuk xk'ot xchi'uk li kuskate,
mu'yuk yich' na'el k'usi k'ot ta pasel ta stojol,
mujnatik jayib sjavilal la sta
mu xkojtikinbetik smamobtak,
mujna'tik k'usi yan albat
yu'un li jk'opojel likemiktal ta xokol vinajel,
va oxib snopbenal sjol sjamalul vinajel,
va oxib tonetik bajemiktal ta mu'yuk spajeb vinajel
oxib xik' xojobalileletik,
oxib alk'op sventa tsatsalil.

Agustina Gómez Chechev,
mujer elegida de los dioses,
se perdió en algún vacío del espacio,
en el andar de los hechos,
en la mitad del camino,
de la semana;
no llegó con Cuscat,
no supimos de ella,
no sabemos cuántos años cumplió,
no conocemos a sus nietos,
no sabemos qué más le dijeron
aquellas voces venidas del espacio,
estas tres piedras caídas del infinito cosmos,
esas tres memorias del universo,
tres alas de luz,
tres insignias de la resistencia.

Agustina Gómez Chechev,
chosen woman of the gods,
disappeared in some space vacuum,
in the walk of the facts,
in the middle of the path,
of the week;

did not arrive with Cuscat,
we didn't know about her
we don't know how old she turned
we don't know her grandchildren,
we don't know what else they told her
those voices coming from space,
these three stones fallen from the infinite cosmos,
those three memories of the universe,
three wings of light,
three badges of resistance. (66–67)

The leader, receiver of the message, receiver of the stones, fades into time and space. Perhaps the three stones are Chechev's *nahual*, connecting to the verse at the beginning of the songs, when Chechev first encounters the stones and picks them up as if they are extensions of her heart. In *Recovering Lost Footprints* (2017–18, 2:188), Arturo Arias's analysis of this rebellion concludes that Chechev "became the three stones of the Cosmos . . . which evokes the three stars of the constellation of Orion." With the beautiful lines of this song, I would add, the narrative grants Chechev eternal life, absorbed into the cosmos, living everywhere, whispering her truth to those willing to listen.

The authorities never caught up to Cuscat and Chechev, though they found their ends on separate paths; death found them on their own terms. Their triumph, however, must be accompanied by the crude reality of the number of lives lost. And in this song, the narrative emphasizes the battles and the 931 lives lost. This count of 931 excludes Cuscat and Chechev, giving them their own space in history. The song's repetition of the number of lives lost, 931, magnifies the denouncement and the reminder of losses and victories, sorrow and pain, in the defense of dignity.

López Díaz' s epilogue reflects on the cycles of life. Death is not the end, just another cycle in the infinite circle of life, and telling the histories of peoples means that the dead do not die in oblivion. These lines resonate with the actions of the Zapatistas, who said that they rose up so that their dead would not keep dying. Days after the 1994 uprising, the "Dying in Order to Live" communique was released, where the EZLN notes that in the preceding ten years, "15,000 indigenous have died of curable diseases . . . charity resolves nothing but for the moment, and again death visits our homes." And so,

Zapatistas rose up, with death close behind, but this time on their own terms so they could have a dignified death. They rose up and faced death, "so that our people awaken from this dream of deceit that holds us hostage" (EZLN communiqué, January 6, 1994; EZLN 2001b). This sentiment is present in the lines of this last song, where, despite the number of losses, all those who were massacred will somehow live on.

Kuxulik ta sat k'aka'l,
ta xbak'ik ta sbatlej smamalil vinajel,
ta xik' xojobal,
ta sbel sjol y'onton ik'.

Viven en los ojos del tiempo,
vibran en la eternidad del cosmos,
en las alas de la luz,
en la memoria del viento.

They live in the eyes of time,
they vibrate in the eternity of the cosmos,
on the wings of light,
in the memory of the wind. (68)

And just like this, as long as the stories live in the memories of the peoples, the rebels remain alive. The archives of histories keep on talking to denounce the massacres and proclaim that death will not banish them.

Conclusion

In the presentation of *The interminable wound*, author Ulises Córdova (2006) connects Diego Torres Sánchez's retake of this history to the sense of possibilities inspired by the 1994 insurgency. In a similar vein, editor José Antonio Reyes Matamoros (2006) presents Luis López Díaz's "Thirteen songs" by noting that it took over 137 years for this rebellion to find an interlocutor. The 1994 EZLN uprising, Reyes Matamoros adds, gave way to fractures in the system, allowing Indigenous voices to reemerge and tell the stories that rebuild histories. Accordingly, the narrative of the poems lives in the memory of the communities, and the poets' work is to rescue those fragments of history to rebuild the Tsotsil and Tseltal role in these historical rebellions. *Kab'awilian* practices and a process of *caracoleando* framed the poets' actions as they drew from existing historical records and shifted the lens to let Tsotsil and Tseltal voices reemerge. Furthermore, the poets' retelling of these historical rebellions connects to Burdette's (2019) concept of "insurgent poetics" as the poetry demonstrates that in the rebellions, the rebels struggled to defend Maya ways of life. And even more, as Burdette also develops in her analysis of Indigenous literary production in the Americas, the written word proves to be the most enduring weapon in defense of Indigenous autonomy.

In the development of the poetry, both poets grounded the narrative in the communities, decolonizing their histories. And in choosing to write about this rebellion in the aftermath of the EZLN uprising, they link the histories of rebellions in Chiapas. Thus, both poets engage their communities (Tsotsil and Tseltal), unify these voices, and retell these histories of rebellion in a way that further affirms Indigenous people's resistance and resilience in the face of colonial projects. Their words affirm their affinity with the world around, philosophizing about cosmic relations with their environment, and asserting their continuation as Maya peoples. In relation to the role of women in history, the poetry affirms their contribution to legacies of duality, a sense of equilibrium in the universe, and the empowerment that emerges when truths of histories are shared. The poetry is not a rewrite of history, but a new perspective, a new reading that places the main receptors of these histories, the Tseltal and Tsotsil peoples, at the center. Their work contributes to the "interminable wound" that the rescuing and recoding of Indigenous histories require. The writing process, however, gives way to a healing process for the authors and the communities.

CHAPTER 4

"A World Where Many Worlds Fit"

Zapatismo and the Reconstruction of Maya Worlds in Chiapas

> In our dreams we have seen another world, an honest world, a world decidedly more fair than the one in which we live. . . . And in this world there was reason and goodwill in the government, and the leaders were clear-thinking people; they ruled by obeying. This world was not a dream from the past, it was not something that came to us from our ancestors. It came from ahead, from the next step we were going to take.
>
> —EZLN COMMUNIQUÉ, MARCH 1, 1994

The emergence of the Zapatista Army of National Liberation (EZLN or Zapatistas) in January 1994 set forward a new discourse on the relations between the state and the peoples of Mexico, new ways of thinking these relations, and new ways of being in this relation. The EZLN's "dream" or new vision of the world is not about returning to a past that is gone, or extracting a model that was in place in the past, but about shaping and slowly materializing a future in every step the Zapatistas take in their struggles. "Now we follow our path toward our true heart to ask it what we must do," they add, emphasizing that in order to move forward, a process of questioning, reflecting, and acting is necessary to begin to build "another world" (EZLN communiqué, March 1, 1994; EZLN 2001c).

In this chapter, I turn to the six declarations of the Lacandon Jungle released to date. These are testimonies of the struggles of the EZLN to slowly dismantle existing relations in Mexico between political systems and Indigenous peoples (Rabasa 2010). The declarations reveal goals, philosophies, and periods of trial and error in the trajectory of this insurgency and its efforts to create something different and new. The declarations do not reveal a defined vision of this new world, but rather show a revolutionized process toward change of an insurgency that asks rather than answers, proposes rather than dictates, and listens rather than pronounces (Esteva 1995; Gilly 1997; Holloway and Peláez 1998; Rabasa 2010; Volpi Escalante 2004). The EZLN exposes in its ongoing struggles something beyond a paradigm shift in the existing relations of Indigenous peoples and the state of Mexico. It exposes the necessity of an ontological shift that speaks of processes of thinking and enacting toward visions of change. Moreover, the persistence of its struggles reveals that anything short of this change is unimaginable.

In my analysis of the six declarations following the gaze of *caracoleando*, the Zapatistas' worldviews emerge not just as an extension of their Maya past, but also as a process of recapturing fragments of the past to shape their future. In tracing the early steps of the EZLN's formation and public emergence in 1994, this chapter shows that its actions have been nurtured and sustained by Maya knowledge systems that are always in a process of dialogue and transformation. The connections that I present between the EZLN and Maya philosophies are in line with the research of scholars in Indigenous studies (Arias 2017–18, vol. 2; Chacón 2006, 2014, 2018; Hernández-Ávila 2017; Morales López 2004; Soto 2015; Valle Escalante 2009). What I add to this established connection is a focus on the EZLN's literary production as I trace the shared worldviews. The following questions guide my analysis in this chapter: What do the six declarations of the Lacandon Jungle reveal about the worldviews of the EZLN? What does the articulation of these worldviews reveal about the EZLN's ways of doing revolution? How does the articulation of these worldviews contribute to the EZLN's struggles to claim space as Indigenous peoples and Mexicans? My analysis suggests that the EZLN's written and oral delivery of the declarations as well as the symbolic actions articulated in the declarations offer new ways of thinking of Indigenous and Mexican identities. Moreover, I suggest that in offering new ways of thinking of identity, the EZLN is challenging new relations with the Mexican state. I further suggest that in the process of creating and giving life to something new, the EZLN is also rewriting the past to give way to new futures for all peoples of Mexico.

The EZLN and Maya Worldviews

Scholars of Mesoamerican literary traditions trace Indigenous peoples' trajectories as recorders of knowledges across millennia. The arrival of Spanish colonizers positioned the written text following the Latin alphabet as the main source of knowledge, decentering in the process Indigenous peoples' legacies of recorded knowledges in the form of glyphs, stelae, textiles, baskets, and other arts. This displacement was undertaken with complete determination to push Indigenous peoples' knowledge expressions outside the official archive (Chacón 2018; Montejo 1998, 2021; Morales López 2004; Valle Escalante 2009; Worley and Palacios 2019). The arrival of the Spanish thus disrupted Indigenous peoples' knowledge production, but adaptability to change, one of the strongest weapons of survival among Indigenous peoples, shifted their gaze to new practices (Varese 2006). Such an ability to adapt does not replace existing practices of knowledge production but rather enhances them.

In his general introduction to *In the Language of Kings* (2001, 13), Miguel León-Portilla, Mexican anthropologist and visionary in the establishment of Mesoamerican studies, writes about literary production in Mesoamerica in terms of cycles. Following the initial genocidal contact with Spanish colonizers, the colonial period was witness to the "blossoming of Mesoamerican literature." Young scribes learned their trade from friars and in church-run schools established by the Spanish, adapted to change, and began recording stories. Once scribes gained access to the writing system, they not only recorded what the new colonial power was asking them to do, but also found ways to bring in their own voices when recording the invasion of the Spanish and the experiences of Indigenous populations (see León Portilla 1989, 1990b). Ángel María Garibay, teacher and mentor to León-Portilla, explains this path of survival for Indigenous literatures, noting that "the indigenous word remained in the luminous prison of the alphabet" (cited in León-Portilla 2001, 26). Although the colonial power exerted strong control on the narratives produced, once the scribes had hold of the pen, they ingeniously influenced the narratives. This connection of recording histories and engaging in subversive writing shifted during the postindependence period. The general policy in the nineteenth century was to silence voices of dissent because the government was interested in unifying the state (Varese 2006). Mesoamerican communities at this time nurtured oral traditions to continue transferring knowledges to young peoples. With limited access to writing and written records, Indigenous peoples found in oral traditions dissident voices, maintaining their knowledges as communities.

Subcomandante Marcos, EZLN spokesperson, asserts the connection between the survival of Indigenous knowledges and oral tradition when he introduces El Viejo Antonio, Maya elder from Las Cañadas—the cradle of the EZLN—as central figure in the narrative of the EZLN's formation. In *Relatos de el Viejo Antonio* (2002, 205), a compilation of El Viejo Antonio's stories penned by Marcos, he writes, "Es el Viejo Antonio el que da los elementos indígenas que tienen el lenguaje Zapatista cuando se dirige hacia afuera" (It is old Antonio who gives the Indigenous elements to the Zapatista language when directed outward). The compiled stories reveal the survival of Maya peoples' knowledges through the practice of oral tradition, and the interactive roles of orality and written text as methods of survival and endurance.

An affirmation of the wealth of knowledges sheltered and nurtured in the communities and their importance in the formation of the EZLN is also present in the work of Carlos Montemayor (2000, 135–36), Mexican scholar and expert on Indigenous literary and cultural traditions of Mexico, who writes that "el EZLN fue el primer movimiento que podríamos llamar de 'indianización' de un proyecto ideológico occidental" (the EZLN was the first movement we may refer to as the "Indianization" of a Western ideological project). He reads the uprising and the Zapatista philosophy as rooted in the knowledges of the communities, and the EZLN vision and direction as a continued connection to these communities. The "Indianization" of the EZLN, however, was a process, not a given, part of the first stumbling steps of the EZLN.

In *Understanding the Chiapas Rebellion* (2004), Nicholas P. Higgins writes about the early history of the EZLN. He writes that the mestizo men who arrived in the Highlands of Chiapas in the 1970s came charged with leftist philosophies and ideas of guerrilla organizing that were not always relevant to the Indigenous peoples of Chiapas. In *Lacandonia al filo del agua* (Lacandonia at the edge of water, 1996, 154), Mexican anthropologists Xóchitl Leyva Solano and Gabriel Ascencio Franco trace the arrival of these leftist political organizers to a wave of internal migration that occurred after the 1968 social unrest in Mexico. Leyva Solano and Franco refer to this wave of activists as the "nueva izquierda" (new left) movement, with a core philosophy of "ir al pueblo, servir al pueblo" (go to the people, serve the people). The Indigenous communities these leftist groups encountered upon their arrival in Chiapas had already spent decades organizing in defense of their lands and ways of life, with mixed results (Harvey 1998; Nash 2001). Higgins (2004, 158–59) notes in his work that during the early conversations between the groups, a lot of miscommunications took place: "tu palabra es muy dura, no la entendemos" (your word is very tough, we don't understand it) was the local response to the leftist rhetoric. The tensions that arose led to new approaches in communication. The mestizo men had to make some adjustments to their role in organizing, particularly, they had to learn to speak less and to listen more, and to slowly become "part of the mountain." During the period of underground organizing, the mestizo members of the EZLN got to hear for the first time the endless stories that are part of Maya oral tradition, and they witnessed the intimate relations that the communities have with their environment and human and other-than-human worlds, in particular their respect for elders.

What unfolded in these relations during the early years of organizing references the Zapatista philosophy that invites peoples to reflect on the conditions of their lives and their communities and to walk toward the possibilities of change (Eichert, Rowley, and Sandberg 1999). Jacinto Arias Pérez (1975, 14), Maya Tseltal scholar, adds to this understanding of Maya worldviews in the Highlands of Chiapas when he notes that this relation is not something that can be communicated or learned directly per se, but rather something that is awakened in the mind and that is relevant to the communities. José Daniel Ochoa Nájera (Tseltal) (2011) engages with Arias Pérez's position when he notes that the heart is the driving force in the actions among human and other-than-human worlds. Manuel Bolom Pale (Tsotsil) (2010, 9) captures this relation in the concept of *k'anel*, which he defines as a "vitalidad y centro, núcleo o esencia de todo aquello que existe de los sujetos; dicho elemento actúa como un motor de los hechos a parir de la emoción, el conocimiento, la memoria, la voluntad, el lenguaje, la identidad individual y colectiva" (vitality and center, nucleus or essence of everything that exists of the subjects; this element acts as a motor of the facts from emotion, knowledge, memory, will, language, individual and collective identity). *K'anel* thus speaks of life-giving relations rooted in *convivencias* or living exchanges with the communities and all that surrounds them (humans and other-than-human worlds), because it is in these interactions that people grow and acquire knowledge. And María Mayo Mendoza's (Ch'ol) (2015) concept of *cholel* also speaks of knowledges acquired through the trajectories followed in life. From this perspective, the learning process is interactive, nurtured by peoples' lived experiences, which awaken their consciousness and ground them in their communities. Thus, in order for EZLN members to become "part of the mountain," new ways of communicating, learning, and relating to one another and the collective emerged to give life to the EZLN.

The intimate relationship the EZLN established with communities in the Highlands of Chiapas when Zapatistas took their first steps in 1983 anchored the EZLN within Maya worldviews. The EZLN's actions speak of cycles in the organizing process, as the groups of newly arrived mestizos and Maya leaders learned from each other and moved toward new visions of organizing in Chiapas. This process of "Indianization" (Montemayor 2000) disrupts the official history of the Mexican mestizo, where the Indigenous past mixes with the Spanish European to give rise to the mestizo identity (Saldaña-Portillo 2001; Saldaña-Portillo and Trujillo 2021). This process also moves away from binary (Indigenous-mestizo) and essentialist positioning of Indigenous identities (Valle Escalante 2009), which follows a linear progression toward a mestizo identity. The affirmation of Mexican and Maya identities that emerges in the first three declarations of the Lacandon Jungle is thus in line with these new directions and visions of giving life to something different, visions at the core of the insurgency.

Transformation of a Revolutionary Movement

The EZLN burst into the public eye and declared war on the Mexican Army on January 1, 1994. Within the first year of the uprising, the first three declarations of the Lacandon Jungle were released. These three declarations established a close connection between the EZLN and the struggles of all Mexican peoples. The predominantly Indigenous constitution of this rebel insurgency was established from the very beginning. Chiapas has a high concentration of Indigenous peoples and a long trajectory of Indigenous mobilization in the region; thus, there was no doubt of the strong Indigenous presence in the rank and file of the EZLN. What was necessary at this time, however, was to strongly claim the Mexicanness of the EZLN. This was its focus in the first year of the uprising.

Shifts in state policies and constitutional changes facilitated the EZLN's position during these early steps of the uprising. In 1990, Mexico ratified Convention 169 of the International Labour Organization (ILO), which "sets forth a broad range of economic, political, land-related, social, and cultural rights for indigenous peoples" (Stephen 2002, 341; see also Speed 2008). In 1992, Mexico completed revisions to Article 4 of the Mexican Constitution, recognizing the plural composition of the state. Though Mexico's interest in the endorsement of ILO 169 and the subsequent change to the Mexican Constitution were guided by economic interest and the neoliberal agenda that had spread in Latin America since the 1980s, these changes also opened space for the articulation of Indigenous peoples' rights (Speed, Hernández Castillo, and Stephen 2006, 204).

Two weeks after the declaration of war, the EZLN had agreed to a cease-fire and was calling for open dialogues with representatives of the Mexican government. When the dialogues came to a halt, the EZLN sent out an invitation for a National Democratic Convention to be held in Zapatista territory in August 1994 to discuss new directions for Mexico. The EZLN built a space for Zapatistas and civil society to come together in dialogue. They called this place, not coincidently, the Aguascalientes of Guadalupe Tepeyac. The name Guadalupe Tepeyac was attributed to a nearby Tojolabal community, though the historical context is larger than the community's name. Guadalupe makes reference to the Virgin of Guadalupe, *la Virgen morena* (brown-skinned Virgin), *reina de México* (queen of Mexico). Tepeyac is the name of the hill in central Mexico where the Virgin appeared to the Nahua man Juan Diego in the sixteenth century. This event is interpreted as the moment when Mexico's colonial power recognized Indigenous peoples' presence, since it was an Indigenous person that the Virgin of Guadalupe chose as witness to her apparition. But also, this is the moment when Indigenous peoples made their "first divinity of the Christian religious pantheon" (Florescano 1994, 144). The dark skin tone of the Virgin of Guadalupe is important too, because Indigenous peoples were able to find a likeness in the symbolism of the Catholic Church. Moreover, in reclaiming this religious historical moment in the naming of the Aguascalientes, the EZLN recalled the religious past that humanizes Indigenous presence in Mexico.

Aguascalientes (lit. hot waters) is also the name of a state in northern Mexico, where, in 1914, then president Venustiano Carranza held the Convención de Aguascalientes, which brought together leading forces in the Mexican Revolution, including Emiliano Zapata and Francisco Villa. Though no notable outcome came out of the convention, the 1917 Mexican Constitution, drafted under the guidance of Carranza, captured goals addressed during this meeting. The most notable item for the EZLN was the inclusion of Article 27 in the Constitution, which captured the essence of Zapata's struggle for "land for those who work it." The EZLN evoked the spirit of this historical convention by invoking its name in 1994 for the first space where national and international civil society, as well as prominent Mexican intellectuals, would come together with the leadership of the EZLN to discuss a new direction for Mexico. More importantly, Zapatistas positioned themselves as directors of the processes of unity and the creation of a new vision for a new state (Aguilar Camín and Meyer 1993; Gilly 2005; Gossen 1996; Knight 1986).

Amid the reclamation of the name Aguascalientes, and the recalling of its history, a process of *caracoleando* unfolds; the EZLN is changing its relation to a past historical event, which in turn changes the future that it is constructing. Michel-Rolph Trouillot (1995, 15) writes: "the past does not exist independently from the present." In this context, according to Trouillot, the past has content only in relation to the present because it is from this space that memories are collected. The act of reclaiming the name Aguascalientes not only links the EZLN directly to the history of Mexico, but transforms that historical past into something from which to build a future. This act of rescuing the spirit of this pivotal moment in Mexican history links to the EZLN's position of questioning and reflecting, which manifests in constant shifts in the direction of their struggle. The EZLN decided to look back, transform its own relation to this part of Mexican history, and re-create the path toward the building of a new vision for Mexico.

The Aguascalientes of Guadalupe Tepeyac, built by the EZLN for the meetings and dialogues, resembled a ship large enough to sit ten thousand people. References to navigating through high and low tides circled in the days leading up to the August convention (EZLN 1998a, 1:301). A heavy storm greeted all participants the first evening of the convention, materializing this analogy of a ship in high seas. The tide almost turned the direction of the ship around when the ropes at one end of the boat came undone. The participants, however, came together in shared camaraderie to keep sailing ahead toward tides of change. Mexican scholar Antonio García de León wrote days later about this historical event and referenced the ship as follows: "por eso la vieja paradoja renace . . . de que mientras más pasajeros se suban menos tiende a hundirse, de que hace falta peso y variedad para que la nave . . . pueda llegar. . . . Porque contra viento y marea la nave va (so the old paradox revives . . . that the more passengers climb on board the tendency to sink lessens, that weight and diversity is necessary for the ship . . . to arrive. . . . Because against all odds the ship sails)" (EZLN 1998a, 1:330). The historical reference here is clearly noted. The Spanish colonizers arrived in the Americas on ships. Now, the EZLN had built a new ship and was reclaiming this moment in time, a moment when the history of Mexico began and the destiny of Indigenous peoples was forever changed. The EZLN claimed ownership of this historical past and rewrote it to create different results and build new futures.

Indigenous and Mexican: Reemergence and Reclamation of Identities

The predominantly Indigenous constitution of this rebel insurgency was established from the moment the EZLN made itself known to the world on New Year's Day 1994. What was necessary during the early steps of the insurgency was to establish close connections between the EZLN and the struggles of all Mexican peoples. This position is in line with its defense of Indigenous autonomy and a dignified life for all peoples of Mexico, which the EZLN captured in the declarations through the language of democracy, liberty, and justice for all. In the first three declarations, released during the first year of the uprising, the EZLN's focus was on establishing its Indigenous and Mexican constitution, disrupting in this way official histories of Mexican mestizo identity, and forcing the gaze toward the building of new relations with the state.

The First Declaration of the Lacandon Jungle (EZLN 1994a, 1994b), released in January 1994, declared war on the Mexican Army. The language in the declaration focuses on the EZLN's quest to restore Indigenous peoples' relations with the state. The collective "we" (we are Mexican and Indigenous) is present from the beginning of this declaration: "We are the inheritors of the true builders of our nation," a statement that I read as claiming a connection to an Indigenous past and denouncing its long lack of recognition. The declaration continues, "[we are] the dispossessed, we are millions and we thereby call upon our brothers and sisters to join this struggle as the only path, so that we will not die of hunger due to the insatiable ambition" of those in power. The collective tone of "the dispossessed, we" references "Mexican brothers and sisters" affected by centuries of oppression. For five hundred years "we" have struggled, the Zapatistas state, but on January 1, 1994, a new cycle starts and a new way of rebelling emerges: "today, we say 'ENOUGH IS ENOUGH.'" The EZLN does not announce here what this new cycle will look like, but the cry of "enough" cuts through existing relations of the state with its "dispossessed," those who, in the language of this declaration, include Indigenous peoples and their Mexican brothers and sisters.

The EZLN (1994a, 1994b) legitimizes its declaration of war by citing Article 39 of the Constitution, which states that sovereignty of the state resides in the people, who have the inalienable right to "alter or modify their form of government." This declaration of war is in response to the state's "undeclared genocidal war," exerted on peoples of Mexico for over five hundred years. The EZLN positions its declaration of war within the Geneva Accords and agrees to honor international laws of war. Its members pledge allegiance to Mexico as their homeland and recognize the national symbolism of "the beloved tri-colored flag," which they state is "respected by our insurgent fighters." The EZLN sees the declaration of war as necessary to begin restoring relations in Mexico (people, government, history) and respect and dignity for all peoples of Mexico.

The Second Declaration of the Lacandon Jungle (EZLN 1994c, 1994d), released in June 1994, opens with a 1914 statement from the revolutionary leader Emiliano Zapata, whose name is central to the EZLN because of his position in defense of Indigenous peoples and their right to land. In the statement, Zapata notes the importance of fighting for peoples' right to elect governing bodies that represent them and respect them as citizens of a sovereign nation. These words resonate with the EZLN's goal of establishing a system that serves the needs and interests of the people of Mexico to restore order, the rule of law, and peoples' relations with the state (EZLN 1994a, 1994b).

In the introduction to *Memoria indígena de la revolución en Chiapas* (Indigenous memory of the revolution in Chiapas, 2010), editor Enrique Pérez López notes that according to official history, the revolutionary wars never reached Chiapas (see chapter 3 for more here). The stories compiled in this anthology, however, reveal the active engagement of Maya communities during this revolutionary period, specifically in the struggle for the distribution of land and the end of labor exploitation. The revolution achieved both goals successfully. In 1914, Carranza ended the system of servitude and debt peonage that was rampant in Chiapas. In 1917, the newly enacted Mexican Constitution included Article 27 on agrarian reform. By 1994, however, large numbers of Indigenous peoples of Chiapas, coffee and corn growers, were facing poverty, lack of access to land, labor abuse, exploitation, and hunger (EZLN 1994a, 1994b).

The EZLN calls on this moment of revolutionary struggle to remind people (Indigenous and non-Indigenous) that this fight (as outlined in Zapata's words) has been fought and won before (Articles 27 and 39 of the Constitution, the end of the servitude system). In the recalling, the EZLN rescues a past in order to emphasize the urgency of honoring the Constitution of 1917 (a position more clearly articulated in the Third Declaration). This position represents a shift to the long legacy of struggles in Mexico (which is also named in the First Declaration). The EZLN is looking outward, into a new future, demanding the restoration of this overdue commitment of the state to its peoples to build a new tomorrow.

The Second Declaration does not indicate what this new vision is; instead, the EZLN (1994c, 1994d) extends an invitation to all "the honest elements of Civil Society to a National Dialogue for Democracy, Liberty and Justice for all Mexicans," as a way to begin to materialize that vision. The defense of autonomy and ongoing search for alternative ways of organizing socially, politically, and economically (later declarations engage more with these positions) speak to the EZLN's cry for democracy, liberty, and justice. When Zapatistas call for the respect and reestablishment of the Constitution of 1917, they are taking one step toward their vision of a new state. The EZLN is also very clear in noting that this vision will not be able to take shape within the current system: "we are not proposing a new world, but rather a much earlier stage: the entryway to the new Mexico." Here, it critiques a system that imports solutions to develop Mexico, such as the North American Free Trade Agreement (NAFTA), and advocates instead for the affirmation of histories and knowledges stored in the communities.[1] The EZLN thus highlights its invitation to an ongoing project of change, a process that continues to dismantle the current political, economic, and social systems of Mexico. What is unearthed every step of the way is what directs its next step forward.

The sense of collectivity and unified voice from the First Declaration continue in the Second Declaration. "'Para todos todo' . . . mientras no sea así, no habrá nada para nosotros" (For everyone, everything . . . until it is so, there will be nothing for us) (EZLN 1994c, 1994d). The EZLN reveals with these words its commitment to and insistence on the struggle that it is waging. The ambiguous use of language places Zapatistas simultaneously as part of and outside the whole that is "everyone." They are able to move in the liminal spaces of their identities, demonstrating with these statements that they are two sides of one whole: "Don't surrender! Resist! Resist with dignity in the lands of the true men and women! Let the mountains shelter the pain of the people of this land. Don't surrender! Resist! Don't sell-out! Resist!" In this statement, they move between claiming their Indigenous identity as "true men and women," peoples of maize, and speaking "the word of the heart" rooted in their Indigenous ancestral land. "We reject the manipulation and the attempts to separate our just demands from the demands of the Mexican people. We are Mexicans," they state in this declaration, recalling through their word the plural constitution of Mexico (Article 4, ILO 169). The EZLN moves through these layers of identity, navigating liminal spaces and emerging stronger to reach out to Mexican and Indigenous brothers and sisters.

The Third Declaration of the Lacandon Jungle (EZLN 1995a, 1995b), released in January 1995, has a strong reflective tone, looking inward into the EZLN's actions of the previous year, from engaging in war with the Mexican Army to employing dialogue and diplomacy to achieve its goals. In this declaration, the EZLN clearly articulates for the first time a demand for autonomy. This demand is not one of exclusion and separation but a call to work together toward the recognition and incorporation of Indigenous peoples into the state agenda and for a dignified life for all. Explaining this demand has been an ongoing struggle for the EZLN. In the words of El Viejo Antonio, such an idea is connected to the story of the first gods, Ik'al and Votán, two sides of one whole who were able to create movement once they began asking questions and listening to each other. The idea also connects to Maya concepts of duality, equilibrium, and complementary roles. One very simple way to explain these concepts is through day and night: both are essential to humans' survival.

The EZLN (1995a, 1995b) explains this demand in this declaration and places the defense of autonomy at the heart of its struggles.

> The indigenous question will not have a solution if there is not a RADICAL transformation of the national pact. The only means of incorporating, with justice and dignity, the indigenous of the Nation, is to recognize the characteristics of their own social, political and cultural organization. Autonomy is not separation; it is integration of the most humble and forgotten minorities of contemporary Mexico. This is how the EZLN understood the issue since its founding, and this is how the indigenous communities who make up the leadership of our organization have defined it.

In the process of defending autonomy, Zapatistas center themselves as citizens of Mexico with the right to change the course of their lives within the law (rights granted by Article 39 of the Constitution). The EZLN's position in defense of autonomy, the language in this declaration reveals, is not an Indigenous struggle or a Chiapas struggle but a struggle to defend the rights of all peoples of Mexico. The language also reveals the idea of plurality, which the EZLN has defended since its beginnings, and the importance of recognizing "difference" as something that is not separate and that contributes to the formation of a unified whole. This declaration also connects to what Higgins (2004) narrates as an early step in the journey of the EZLN, a time when non-Indigenous and Indigenous peoples came together to form the EZLN and create a new language of understanding. The two created a whole with two sides, just like in the story of Ik'al and Votán (Marcos 2001). This is what the EZLN means by its demands for autonomy, the "incorporation" and "integration" of both Indigenous and Mexican parts.

The Third Declaration also engages in dismantling the Mexican state through a denouncement of the corrupt system. The EZLN (1995a, 1995b) elaborates on this point by stating that the federal government should step down, that the Mexican Constitution as drafted on February 5, 1917, should be reinstated, and that a transition government should be put in place. The language devoted to any transition of power is vague: the EZLN invites civil society to take on this task and makes a show of support for such action, but it avoids laying out definite points to follow. These gaps can be read as in keeping with the EZLN's position of not dictating any actions but rather giving space for others to contribute to the transformation of Mexico. The EZLN is also showing here that the path it is following is taking shape as this path is walked and, in this way, that everyone who chooses to support the EZLN is contributing toward its goals of autonomy and self-determination.

The EZLN pulls fragments of Indigenous histories to assert Zapatistas' Maya identity, and fragments of Mexican history to assert their Mexicanness. "We are Mexicans," Zapatistas claim in the Third Declaration, adding that "there will be no real solutions in Chiapas until the situation in Mexico as a whole is resolved" (EZLN 1994c, 1994d). Their demand for change is framed within their demand for autonomy, which seeks to attain democracy, liberty, justice, and a dignified life for all Mexicans. The absence of such demands has affected Indigenous peoples the most, they write—"we are the inheritors of the true builders of our nation. The dispossessed, we are millions and we thereby call upon our brothers and sisters to join this struggle as the only path, so that we will not die of hunger" (EZLN 1994a, 1994b)—but as their trajectory has demonstrated, their struggle touches on everyone in Mexico and as such all must participate in the change together. Whatever the new nation will look like is up to all willing to join in the struggle, unlayering the limitations of a system that does not meet all the needs of the peoples of Mexico, giving rise to something new and fresh that they cannot yet name.

The Flower of the Word and New Directions of the EZLN

The Fourth and Fifth Declarations, released in 1996 and 1998, respectively, align the EZLN within the histories of Indigenous struggles in Mexico and loudly reclaim an Indigenous vision. Notably, when I reviewed existing English translations published online and in print of these two declarations (as well as the Sixth Declaration, as I will discuss), I found selected pieces of the original Spanish that were omitted in the English versions. These omissions go beyond translation nuances and result in silencing sections of these declarations. In an attempt to restore these silenced sections, I present here my own English translations as part of my narrative and analysis of the declarations.

The Fourth Declaration of the Lacandon Jungle (EZLN 1996a, 1996b), released in January 1996, exactly two years after the uprising began, establishes a clear and firm relation between the EZLN and Maya Indigenous ideology. The Zapatistas had articulated their Indigenous worldviews in the three previous declarations, calling themselves peoples of maize and members of the *pueblos originarios* (originary peoples), establishing their struggle as one of the most forgotten and neglected, and claiming the importance of pluralism and difference. In this declaration, however, the EZLN's position is loudly stated. "When the homeland speaks its indian heart, it will have dignity and memory," they write in response to what they call an all-out war against the Indigenous presence in Mexico. "They do not want Indians," the EZLN writes, denouncing policymakers: "they want us dead." Thus, Indigenous peoples of Chiapas rise up to "fight against this loss of memory, against death and for life." Their ongoing practice of recording their histories is a strategy to sustain their memory and reclaim their place in the histories of Mexico. "The Zapatista war is only a part of that great war which is the struggle between a history which aspires for a future and an amnesia which has foreign vocation," the EZLN writes. Zapatistas contribute to this fight against oblivion not only in the actions of the uprising, but in the way they record their histories. They engage in a practice of collecting fragments of their history and the history of Mexico, and they work toward change through a process of rewriting.

The EZLN (1996a, 1996b) thus recenters the insurgency within the long trajectory of Indigenous struggles in Mexico. The Fourth Declaration reads: "The arrogant wish to extinguish a rebellion which they mistakenly believe began in the dawn of 1994. But the rebellion which now has a dark face and an indigenous language was not born today. It spoke before with other languages and in other lands. This rebellion against injustice spoke in many mountains and many histories. It has already spoken." The declaration then proceeds to list up to sixty-three Indigenous languages of Mexico, noting that before the EZLN, other struggles spoke other languages. Rebellion is about dignity, the EZLN claims, and so Zapatistas rebel "por el miedo a morir la muerte del olvido" (for fear of dying the death of oblivion) (my translation). What the EZLN is doing here is claiming a direct connection between Indigenous struggles and Indigenous languages. But even this position is not adopted in isolation, as it also adds that these struggles that spoke other Indigenous languages "habló y habla la castilla" (spoke and speak the Castilian language) (my translation), meaning that these struggles also spoke the dominant language (Spanish). The EZLN thus claims with this statement that Zapatistas' Indigenous identities connect them to their Indigenous languages and yet cannot be separated from the Spanish language, which connects them to their Mexican identity.

The EZLN (1996a, 1996b) claims in this declaration that its struggle against oblivion and in defense of dignity is the word. The Fourth Declaration reads: "Nuestra palabra, nuestro canto y nuestro grito, es para que ya no mueran más los muertos" (Our word, our song and our cry, is so that our dead will no longer die) (my translation). Zapatistas are here raising their voice to claim presence and recognition, to not let their dead die, and to return their sense of dignity. Their loud cry against oblivion is also a cry to be remembered. The poet Enriqueta Lunez (Tsotsil) (2007, 47–48) captures this process of raising one's voice to become stronger and bring together all parts of the self in her poem "J-ilol: Rezador" (The one who prays). The poem is analyzed in chapter 2. "Clamor insoslayable" (Unstoppable clamor) is the opening line to a prayer offered to bring the soul and body of a person together. The line is a cry to reunite detached parts of the self to unify the person. Just like the subject in Lunez's poem, Zapatistas raise their voice to give way to a process of reconstructing the past (not let dead people die), to bring together fractured parts of the self (Indigenous and Mexican), and to transform their future.

This process, the EZLN (1996a, 1996b) states, has to be fiercely defended. They write the following toward the end of the declaration: "La palabra se hace soldado para no morirse en el olvido" (The word becomes a soldier to not die in oblivion) (my translation). The word becomes the weapon to reshape relations that place Indigenous peoples "in oblivion." The poet Andrés López Díaz (Tsotsil) (2006c) speaks to this relation directly in his poem "Ta'lo xa: Basta" (Enough), analyzed in chapter 1, when he writes about the importance of elevating his language in song to give way to processes of transformation. The transformation the poet writes about in the poem is that of historical oppression and abuse against him and his peoples. "My warrior spirit contains / prayers" he writes as part of that loud transformative cry that relies on words and language to say *Enough*. The EZLN and Maya poets elevate their word and song to reshape the memory of Mexico, rewrite the past to dignify their present identity, and push open their place in the future.

The Fifth Declaration of the Lacandon Jungle (EZLN 1998b, 1998c), released in July 1998, is a direct response to the failed attempts to reach an agreement with the Mexican government on the EZLN's demands for autonomy. The San Andrés Accords, signed in February 1996, were never enacted into law, and so the demands for autonomy for Indigenous peoples of Mexico were legally denied. In this declaration, the EZLN highlights the importance of speech, of a language of silence, of a language of peace and dignity: "The time has now passed for the war of the powerful to speak, we will not let it speak more. It is now the time for peace to speak, which we all deserve and need, peace with justice and dignity." Zapatistas spoke their true word when they met with representatives of the government, but the representatives did not keep their word and violated the rights of Indigenous peoples when, under the direction of President Ernesto Zedillo, the San Andrés Accords were not enacted into law. The Zapatistas decided to terminate any form of dialogue with the government and to remain silent before them. The language of silence is also a shield of protection to maintain the strength of the struggle.

In the Fifth Declaration, the EZLN (1998b, 1998c) reaffirms its ongoing struggle for democracy, liberty, and justice in Mexico and for the recognition of Indigenous peoples. This they demand "with the indigenous heart which is the dignified root of the Mexican nation." The EZLN also calls on all peoples of Mexico and beyond to support the rights of Indigenous peoples: "There will be no transition to democracy, nor State reform, nor real solutions to the primary problems of the national agenda, without the Indian peoples. A better and new country is necessary and possible with the indigenous. Without them there is no future at all as a Nation." The EZLN is once again reaffirming Zapatistas' Mexican and Indigenous identity, and the importance of a unified struggle. It is denouncing the actions of the government, stating that this violation is not just against Indigenous peoples, but against all peoples of Mexico. This position is in agreement with the work of Mexican anthropologist Guillermo Bonfil Batalla in his groundbreaking book *México Profundo* (1990, 2004), where he states that Mexico will continue in its crippled state, unable to walk forward as a nation, if Indigenous peoples are not pulled in as part of the state agenda. This is the Indigenous identity that reemerges and is reclaimed throughout the Fifth Declaration.

The EZLN (1998b, 1998c) thus positions its achievements and failures as having an impact in all of Mexico, bringing in, in this way, the voices and support of all Indigenous peoples, a strategy that has worked successfully. The Zapatistas' fight is not just theirs, but they are at the forefront, facing the casualties that war brings, and they do not pull themselves from this position, but rather claim louder, "for everyone, everything, nothing for ourselves."[2] This play of words, which captures the spirit of their fight for all whom the state has historically denied, speaks of the collectivity that is so central to Indigenous peoples' belief systems. The EZLN is reclaiming space in the discourse of the Mexican state, restating the Zapatistas' position as an insurgency, highlighting the demands of their struggles, recalling all the forces of support, and reminding all those who are listening that "we are here" and "we are resisting."

The government's refusal to enact the San Andrés Accords into law as originally agreed led the EZLN to a period of silence after the Fifth Declaration. The use of silence as a shield of protection is a weapon the EZLN had also deployed in the past as a defense against the government's aggression. In 2003, the EZLN emerged from this period of silence with a new vision for the direction of the insurgency.

(Re)Birth of the *Caracoles*

In August 2003, the EZLN decided to change the name of the Aguascalientes, its center of social, political, and economic activity, now dubbing such centers *caracoles* (conch shells). When the EZLN chose the name of

Aguascalientes, it was establishing its connection to the history of Mexico. When the EZLN chose the new name, conversely, it was recentering itself within Indigenous worldviews. This new name is rooted to the EZLN's own history and place, clearly aligning with the trajectory and vision of an insurgency where *la palabra* (the word) and language are so important. The name *caracol* captures the process of building something different and new, and frames the EZLN's vision of a "new world."

Importantly, the new name in fact recalled the historical moment when the EZLN established the first Aguascalientes. In a 1996 communiqué, Subcomandante Marcos reflected on a conversation he had held with Comandante Tacho when the Aguascalientes Guadalupe Tepeyac was first completed, in June 1994. As they stared into the meeting compound, Comandante Tacho pointed out that the space had taken the shape of a *caracol*. In response to Marcos's stupefaction, Tacho "sketch[ed] in the mud with a stick . . . the location of all the buildings," and the image that emerged was that of a conch shell. At one end was the very first building the EZLN had constructed back in 1983, where all the early planning for the revolution had taken place, and which continued to be in use in 1994. At the other end was the library, which had been more recently constructed. "So there you have the Maya conch. A spiral with no beginning or end" (EZLN communiqué, October 23, 1996; EZLN 2001d).

The symbol of the *caracol* captured in the name speaks to the shifts in the EZLN's vision and ongoing quest to build something new. This concept of the *caracoles* also connects to the cycles of time that are central to timekeeping in Maya worldviews. The EZLN is engaging with the reading of time as something cyclical, linked to the idea of renewal. The Aguascalientes of Guadalupe Tepeyac was destroyed in February 1995, when the Mexican Army violated an agreement with the EZLN to not enter their territory. The library that Marcos and Tacho make reference in the story was destroyed during this invasion. The EZLN, however, responded with the construction of five new Aguascalientes in 1996 (EZLN 1996a, 1996b), and with the change in name in 2003, further improvements to the organizational structure of these spaces were announced, reflective of that spiral in motion that is the *caracol*.

Captured in this idea is the constant movement and reflection connected to questioning and dialoguing that have been part of the EZLN since the beginning. "The 'Caracoles' will be like doors for going into the communities and for the communities to leave. Like windows for seeing us and for us to look out. Like speakers for talking our word far, and for listening to what is far away. But, most especially, for reminding us that we should stay awake and be alert to the rightness of the worlds which people the world" (EZLN communiqué, July 21, 2003; EZLN 2004). The EZLN has navigated this process with certainty. It has experienced some setbacks along the way, but it has always pushed forward in the struggle, transforming ways of doing revolution and giving rise to a new vision for Mexico. This new way of doing revolution reveals that the EZLN has closely analyzed the successes and failures of guerrilla movements in Latin America and, instead of following those older patterns, decided to propose something different (Esteva 1995; Gilly 1997; Holloway and Peláez 1998; Volpi 2004). This "different" is what is so difficult for some to understand, but what the EZLN has been outlining in its declarations, communiqués, letters, and audio and video releases since 1994.[3]

"Another World Is Possible"

The Sixth Declaration (EZLN 2005a, 2005b), released in June 2005, documents the historical developments of the EZLN and the transformation of Indigenous peoples and Mexico since 1994. This declaration also reflects on the EZLN's eleven years in the public eye. It opens with the following:

> Ésta es nuestra palabra sencilla que busca tocar el corazón de la gente humilde y simple como nosotros, pero, también como nosotros, digna y rebelde. . . . Ésta es nuestra palabra sencilla para dar cuenta a todos los corazones que son honestos y nobles, de lo que queremos en México y el mundo. Ésta es nuestra palabra sencilla, porque es nuestra idea el llamar a quienes son como nosotros y unirnos a ellos, en todas partes donde viven y luchan.
>
> This is our simple word, which seeks to touch the hearts of humble and simple people like us, but also, like ourselves, dignified and rebellious. . . . This is our simple word to account for all the hearts that are honest and noble of what we want in Mexico and the world. This is our simple word, because it is our idea to call on those who are like us and to join them, everywhere they live and fight. (my translation)

With these lines and the narrative in this declaration, the EZLN recaptures oral traditions that carry responsibility and risk and that recognize the power in the telling of the story. The declaration recalls the formation of the EZLN and their desire to fight for Indigenous peoples of Chiapas and Mexico, and then extends this vision to encompass a "fight along with everyone who was humble and simple like ourselves and who was in great need and who suffered from exploitation and thievery by the rich and their bad governments here, in our Mexico, and in other countries in the world." It describes the EZLN's struggle to defend Indigenous autonomy and the failure to enact the San Andrés Accords into law: "And so the political class not only closed, one more time, the door to the Indian peoples, they also delivered a mortal blow to the peaceful resolution—through dialogue and negotiation—of the war." When the EZLN agreed to a cease-fire early in 1994, Zapatistas embraced the word "as their strongest weapon," following legacies of diplomacy Indigenous peoples have astutely practiced for over five hundred years in defense of their ways of life. The power of the word has guided their struggles and dialogues with the government, but as the EZLN reiterates in this declaration, the word has fallen on deaf ears with the government.

In response to the rejection of the San Andrés Accords, the autonomous communities in Chiapas continued to bloom by establishing educational and health centers. A number of land takeovers have been organized and undertaken since 1994 as well, giving the Zapatistas more land, arid land in particular, to better feed themselves and their families.[4] These improvements, as the EZLN (2005a, 2005b) carefully notes in its narrative, are only possible "if the indigenous join together with workers, campesinos, students, teachers, employees . . . the workers of the city and the countryside." Thus, when Zapatistas call on the peoples of Mexico, the dispossessed ones, to engage in the political developments of the country, they are leading by example.

The EZLN reinforces its anticapitalist stance by referring to capitalism as a reconquest of Mexico, where Indigenous communities are seen as obstacles in the plans for development. The EZLN (2005a, 2005b), however, is quick to highlight that just like "there is a neoliberal globalization, there is a globalization of rebellion." These "rebellions and resistances" fight against systems of oppressions and "struggl[e] for humanity." The "globalization of rebellion" also connects to the EZLN philosophy of Zapatismo, defined as an invitation to reflect on the needs of peoples and the actions required to create change or form a new world (Eichert, Rowley, and Sandberg 1999). The EZLN names in the Sixth Declaration the "persecuted and despised . . . like women, young people, indigenous peoples, homosexuals, lesbians, transsexual persons, migrants and many other groups who exist all over the world." Members of these communities did not line up directly behind the EZLN. They reflected on their own needs and formed their own ways of organizing, accepting with their actions the EZLN's invitation to join in its effort and thus become part of the globalization of rebellion.[5]

Connected also to the globalization of rebellion is an idea that the EZLN (2005a, 2005b) has been pushing since the beginning of the uprising: "another world is possible." Activists, the disposed, the marginalized, and the ones fighting against oblivion materialize this vision "through actions, not just words." In this statement, the EZLN is really dressing "the word" as a soldier charged with a weapon to lead actions. In a communiqué released on October 26, 1999, the EZLN (2001f) writes:

> O sea que cuando los zapatistas dicen "queremos un mundo donde quepan muchos mundos" no están descubriendo nada nuevo, simplemente están diciendo lo que ya dicen los "otros" y "diferentes" que caminan los mundos de abajo. Los zapatistas decimos "yo soy como soy y tú eres como eres," construyamos un mundo donde yo pueda ser sin dejar de ser yo, donde tú puedas ser sin dejar de ser tú, y donde ni yo ni tú obliguemos al otro a ser como yo o como tú. O sea que cuando los zapatistas dicen "un mundo donde quepan muchos mundos" están diciendo, palabras más o palabras menos, "cada quien su pedo."
>
> In other words, when the Zapatistas say, "we want a world where many worlds fit," they are not uncovering anything new, they are simply saying what the "others" and "different ones" who walk the worlds from below are already saying. We Zapatistas say: "I am as I am and you are as you are." Let's build a world where I can be, and not have to cease being me, where you can be, and not have to cease being you, and where neither I nor you will force another to be like either me or you." So when the Zapatistas say, "a world where many worlds fit," they are saying, more or less, "Everyone do your own thing." (my translation)

In the unification of struggles outlined here, the recognition of difference is at the base of the vision the EZLN continues to trace. When Zapatistas claimed their Mexicanness early in the uprising, they were highlighting this idea of a "different" way of being Mexican (Indigenous and Mexican); when they called on their "Mexican brothers and sisters," they were calling on those who are disposed and hiding in the shadows to claim their place as part of the state and help restore this relation.

The process of recapitulating their story in the Sixth Declaration and circulating it at such an important moment in the history of Mexico, in the middle of the 2006 presidential campaign, speaks to Zapatistas' insistence on working toward change, toward something different from what the existing system can offer.[6] They say that they wanted change for Indigenous peoples of Chiapas but realized early in their organizing that they wanted to do more, restoring dignity for all Indigenous peoples of Mexico and, for that matter, for all peoples of Mexico. They understood early on that as both Indigenous and Mexican they could not separate the struggles but rather had to work on connections and unification for change. "Our struggle is national," the EZLN (2005a, 2005b) repeated in this declaration, a struggle for "justice, democracy, and liberty for all peoples of Mexico."

The trajectories of the EZLN are *caracoleando* in practice. Thus, its amorphous vision, its inability to define the real goals of the movement, and the constant moving around that has been seen as a negative characteristic of the EZLN are all but part of a long trajectory that Indigenous peoples have been practicing in their struggles to defend their ways of life and ways they relate to the world. These actions are reflective of and adaptive to new challenges, but always rooted in communities' belief systems and calls for autonomy and self-determination.

Conclusion

The six declarations demonstrate that on January 1, 1994, the EZLN took the first step toward building new relations between Indigenous peoples and the state, as well as among all Indigenous peoples of Mexico. This whole process is an act of *caracoleando*, as the EZLN draws on old practices, knowledges, and understandings of the world informed by Maya worldviews to build new directions in relation to the state and among Indigenous peoples. In its building process, the ELZN (2005a, 2005b) embraces the notion of "un mundo donde quepan muchos mundos" (a world where many worlds fit), a world that it is helping bring to life while pursuing its practice of "caminando y preguntando" (walking and asking). In the EZLN's struggles, the path toward change is not fixed; rather, that journey unfolds through questioning and reflecting. The close readings of the declarations and communiqués in this chapter reveal the actions that the EZLN has taken since 1994. They are transforming ways of doing revolution, because in the quest toward its vision, the process is more important than the goalpost. The declarations do not reveal how exactly to reach that change, but they demonstrate how to question and challenge a system. In this process, the role of Indigenous peoples is enhanced, the elements of this vision revealed, and the urgency of the need for change emphasized.

The art of storytelling that the EZLN has captured so vividly over the years through its declarations and communiqués connects their actions to legacies of oral tradition. Such trajectories are also present in the collapsing of time and the connection to place the EZLN enacted in the naming of the first Aguascalientes, and subsequent renaming of the Aguascalientes to *caracoles*. The EZLN's recorded history shows that the insurgency emerges from members' dual relations with the world as Indigenous and Mexican. Their strategic positionality of claiming their Mayaness (members of communities that have lived in this Maya region for millennia) as well as their Mexicanness (members of a nation with constitutional laws that have been in place since 1917 to protect them) challenges the relations the state has with Mexican and Indigenous peoples. In their pursuit and defense of Indigenous autonomy and self-determination, they affirm their rights of liberty, justice, and democracy and claim their right to a dignified life. In the process of challenging these relations, the EZLN is carving open spaces in which to be Indigenous and Mexican.

Conclusion

Caracoleando *Among Worlds*

> When the men and women of maize look at this world and its pain, they also see the world that must be created and they make a path to get there. They have three gazes: one for what came before; one for the present; and one for what is to come. That is how they know that what they are planting is a treasure: the gaze itself.
>
> —EZLN COMMUNIQUÉ, DECEMBER 24, 2020

In the summer of 2022, I was invited to accompany members of the luk' upsíimey/North Star Collective for what they called the "Niimiípuu/Mayan Connections—Language Revitalization in Chiapas."[1] The collective, which constitutes Niimiípuu/Nez Perce tribal members, scholars, writers, teachers, performers, and artists, came together with Maya writers, poets, and language and cultural workers in what is considered to be the first intellectual exchange of its kind. In my role as translator, I facilitated exchanges in the poetry readings and panel conversation on Maya and Niimiípuu worldviews. When we visited the EZLN autonomous community in Oventic, I also facilitated exchanges between Niimiípuu members and EZLN community members on the recognition of struggles and affirmation of Indigenous autonomy and Native sovereignty, as well as expressions of solidarity with each other.

I think of this *acompañamiento* like a living experience of what this book is all about—*caracoleando* among worlds. As stated in my note on translation at the beginning of this book, the translation process involves moving among languages, following constant flows, exchanges, and reflections. A process of coiling in and out among the participants' languages, positionalities, and perspectives unfolded through the exchanges in the 2022 project, bringing into perspective trans-Indigenous concepts as worldviews were exchanged without recourse to direct comparison, focusing on dialogues of "unexplored possibilities" nurtured through mutual interest and understanding, and strengthening *conocimientos* (knowledges) among all participants (C. Allen 2012, xv). My *acompañamiento* of the "Niimiípuu/Mayan Connections," and witnessing of its exchanges, also feels like the materialization of the trans-Indigenous methodology I have been pursuing in my research and now present in this project on the literary trajectories of contemporary Maya writers, poets, and artists of Chiapas.

Framing this book within U.S. Native scholarship, presenting the literary trajectories of Maya writers of Chiapas in their Native tongue and Spanish, and following a trans-Indigenous framework that places these Maya works in conversation with Indigenous and non-Indigenous scholars of the Americas is my contribution to bridging the gap between Native American and Indigenous studies. Further, my analysis incorporates textual and visual narratives that cross geopolitical and literary borders, collapse political divisions imposed by colonial settler states, and push back on imposed literary genres that do not always allow for the multimedia platforms Indigenous peoples apply in the production and recording of their knowledges. The dialogues that ensue as part of the analysis of the contemporary Maya literature of Chiapas in this book contribute to bridging the unexplored characteristics of the literatures and English-Spanish language barriers.

The introduction presented the growing number of Indigenous studies publications grounded in Latin American experiences, and the dialogues the literatures are creating within and among these Indigenous knowledge systems. This book not only follows the trajectories of these creative thinkers but also positions its gaze within decades-long trajectories of U.S. Native scholars, also visionaries, in this discipline. Centering the focus on the literature in Chiapas, home of the 1994 Zapatista Army of National Liberation (ELZN) uprising, also highlights a central tenet of Native American and Indigenous studies: the gains within the discipline have always been a collaboration among intellectuals, activists on the ground, and artists, reflecting a strong sense of passion and love among them. The EZLN uprising has demonstrated the value of these collaborative efforts, first by taking on arms, then by laying them down and pursuing goals that follow the power of the word and diplomacy. Noting the impact of the insurgency among Maya peoples of Chiapas, Tojolabal scholar, artist, cultural promoter, and visionary María Roselia Jiménez Pérez stated that she was not strong enough to join the Zapatistas in the armed struggle but willingly stood alongside them in their ongoing struggle in defense of Maya ways of life (pers. comm.).

Calling on Indigenous voices, this book demonstrates that in the process of defending Maya ways of life to ensure the continuances of their peoples, Indigenous writers must critically rescue, restore, and reclaim knowledges buried in their communities. The authors are engaged in a process of *caracoleando*, demonstrating that this is a journey to their past, a validation of their present, and a reconstruction of their future. The conversations developed in chapters 1, 2, and 3 on the reconstruction of Maya worldviews in literary productions further draw on this concept of *caracoleando*, where writers and artists collapse notions of time and space to rescue fragments of their knowledge systems and piece together these fragments to restore their relation with the world. These Indigenous writers and artists engage in *caracoleando* through time and space, transforming histories and moving through the layers of their identities to assume control of the direction of their lives.

The paradigm shift brought about by Indigenous intellectuals in the late 1970s and early 1980s—as they transformed from agents of acculturation to promoters of their own culture, history, and language—is part of the politics of inclusiveness that the EZLN and Maya intellectuals continue to affirm in their literatures. Indigenous intellectuals proposed that their Indigenous identities as Ch'ol, Mam, Tsotsil, Tseltal, and Tojolabal did not have to be separated from their Mexican identity. This idea emerges strongly in the works of Maya writers, poets, and artists of Chiapas, who seek to be seen and heard as both Indigenous and Mexican. Zapatistas also share this stance in their struggles to defend Indigenous autonomy not through compartmentalization but through the creation of spaces where they can articulate themselves as Indigenous and Mexican.

This position challenges notions of identity in Mexico as a nation that ascended from its colonial and Indigenous past to become "Mexico mestizo." The revelatory standing of Indigenous intellectuals (both within the EZLN and within the Indigenous intellectual movement) rests in the ease with which this position is presented. In other words, in their efforts to reclaim their place, their voice, and their history within the official narrative of Mexico, their Indigenousness emerges always in relation to their Mexicanness. "We are all Mexicans, but each lives and feels his/her Mexican-ness differently," is a stance Zapatistas took during their first steps as an insurgency (quoted in Nash 2001, 147). The voices in the literary and art productions and the declarations and communiqués of the EZLN examined in this book present a sense of identity that recognizes multiple layers of the self and the spaces Indigenous people navigate as both Mexican and Indigenous. The concept of *caracoleando* speaks to Indigenous peoples' dynamic relational identity, formed as they navigate the multiple layers of their identity and worldview.

As I bring this book to a close, I too reflect on my entry into Chiapas as a field of study, first as an activist in solidarity with the EZLN and later as an academic researcher tracing the trajectories of the contemporary literary movement in Chiapas. In bringing this book to fruition, I started my research with the EZLN, spiraled out to contemporary Maya literature, and finally spiraled back to the EZLN in the last chapter. Returning to the literature of the EZLN has meant turning my gaze back to where this research began, rereading the declarations and communiqués through the gaze of *caracoloeando.*

Lastly, Mexico is faced with this challenge of recognizing the diversity of needs of peoples, Indigenous and non-Indigenous, and of understanding that despite its tactics of repression, peoples' voices cannot be silenced. The EZLN has stated, "Dignity cannot be studied; you live it or it dies" (EZLN communiqué, July 5, 1995; EZLN 2001a), meaning that dignity cannot simply be an object of analysis; it must be a part of everyday life, something that is lived, felt, and practiced. The EZLN and Indigenous intellectuals embody this sentiment through their ongoing struggles in defense of their ways of life and, as such, continue their process of *caracoleando* toward change.

NOTES

Preface

1. Zinapécuaro is located in the northeastern part of the state of Michoacán.

2. The project of *mestizaje* dates back to the sixteenth century, when Spanish colonizers promoted the mixing of Spanish colonizers with Indigenous communities of the Americas as part of their colonial project. The arrival of enslaved Africans expanded the mixing to Black communities.

3. Guillermo Bonfil Batalla writes in *México Profundo* (2004, 24) about the project of *mestizaje* in Mexico: "de-Indianization, has been called 'mixture' [*mestizaje*], but it really was, and is, ethnocide."

4. For more information on Indigenous self-identification, see United Nations (2007) and NAISA (2015).

5. Additional readings on this subject include María Eugenia Cotera and María Josefina Saldaña-Portillo's "Indigenous but Not Indian?" (2014), Saldaña-Portillo's *Indian Given* (2016), Gloria E. Chacón's *Indigenous Cosmolectics* (2018), and Maylei Blackwell's "Geographies of Indigeneity" (2017).

6. Bonfil Batalla (2004) writes about the necessity for Mexico to recognize its Indigenous presence and communities in order to survive as a nation. Indigenous communities, he writes, have historically been pushed into the depths of Mexico or Mexico *profundo* and removed from state projects.

7. Over almost three decades in the public eye, the EZLN has articulated this idea of a better world for Indigenous peoples and all peoples of Mexico. Its anti-globalization and anti-capitalist stance is at the center of its focus on the well-being of all humans and their relations with the world around. Chapter 4 elaborates on this position further.

Introduction

1. CELALI was established in 1997 as a result of dialogues between representatives of the Zapatista Army of National Liberation (EZLN) and the Mexican government.

This state-funded center is the first center to be run by and for Indigenous peoples of Chiapas. I present a larger history of the establishment of the center later in this introduction.

2. Zapatistas burst into the public scene on January 1, 1994, declaring war on the Mexican Army and taking over seven cities in the state of Chiapas using armed force. In their declaration of war, they demanded from the government, among other things, food and shelter, as well as access to land, health services, and education. Chapter 4 is devoted to the philosophies of the insurgency.

3. The EZLN and representatives of the Mexican government gathered in the community of San Andrés Larráinza, renamed San Andrés Sakamch'en de los Pobres by the EZLN, to agree on and sign what became known as the San Andres Accords. This is the only official document that recognizes the autonomous demands of the EZLN. CELALI was established based on one point in the accords promoting Indigenous cultures and traditions. Though the accords were signed in 1996, the government has to date failed to bring the accords into law.

4. I also write as a member of the Chiapas Support Committee, a nonprofit organization that was based in Oakland, California, through 2007; a member of the Acción Zapatista collective, based in Berkeley and Davis, 2006–9; and cofounder of the Semilla de Corazón collective, also based in Oakland and established in 2007.

5. There are thirteen different Maya language groups in Chiapas. In this book project, I work with Tsotsil, Tseltal, Mam, Ch'ol, and Tojolabal artists and writers. Some of the writers and artists speak more than one Maya language, but the common language among them continues to be Spanish. The EZLN consists of members of these five main language groups too, and Spanish is also their common language. Since its inception, the EZLN has stated the position of its insurgency and developed its philosophy of Zapatismo through the release of several hundred communiqués and six declarations of the Lacandon Jungle. The literature circulates through its own media outlets as well as national and international venues.

6. The choice to work with the Spanish term is in line with the language the EZLN uses in its literature and in the promotion of its philosophy. The EZLN's position echoes the notion of "reinventing the enemy's language," which U.S. Native scholars have applied in their literary production (Harjo and Bird 1997).

7. Mexican, Latin American, and U.S. scholars have been writing about Indigenismo for decades. The project of Indigenismo in Mexico was established through the Secretaría de Educación Pública (Secretariat of Public Education) in the late 1920s and had at its base the implementation of a state-dictated curriculum to spread a homogenous national consciousness and teach children how to become Mexicans (Aguirre Beltrán 1973; Bonfil Batalla 1990, 2004; Modiano 1973, 1974; Pérez Pérez 2003). This erasure of an Indigenous presence was vital as Indigenous peoples were considered deadweight to the progress and solidification of the nation (Bonfil Batalla 1990). The vision of these projects was further formalized with the establishment of the Departamento Autónomo de Asuntos Indígenas (Autonomous Department of

Indian Affairs) in 1936, and the Instituto Nacional Indigenista (National Indigenous Institute) in 1948 (Bonfil Batalla 2004, 117). Rural areas were the targets because educational institutions up to that time were concentrated in major cities and because rural areas had a higher concentration of Indigenous peoples.

8. On March 25, 2006, Jacinto Arias Pérez received an honorary doctoral degree from the Universidad Intercultural de Chiapas (Intercultural University of Chiapas), in recognition of his long trajectory as an anthropologist in defense of Indigenous languages of Mexico (Henriquez 2006).

9. This history reflects that of Native Americans entering the boarding school system and leaving with a stronger sense of Native identity; see, e.g., Standing Bear (1978), Ortiz (1998), and Warrior (2005).

10. The Harvard Chiapas Project was founded by anthropologist Evon Z. Vogt in the 1950s to study Maya peoples of Chiapas. Vogt trained dozens of anthropologists, including Victoria Bricker, George Collier, Jane Collier, and Robert Laughlin; see Vogt (1994) for more information on the trajectories of this project.

11. FOMMA is now part of the Hemispheric Institute of Performance and Politics and funded mainly by New York University. See Hemispheric Institute (n.d.) for more information on the histories of the center.

12. This close collaboration has been visible during my visits to these centers since 2008, and also shared by some members in conversation with me.

13. Culturas Populares was a government-run program established by Mexican anthropologist Guillermo Bonfil Batalla in the 1980s to empower Indigenous intellectuals and train them as cultural promoters. It was intended to help them steer away from assimilationist policies and engage instead with Indigenous knowledge systems. See Varese, Delgado, and Meyer (2008).

14. NAFTA is now known as the United States–Mexico–Canada Agreement (USMCA), after renegotiations among the three governments in 2019.

15. In most of Latin America, October 12 is observed as Día de la Raza, which is known as Columbus Day or Indigenous Peoples' Day in the United States (where it is observed on the second Monday in October). Official celebrations in Latin America recognize this day as the "discovery" of America by Christopher Columbus.

16. See the conversation on "participatory Indigenismo" (Sánchez 1999; Taylor 2009), which also speaks to notions of "Indio Permitido" (Hale 2004), for longer histories on state-Indigenous relations.

17. The term *kaxlanes* is also derived from the Spanish "Castilian," meaning European, outsider, or someone not from the communities; see also Mora Bayo (2017).

18. In *Racial Revolutions: Antiracism and Indian Resurgence in Brazil* (2001), U.S. anthropologist Jonathan W. Warren writes about ways Afro-Indigenous communities in northeastern Brazil are piecing their Indigenous identities together by rescuing fragments of their buried histories and knowledges. Language and cultural and spiritual practices that have barely survived over time are being rescued and put into practice to piece together their Indigenous identities.

Chapter 1

An earlier, shorter version of this chapter was published in 2017 as "Rebuilding a Mayan World: Awakening, Presence, and Possibilities," *TRANSMODERNITY: Journal of Peripheral Cultural Production of the Luso-Hispanic World* 7 (1): 166–88.

1. Prior to the release of the first declaration, the EZLN released a series of communiqués introducing *El Despertador Mexicano*, which was to capture the voice and actions of the EZLN (*enlace Zapatista*).

2. The project of Indigenismo in Mexico was established through the Secretaría de Educación Pública (Secretariat of Public Education) in the late 1920s in order to implement a state-dictated curriculum that would spread a homogenous national consciousness (Aguirre Beltrán 1973; Bonfil Batalla 1990, 2004; Modiano 1973, 1974; Pérez Pérez 2003). See note 7 in the introduction for more extensive historical context of the concept.

3. In 1996, the EZLN and representatives of the Mexican government gathered in the community of San Andrés Larráinza, renamed San Andrés Sakamch'en de los Pobres by the EZLN, to agree on and sign what became known as the San Andrés Accords. This document, which would also lead to the establishment of CELALI, is the only official document to recognize the autonomous demands of the EZLN. To date, the government has still failed to bring the accords into law as agreed when first signed.

Chapter 2

1. I am choosing to use this spelling of the *Popol Vuh* following the edition by Delia Goetz and Sylvanus G. Morley (1950), from the Spanish edition by Adrián Recinos (1947). Recinos's Spanish translation is from the original "Ximenez manuscript in Quiché" (1947). In 2009, CELALI published a Spanish-Tsotsil edition of the *Popol Vuh*. This translator relied on Recinos's Spanish edition in the development of the text. Spanish in this project was the common language to bring this Quiché text to the Tsotsil communities of Chiapas. My references to the *Popol Vuh* in this book project are informed by these three editions.

2. Laughlin is part of the Harvard Chiapas Project, founded by anthropologist Evon Z. Vogt in the 1950s to study Maya peoples of Chiapas; see Vogt (1994) for more information on the trajectories of this project.

3. Subcomandante Marcos was the spokesperson of the EZLN from 1994 until 2014, when he changed his nom de guerre to Subcomandante Galeano in honor of a slain teacher. He has been the source of much journalistic and literary attention since the early years of the EZLN as the most visible mestizo member of the insurgency.

4. Venustiano Carranza assumed the presidency of Mexico in 1914. He banned the system of servitude, which affected Chiapas directly since large landowners there relied on this system to keep workers (mostly Indigenous people) laboring under

slave-like conditions in their large coffee- and cornfields. Emiliano Zapata led the revolutionary factions in the south of Mexico, and his quest for land reform resonated (and continues to resonate) among Indigenous peoples and tenders of the land. Large landowner ladinos of Chiapas wanted to keep the ideas of these two revolutionaries as far away from Chiapas as possible. The Jacinto Arias Pérez poem that I discuss in this section speaks directly to this history; see Pérez López (2010, 18–22).

5. The removal from power of Porfirio Díaz, who had held office for over three decades, was one of the main objectives of the Mexican Revolution of 1910. Madero, Carranza, Villa, and Zapata are all heroes of the revolution, each one following his own ideals of change. Zapata's goal, "land for those who work it," was captured in Article 27 of the Mexican Constitution of 1917.

6. Lázaro Cárdenas assumed the presidency in 1934 and is historically credited with the wide implementation of land reform dictated by the Mexican Constitution of 1917. His efforts in favor of Indigenous rights in Mexico are also historically recognized.

Chapter 3

1. In the early eighteenth century, the Zendales region constituted what is now known as the Eastern Highlands of Chiapas.

2. Agustina Gómez Chechev found the three sacred stones in 1867, which is why the Tsotsil Rebellion is linked to that year. The years that followed, 1868–70, were marked by the spread of violence as a result of the shrine established for the adoration of the three stones.

3. Though Chiapas was officially annexed to Mexico in 1824, the dispute between Mexico and Guatemala over the annexation would last through the second half of the nineteenth century.

4. In the Latin American context, the discourse is always around autonomy and self-determination. Sovereignty is a term reserved for the nation-state only, and in the Latin American colonial experience, we talk about Indigenous communities, not nations.

Chapter 4

An earlier version of chapter 4 with a focus on Indigenous violence was published as "'A World Where Many Worlds Fit': Zapatismo and the Reconstruction of a Mayan World in Chiapas," in *Violence and Indigenous Communities: Confronting the Past and Engaging the Present*, ed. Susan Sleeper-Smith, Jef Ostler, and Joshua L. Reid (Evanston, Ill.: Northwestern University Press, 2021), 261–77. A revised and shortened version of this chapter with a focus on Maya histories has been approved for publication as "The Maya and the EZLN," in *Oxford Handbook of the Maya*, ed. Thomas Garrison, Jeffrey B. Glover, and Brent K. S. Woodfill (Oxford: Oxford University Press, 2024).

1. NAFTA is now known as the United States–Mexico–Canada Agreement (USMCA), after renegotiations among the three governments in 2019.

2. The EZLN (1994c, 1994d) expressed an earlier version of this statement in the Second Declaration: "Para todos todo . . . mientras no sea así, no habrá nada para nosotros" (For everyone, everything . . . until it is so, there will be nothing for us). In the repetition, the ELZN demonstrates the evolution of its language in the declarations.

3. In *Autonomy Is in Our Hearts* (2019), Dylan Eldredge Fitzwater engages in an analysis of the Tsotsil language to understand the road of autonomy for EZLN support communities. He argues that it is in the millennia-old language that the philosophy of the EZLN emerges.

4. Hilary Klein, in *Compañeras* (2015, 83–84), offers a deep analysis of land takeovers and land distribution in Zapatista autonomous communities. In her work, based on 2007 reporting, Klein indicates the difficulty of presenting an exact figure, putting the area of EZLN-occupied lands at "between five hundred thousand and seven hundred thousand hectares (1,235,527 to 1,729,738 acres)" (84). This is an increase from 1994, when the approximate area of EZLN-occupied lands was "sixty thousand hectares (148,263 acres) in the conflict zone" (83).

5. The EZLN's decision to travel across the Atlantic to visit Europe as part of its voyage across five continents, as well as the welcome it received, also speaks to this globalization of rebellion.

6. In 2006, after over seven decades in power, the Partido Revolucionario Institucional (Institutional Revolutionary Party, PRI) lost the presidency to the more conservative Partido Acción Nacional (National Action Party, PAN) candidate. However, PAN lost the presidency to the PRI in 2012, and both parties (the primary political parties in Mexico) lost to a newly established coalition party and its leftist candidate in the presidential election of 2020.

Conclusion

1. The principal investigators for this project were Inés Hernández-Ávila, professor emerita in Native American studies at the University of California, Davis; and Beth Piatote, associate professor in comparative literature and Native American studies at the University of California, Berkeley. For more information on this project, please see "Reclaiming Language, Revitalizing Culture: An Interview with Inés Hernández-Ávila; Artist, Poet, Faculty in Native American Studies" at the UC Davis portal on Public Scholarship and Engagement: https://www.ucdavis.edu/arts/blog/reclaiming-language-revitalizing-culture, accessed June 21, 2023.

REFERENCES

Aguilar, Camín H., and Lorenzo Meyer. 1993. *In the Shadow of the Mexican Revolution: Contemporary Mexican History, 1910–1989*. Austin: University of Texas Press.

Aguirre Beltrán, Gonzalo. 1973. *Teoría y práctica de la educación indígena*. Mexico City: Secretaría de Educación Pública.

Allen, Chadwick. 2012. *Trans-Indigenous: Methodologies for Global Native Literary Studies*. Minneapolis: University of Minnesota Press.

Allen, Paula Gunn. 1986. *The Sacred Hoop: Recovering the Feminine in American Indian Traditions*. Boston: Beacon Press.

Arias, Arturo. 2017–18. *Recovering Lost Footprints: Contemporary Maya Narratives*. 2 vols. Albany: State University of New York Press.

Arias Pérez, Jacinto. 1973. "The 'Numinous' World of the Maya: Contemporary Structure and Change." Master's thesis, Catholic University of America.

Arias Pérez, Jacinto. 1975. *El mundo numinoso de los mayas: estructura y cambios contemporáneos*. Mexico City: Secretaría de Educación Pública, Dirección General de Divulgación.

Arias Pérez, Jacinto. 2010. "Conclusion." In Pérez López 2010, 77–90.

Armstrong, Jeannette C. 1998. "Land Speaking." In Ortiz 1998, 174–94.

Blackwell, Maylei. 2017. "Geographies of Indigeneity: Indigenous Migrant Women's Organizing and Translocal Politics of Place." *Latino Studies Journal* 15 (2): 156–81.

Bolom Pale, Manuel. 2010. *K'anel: Funciones y representaciones sociales en Huixtán, Chiapas*. San Cristóbal de las Casas: Universidad Intercultural de Chiapas.

Bonfil Batalla, Guillermo. 1990. *México profundo: una civilización negada*. Mexico City: Editorial Grijalbo.

Bonfil Batalla, Guillermo. 2004. *México Profundo: Reclaiming a Civilization*. Austin: University of Texas Press.

Brant, Beth. 1991. *Food and Spirits: Stories*. Ithaca, N.Y.: Firebrand Books.

Bricker, Victoria Reifler. 1981. *The Indian Christ, the Indian King: The Historical Substrate of Maya Myth and Ritual*. Austin: University of Texas Press.

Burdette, Hannah. 2019. *Revealing Rebellion in Abiayala: The Insurgent Poetics of Contemporary Indigenous Literature*. Tucson: University of Arizona Press.

Chacón, Gloria E. 2006. "Contemporary Maya Writers: Kabawil and the Making of a Millenarian Literary Tradition." PhD diss., University of California, Santa Cruz.

Chacón, Gloria E. 2014. "Cultivating Nichimal K'op (Poetry) from the Heart: Indigenous Women of Chiapas." *Revista Canadiense de Estudios Hispánicos* 39 (1): 155–80.

Chacón, Gloria E. 2018. *Indigenous Cosmolectics: Kab'awil and the Making of Maya and Zapotec Literatures*. Chapel Hill: University of North Carolina Press.

Chihuailaf Nahuelpan, Elicura. 2009. *Message to Chileans*. Victoria, B.C.: Trafford.

Collier, George, and Elizabeth Lowery Quaratiello. 1994. *Basta! Land and the Zapatista Rebellion in Chiapas*. Oakland, Calif.: Institute for Food and Development Policy.

Córdova, Ulises. 2006. "Presentación." In Torres Sánchez 2006a, 13–17.

Cotera, María Eugenia, and María Josefina Saldaña-Portillo. 2014. "Indigenous but Not Indian? Chicana/os and the Politics of Indigeneity." In *The World of Indigenous North America*, edited by Robert Allen Warrior, 549–68. New York: Routledge.

De Vos, Jan. 2011. *La guerra de las dos vírgenes: la rebelión de los Zendales (Chiapas, 1712); documentada, recordada, recreada*. Mexico City: Universidad Nacional Autónoma de México.

Eichert, Benjamin, Rick Rowley, and Ståle Sandberg, dirs. 1999. *Zapatista*. Santa Barbara, CA: Big Noise Films. 56 min.

Erdrich, Heid E. 2012. *Cell Traffic: New and Selected Poems*. Tucson: University of Arizona Press.

Estes, Nick. 2019. *Our History Is the Future: Standing Rock Versus the Dakota Access Pipeline, and the Long Tradition of Indigenous Resistance*. London: Verso.

Esteva, Gustavo. 1995. *Crónica del fin de una era: el secreto del EZLN*. Mexico City: Editorial Posada.

EZLN (Ejército Zapatista de Liberación Nacional). 1994a. "First Declaration of the Lacandon Jungle." Chiapas and the Zapatista Rebellion (website). January 1, 1994. https://www.struggle.ws/mexico/ezln/ezlnwa.html.

EZLN (Ejército Zapatista de Liberación Nacional). 1994b. "Primera Declaración de la Selva Lacandona." Enlace Zapatista (website). January 1, 1994. http://enlacezapatista.ezln.org.mx/1994/01/01/primera.

EZLN (Ejército Zapatista de Liberación Nacional). 1994c. "Second Declaration of the Lacandon Jungle." School for Chiapas (website). June 10, 1994. http://www.schoolsforchiapas.org/library/declaration-lacandon-jungle-2/.

EZLN (Ejército Zapatista de Liberación Nacional). 1994d. "Segunda Declaración de la Selva Lacandona." Enlace Zapatista (website). June 10, 1994. http://enlacezapatista.ezln.org.mx/1994/06/10/segunda.

EZLN (Ejército Zapatista de Liberación Nacional). 1995a. "Tercera Declaración de la Selva Lacandona." Enlace Zaptista (website). January 1, 1995. http://enlacezapatista.ezln.org.mx/1995/01/01/tercera.

EZLN (Ejército Zapatista de Liberación Nacional). 1995b. "Third Declaration of the Lacandon Jungle." School for Chiapas (website). January 1, 1995. http://www.schoolsforchiapas.org/library/declaration-lacandon-jungle/.

EZLN (Ejército Zapatista de Liberación Nacional). 1996a. "Cuarta Declaración de la Selva Lacandona." Enlace Zapatista (website). January 1, 1996. http://enlacezapatista.ezln.org.mx/1996/01/01/cuarta.

EZLN (Ejército Zapatista de Liberación Nacional). 1996b. "Fourth Declaration of the Lacandon Jungle." School for Chiapas (website). January 1, 1996. http://www.schoolsforchiapas.org/library/declaration-lacandon-jungle/.

EZLN (Ejército Zapatista de Liberación Nacional). 1998a. *EZLN: Documentos y Comunicados.* Vols 1 and 2. Mexico City: Ediciones Era.

EZLN (Ejército Zapatista de Liberación Nacional). 1998b. "Fifth Declaration of the Lacandon Jungle." School for Chiapas (website). July 17, 1998. http://www.schoolsforchiapas.org/library/declaration-lacandon-jungle/.

EZLN (Ejército Zapatista de Liberación Nacional). 1998c. "Quinta Declaración de la Selva Lacandona." Enlace Zapatista (website). July 17, 1998. http://enlacezapatista.ezln.org.mx/1998/07/17/v.

EZLN (Ejército Zapatista de Liberación Nacional). 2001a. "Dignity Cannot Be Studied; You Live It or It Dies (July 5, 1995)." In Ponce de León 2001, 264.

EZLN (Ejército Zapatista de Liberación Nacional). 2001b. "Dying in Order to Live (January 6, 1994)." In Ponce de León 2001, 17.

EZLN (Ejército Zapatista de Liberación Nacional). 2001c. "In Our Dreams We Have Seen Another World (March 1, 1994)." In Ponce de León 2001, 18.

EZLN (Ejército Zapatista de Liberación Nacional). 2001d. "The Spiral from the End and the Beginning (October 23, 1996)." In Ponce de León 2001, 133–37.

EZLN (Ejército Zapatista de Liberación Nacional). 2001e. "Who Should Ask for Pardon and Who Can Grant It? (January 18, 1994)." In Ponce de León 2001, 38–39.

EZLN (Ejército Zapatista de Liberación Nacional). 2001f. "Why We Use the Weapon of Resistance (October 26, 1999)." In Ponce de León 2001, 159–63.

EZLN (Ejército Zapatista de Liberación Nacional). 2004. "Each Caracol Now Has a Name Assigned (July 21, 2003)." In *¡Ya Basta! Ten Years of the Zapatista Uprising,* writings by Subcomandante Marcos, edited by Žiga Vodovnik, 601–5. Chico, Calif.: AK Press.

EZLN (Ejército Zapatista de Liberación Nacional). 2005a. "Sexta Declaración de la Selva Lacandona." Enlace Zapatista (website). June 30, 2005. http://enlacezapatista.ezln.org.mx/2005/06/30/sexta.

EZLN (Ejército Zapatista de Liberación Nacional). 2005b. "Sixth Declaration of the Lacandon Jungle." June 30, 2005. http://www.schoolsforchiapas.org/library/declaration-lacandon-jungle/.

EZLN (Ejército Zapatista de Liberación Nacional). 2006. "Women's Revolutionary Law." In Speed, Hernández Castillo, and Stephen 2006, 3.

EZLN (Ejército Zapatista de Liberación Nacional). 2012. "Comunicado del Comité Clandestino Revolucionario Indígena-Comandancia General del Ejército Zapatista de Liberación Nacional del 21 de Diciembre del 2012." Enlace Zapatista (website). December 21, 2012. http://enlacezapatista.ezln.org.mx/2012/12/21/comunicado.

EZLN (Ejército Zapatista de Liberación Nacional). 2018. "Zapatista Women's Opening Address at the First International Gathering of Politics, Art, Sport, and Culture for Women in Struggle." Enlace Zapatista (website). March 26, 2018. http://enlace zapatista.ezln.org.mx/2018/03/26/zapatista.

Ferm, Deane W. 1986. *Third World Liberation Theologies: An Introductory Survey*. Ossining, N.Y.: Orbis Books.

Fitzwater, Dylan Eldredge. 2019. *Autonomy Is in Our Hearts: Zapatista Autonomous Government Through the Lens of the Tsotsil Language*. Binghamton, N.Y.: PM Press.

Florescano, Enrique. 1994. *Memory, Myth, and Time in Mexico: From the Aztecs to Independence*. Austin: University of Texas Press.

Forbes, Jack D., with Steven James Crum, Inés Hernández-Ávila, George Longfish, Martha J. Macri, Victor Montejo, and Stefano Varese. 2002. "A Hemispheric Approach: Native American Studies at the University of California–Davis." In *Native American in Higher Education: Models for Collaborations Between University and Indigenous Nations*, edited by Duane Champagne and Joseph H. Stauss, 97–121. Walnut Creek, Calif.: AltaMira Press.

Freire, Paulo. (1968) 2000. *Pedagogy of the Oppressed*. New York: Continuum.

García Muñoz, José Osbaldo. 2011. "El arcoíris." In Sánchez Gómez and Córdova Solís 2011, 35.

Gilly, Adolfo. 1997. *Chiapas: la razón ardiente; ensayo sobre la rebelión del mundo encantado*. Mexico City: Ediciones Era.

Gilly, Adolfo. 2005. *The Mexican Revolution*. New York: New Press.

Gómez, Reid. 2003–4. "They Killed the Word." *SAIL: Studies in American Indian Literatures* 15 (3/4): 64–95.

González Esponda, Juan. 2013. *"Ya no hay tributo, ni rey": de profetas y mesías en la insurrección de 1712 en provincial de Chiapa*. San Cristóbal de las Casas, Chiapas: Secretaría de Pueblos y Culturas Indígenas.

Gosner, Kevin. 1992. *Soldiers of the Virgin: The Moral Economy of a Colonial Maya Rebellion*. Tucson: University of Arizona Press.

Gossen, Gary H. 1996. "Maya Zapatistas Move to the Ancient Future." *American Anthropologist*, n.s., 98 (3): 528–38.

Gross, Lawrence. 2003. "Cultural Sovereignty and Native American Hermeneutics in the Interpretation of the Sacred Stories of the Anishinaabe." *Wicazo Sa Review* 18 (2): 127–34.

Gutiérrez, Gustavo. 1972. *Teología de la liberación: perspectivas*. Salamanca, Spain: Ediciones Sígueme.

Gutiérrez, Gustavo. 1973. *A Theology of Liberation: History, Politics, and Salvation*. Ossining, N.Y.: Orbis Books.

Hale, Charles R. 2004. "Rethinking Indigenous Politics in the Era of the 'Indio Permitido.'" *NACLA Report on the Americas* 38 (2): 16–21.

Harjo, Joy, and Gloria Bird, eds. 1997. *Reinventing the Enemy's Language: Contemporary Native Women's Writing of North America.* New York: W. W. Norton.

Harvey, Neil. 1998. *The Chiapas Rebellion: The Struggle for Land and Democracy.* Durham, N.C.: Duke University Press.

Hemispheric Institute. n.d. Website. Accessed January 24, 2024. http://hemisphericinstitute.org/en/.

Henne, Nathan C. 2020. *Reading Popol Wuj: A Decolonial Guide.* Tucson: University of Arizona Press.

Hennelly, Alfred T. 1990. *Liberation Theology: A Documentary History.* Ossining, N.Y.: Orbis Books.

Henriquez, Elio. 2006. "Otorgan en Chiapas *honoris causa* a tzotzil, primero en estudiar un posgrado en EU." *La Jornada,* March 25, 2006.

Hernández-Ávila, Inés. 2003. "The Power of Native Languages and the Performance of Indigenous Autonomy: The Case of Mexico." In *Native Voices: American Indian Identity and Resistance,* edited by Richard A. Grounds, George E. Tinker, and David E. Wilkins, 35–74. Lawrence: University Press of Kansas.

Hernández-Ávila, Inés. 2017. Introduction to Sell and Huet Bautista 2017, 3–20.

Hernández Castillo, R. Aída. 2002. "Zapatismo and the Emergence of Indigenous Feminism." *NACLA Report on the Americas* 35 (6): 39–59.

Hernández Castillo, R. Aída. 2006. "Between Feminist Ethnocentricity and Ethnic Essentialism: The Zapatistas' Demands and the National Indigenous Women's Movement." In Speed, Hernández Castillo, and Stephen 2006, 57–74.

Higgins, Nicholas P. 2004. *Understanding the Chiapas Rebellion: Modernist Visions and the Invisible Indian.* Austin: University of Texas Press.

Holloway, John, and Eloína Peláez, eds. 1998. *Zapatista! Reinventing Revolution in Mexico.* London: Pluto Press.

Hostler, Allie. 2013. "Taking It on the Chin." *Native News Network* (blog). October 30, 2013. https://nativenewsnetwork.posthaven.com/taking-it-on-the-chin-culture.

Huet Bautista, Nicolás. 2016. "The Art of Translation." Workshop, Centro Estatal de Lenguas, Arte y Literatura Indígena, San Cristóbal de las Casas, Chiapas, March 2016.

Klein, Hilary. 2015. *Compañeras: Zapatista Women's Stories.* New York: Seven Stories Press.

Knight, Alan. 1986. *The Mexican Revolution.* Cambridge: Cambridge University Press, 1986.

Kojtom Lam, Antun. 2007a. "J-ilol." In Lunez 2007, 46.

Kojtom Lam, Antun. 2007b. "L'amtabanejetik." In Lunez 2007, 35.

Kojtom Lam, Antun. 2007c. "Nichimetik." In Lunez 2007, 80.

Kojtom Lam, Antun. 2007d. "Ta ba mukinal." In Lunez 2007, 59.

Kojtom Lam, Antun. 2007e. "Vo'ne xatal." In Lunez 2007, 69.

La Farge, Oliver, and Douglas S. Byers. 1997. *El pueblo del cargador del año.* Translated by Víctor D. Montejo and Oscar Velázquez Estrada. South Woodstock, Vt.: Yax Te' Foundation.

Laughlin, Robert M., trans. 1997. *Mayan Tales from Zinacantán: Dreams and Stories from the People of the Bat.* Edited by Carol Karasik. Washington, D.C.: Smithsonian Institution Press.

Le Bot, Yvon. 1997. *Subcomandante Marcos: el sueño zapatista.* Barcelona: Plaza y Janés.

León-Portilla, Miguel. 1989. *Visión de los vencidos: Crónicas Indígenas.* Madrid: Historia 16.

León-Portilla, Miguel. 1990a. *Aztec Thought and Culture: A Study of the Ancient Nahuatl Mind.* Translated by Jack Emory Davis. Norman: University of Oklahoma Press.

León-Portilla, Miguel. 1990b. *The Broken Spears: The Aztec Account of the Conquest of Mexico.* Translated by Lysander Kemp. Boston: Beacon Press.

León-Portilla, Miguel. 1996. *El destino de la palabra: de la oralidad y los códices mesoamericanos a la escritura alfabética.* Mexico City: El Colegio Nacional, Fondo de Cultura Económica.

León-Portilla, Miguel. 2001. General introduction to *In the Language of Kings: An Anthology of Mesoamerican Literature—Pre-Columbian to the Present,* edited by Miguel León-Portilla and Earl Shorris, 8–41. New York: W. W. Norton.

Leyva Solano, Xóchitl, and Gabriel Ascencio Franco. 1996. *Lacandonia al filo del agua.* Mexico City: Fondo de Cultura Económica.

López Díaz, Andrés. 2006a. "A'yej." In López Díaz, Díaz Ruiz, and López Díaz 2006, 2.

López Díaz, Andrés. 2006b. "Jun k'ak'al." In López Díaz, Díaz Ruiz, and López Díaz 2006, 1.

López Díaz, Andrés. 2006c. "Ta'lo xa." In López Díaz, Díaz Ruiz, and López Díaz 2006, 4–5.

López Díaz, Andrés, Angelina Díaz Ruiz, and Luis López Díaz. 2006. *Sbel sjol yo'nton ik': Memoria del viento.* Edited by Armando Sánchez Gómez and José Antonio Reyes Matamoros. Tuxtla Gutiérrez: Chiapas: Consejo Nacional para la Cultura y las Artes.

López Díaz, Luis. 2006. "Oxlajuneb k'ejimol sventa Tsajaljemel: Trece cantos por Tsajaljemel." In López Díaz, Díaz Ruiz, and López Díaz 2006, 23–68.

López Gómez, Josías. 2011. *Te'eltik ants: Mujer de la montaña.* San Cristóbal de las Casas, Chiapas: Centro Estatal de Lenguas, Arte y Literatura Indígenas.

López K'ana, Josías, Juana Karen Peñate Montejo, Ruperta Bautista Vázquez, Nicolás Huet Bautista, and Enrique Pérez López. (1999) 2012. *Palabra conjurada: cinco voces, cinco cantos,* edited by José Antonio Reyes Matamoros. San Cristóbal de las Casas, Chiapas: Centro Estatal de Lenguas, Arte y Literatura Indígenas.

López Sántiz, Adriana del Carmen. 2005. *Jalbil k'opetik: Palabras tejidas.* San Cristóbal de las Casas, Chiapas: Centro Estatal de Lenguas Arte y Literatura Indígenas.

Lunez, Enriqueta. 2007. *Yi' Beltak ch'ulelaletik: Raíces del alma.* Hermosillo, Sonora: Instituto Sonorense de Cultura.

Lunez, Enriqueta. 2012. "La Poesía Indígena debe comprenderse, sentirse y completarse: Enriqueta Lunez." *La Jornada,* August 13, 2012.

Lunez, Enriqueta. 2017. "Mujeres: Enriqueta Lunez." . . . *de Raíz Luna*, hosted by Mardonio Carballo, Canal 22, November 14, 2017.

Lunez, Enriqueta. 2019. *New Moon: Luna Nueva: Yuninal Jme'tik*. Translated by Clare Sullivan. Brooklyn, N.Y.: Ugly Duckling Presse.

Marcos, Subcomandante. 2001. "The Story of Questions." In *Zapatista Stories*, translated by Dinah Livingstone, 91–96. London: KATABASIS.

Marcos, Subcomandante. 2002. *Relatos de el Viejo Antonio*. San Cristóbal de las Casas: Centro de Información y Análisis de Chiapas.

Mayo Mendoza, María. 2015. *Cholel-päk'äbtyak: crecer desde el nosotros*. San Cristóbal de las Casas, Chiapas: Centro Estatal de Lenguas, Arte y Literatura Indígenas.

Menchú, Rigoberta. 1984. *I, Rigoberta Menchú: An Indian Woman in Guatemala*. Edited by Elisabeth Burgos-Debray. New York: Verso.

Modiano, Nancy. 1973. *Indian Education in the Chiapas Highlands*. New York: Holt, Rinehart and Winston.

Modiano, Nancy. 1974. *La educación indígena en los altos de Chiapas*. Mexico City: Instituto Nacional Indigenista y Secretaría de Educación Pública.

Moksnes, Heidi. 2012. *Maya Exodus: Indigenous Struggle for Citizenship in Chiapas*. Norman: University of Oklahoma Press.

Momaday, N. Scott. 1999a. *House Made of Dawn*. New York: Perennial Classics.

Momaday, N. Scott. 1999b. "The Man Made of Words." In *Native American Literature: An Anthology*, edited by Lawana Trout, 635–47. Lincolnwood, Ill.: NTC/Contemporary.

Montejo, Victor. 1998. "The Stones Will Speak Again: Dreams of an Atz'ib' (Writer) in the Maya Land." In Ortiz 1998, 196–218.

Montejo, Victor. 2001. "The Road to Heaven: Jakaltek Maya Belief, Religion, and the Ecology." In *Indigenous Traditions and Ecology: The Interbeing of Cosmology and Community*, edited by John Grim, 175–95. Cambridge, Mass.: Harvard University Press.

Montejo, Victor. 2004. "Mayan Ways of Knowing: Modern Mayans and the Elders." In *A Will to Survive: Indigenous Essays on the Politics of Culture, Language, and Identity*, edited by Stephen Greymorning, 154–70. Boston: McGraw-Hill.

Montejo, Victor. 2005. *Maya Intellectual Renaissance: Identity, Representation, and Leadership*. Austin: University of Texas Press.

Montejo, Victor. 2021. *Mayalogue: An Interactionist Theory of Indigenous Cultures*. Albany: State University of New York Press.

Montemayor, Carlos. 1997. *Chiapas: La rebelión indígena de México*. Mexico City: J. Mortiz.

Montemayor, Carlos. 2000. *Los pueblos indios de México hoy*. Mexico City: Editorial Planeta Mexicana.

Montemayor, Carlos, and Donald H. Frischmann, eds. 2005–7. *Words of the True Peoples: Anthology of Contemporary Mexican Indigenous-Language Writers*. 3 vols. Austin: University of Texas Press.

Mora Bayo, Mariana. 2017. *Kuxlejal Politics: Indigenous Autonomy, Race, and Decolonizing Research in Zapatista Communities*. Austin: University of Texas Press.

Morales López, Micaela. 2004. *Raíces de la ceiba: literatura indígena de Chiapas*. Mexico City: Universidad Autónoma Metropolitana, Unidad Iztapalapa, División de Ciencias Sociales y Humanidades, Departamento de Filosofía.

NAISA (Native American and Indigenous Studies Association). 2015. "NAISA Council Statement on Indigenous Identity Fraud." Approved September 15, 2015. https://naisa.org/about/documents-archive/previous-council-statements/naisa-council-statement-on-indigenous-identity-fraud/.

Nash, June C. 2001. *Mayan Visions: The Quest for Autonomy in an Age of Globalization*. New York: Routledge.

Ochoa Nájera, José Daniel. 2011. *Del lingüicidio al plurilingüismo*. San Cristóbal de las Casas, Chiapas: Centro Estatal de Lenguas, Arte y Literatura Indígenas.

Olszewska, Zuzanna. 2015. *The Pearl of Dari: Poetry and Personhood Among Young Afghans in Iran*. Bloomington: Indiana University Press.

Ortiz, Simon J. 1981. *From Sand Creek: Rising in This Heart Which Is Our America*. New York: Thunder's Mouth Press.

Ortiz, Simon J. 1992. *Woven Stone*. Tucson: University of Arizona Press.

Ortiz, Simon J., ed. 1998. *Speaking for the Generations: Native Writers on Writing*. Tucson: University of Arizona Press.

Ortiz, Simon J. 2006a. "Foreword: Speaking-Writing Indigenous Literary Sovereignty." In Weaver, Womack, and Warrior 2006, vii–xiv.

Ortiz, Simon J. 2006b. "Towards a National Indian Literature." In Weaver, Womack, and Warrior 2006, 253–60.

Past, Ambar, Xun Okotz, and Petra Ernándes, eds. 2005. *Incantations by Mayan Women*. San Cristóbal de las Casas, Chiapas: Taller Leñateros.

Pérez López, Enrique. 2008. "Historia de Chiapas." Lecture, University of California, Davis, Summer Abroad, San Cristóbal de las Casas, Chiapas, August 2008.

Pérez López, Enrique, ed. 2010. *Memoria indígena de la revolución en Chiapas*. San Cristóbal de las Casas, Chiapas: Centro Estatal de Lenguas, Arte y Literatura Indígenas.

Pérez Pérez, Elías. 2003. *La crisis de la educación indígena en el área tzotzil: Los Altos de Chiapas*. Mexico City: Universidad Pedagógica Nacional.

Ponce de León, Juana, ed. 2001. *Our Word Is Our Weapon: Selected Writings, Subcomandante Insurgente Marcos*. New York: Seven Stories Press.

Popol Vuh: ch'ul vun yu'un maya k'iche'etik ta bats'i k'op. 2009. Translated by Mariano Sánchez Pérez, Marcelina Petrona Pérez Vásquez, and Alfonso Miguel Jasso Flores, from the Spanish translation by Adrián Recinos. Tuxtla Gutiérrez: Consejo Estatal para las Culturas y las Artes de Chiapas.

Popol Vuh: las antiguas historias del Quiché. 1947. Translated by Adrián Recinos. Mexico City: Fondo de Cultura Económica.

Popol Vuh: The Sacred Book of the Ancient Quiché Maya. 1950. Translated by Delia Goetz and Sylvanus G. Morley, from the Spanish translation by Adrián Recinos. Norman: University of Oklahoma Press.

Rabasa, José. 2010. *Without History. Subaltern Studies, the Zapatista Insurgency, and the Specter of History.* Pittsburgh, Pa.: University of Pittsburgh Press.

Rader, Dean. 2012. "The Poetry of Participation: On the Work of Heid Erdrich." In Erdrich 2012, xi–xvi.

Reyes Matamoros, José Antonio. 2006. "Presentación." In López Díaz, Díaz Ruiz, and López Díaz 2006, i–vi.

Rocha Vivas, Miguel. 2021. *Word Mingas: Oralitegraphies and Mirrored Visions on Oralitures and Indigenous Contemporary Literatures.* Chapel Hill: University of North Carolina Press.

Rodríguez Gómez, Marlene. 2007. "La luna centellea." In Sánchez Gómez and Reyes Matamoros 2007, 59.

Rus, Jan. 1989. "The Caste War of 1869 from the Indian's Perspective: A Challenge for Ethnohistory." In *Memorias del Segundo Coloquio Internacional de Mayistas, 17–21 de agosto de 1987.* Vol. 2, 1033–47. Mexico City: Universidad Nacional Autónoma de México.

Saldaña-Portillo, María Josefina. 2001. "Who's the Indian in Aztlán? Re-Writing Mestizaje, Indianism, and Chicanismo from the Lacandón." In *The Latin American Subaltern Studies Reader,* edited by Ileana Rodríguez, 402–23. Durham, N.C.: Duke University Press.

Saldaña-Portillo, María Josefina. 2016. *Indian Given: Racial Geographies Across Mexico and the United States.* Durham, N.C.: Duke University Press.

Saldaña-Portillo, María Josefina, and Simón Trujillo. 2021. "Introduction: What Does Mestizaje Name?" *Aztlan: Journal of Chicano Studies* 46 (2): 149–59.

Sánchez, Consuelo. 1999. *Los pueblos indígenas: del indigenismo a la autonomía.* Mexico City: Siglo Veintiuno Editores.

Sánchez Gómez, Armando. 2011. "Tepnax la jnop: Poco aprendí." In Sánchez Gómez and Córdova Solís 2011, 57.

Sánchez Gómez, Armando, and Carlos Córdova Solís, eds. 2011. *Snojk'ental beel ta Yaxinal u Nichimal k'op: Versos y huellas bajo la luna: Poesía Maya; Sendero de Valores Universales.* San Cristóbal de las Casas, Chiapas: Escritores Tseltales, UNEMAZ, A.C., Programa Escuelas de Calidad.

Sánchez Gómez, Armando, and José Antonio Reyes Matamoros, eds. 2007. *Sab xojob: Vapor de luz.* San Cristóbal de las Casas, Chiapas: Unidad de Escritores Mayas-Zoques, Comisión Nacional para el Desarrollo de los Pueblos Indígenas.

Sell, Sean S., and Nicolás Huet Bautista, eds. 2017. *Chiapas Maya Awakening: Contemporary Poems and Short Stories.* Norman: University of Oklahoma Press.

Shook, David, and Victor Terán, eds. 2015. *Like a New Sun: Six Contemporary Mexican Poets Writing in Indigenous Languages.* Los Angeles: Phoneme Media.

Silko, Leslie Marmon. 1996. *Yellow Woman and a Beauty of the Spirit: Essays on Native American Life Today*. New York: Simon and Schuster.

Silko, Leslie Marmon. 1998. "Interior and Exterior Landscapes: The Pueblo Migration Stories." In Ortiz 1998, 2–24.

Silko, Leslie Marmon. 2010. *The Turquoise Ledge: A Memoir*. New York: Viking.

Smith, Linda Tuhiwai. 2005. *Decolonizing Methodologies: Research and Indigenous Peoples*. London: Zed Books.

Soto, Silvia. 2015. "Unstoppable Clamor: The Re-Construction of a Mayan World in Chiapas." PhD diss., University of California, Davis.

Speed, Shannon. 2008. *Rights in Rebellion: Indigenous Struggles and Human Rights in Chiapas*. Stanford, Calif.: Stanford University Press.

Speed, Shannon, R. Aída Hernández Castillo, and Lynn M. Stephen. 2006. *Dissident Women: Gender and Cultural Politics in Chiapas*. Austin: University of Texas Press.

Standing Bear, Luther. 1978. *Land of the Spotted Eagle*. Lincoln: University of Nebraska Press.

Stephen, Lynn. 2002. *Zapata Lives! Histories and Cultural Politics in Southern México*. Berkeley: University of California Press.

Talamantez, Inés. 1990. "An Insider's Point of View." *Center for the Study of Women in Society Annual Review*, 20.

Taylor, Analisa. 2009. *Indigeneity in the Mexican Cultural Imagination: Thresholds of Belonging*. Tucson: University of Arizona Press.

Tello Díaz, Carlos. 1994. *La rebelión de las cañadas: origen y ascenso del EZLN*. Mexico City: Ediciones Cal y Arena.

Torres Sánchez, Diego. 2006a. *Ma'yuk slajibal te ejchenil: La herida interminable*. San Cristóbal de las Casas, Chiapas: Centro Estatal de Lenguas, Arte y Literatura Indígena.

Torres Sánchez, Diego. 2006b. "Yokinel Ch'ich'elil 1712: Sangriento 1712." In Torres Sánchez 2006a, 20–89.

Trouillot, Michel-Rolph. 1995. *Silencing the Past: Power and the Production of History*. Boston: Beacon Press.

United Nations. 2007. *Declaration on the Rights of Indigenous People*. Resolution 61/295. Adopted September 13, 2007.

Valle Escalante, Emilio del. 2009. *Maya Nationalisms and Postcolonial Challenges in Guatemala: Coloniality, Modernity, and Identity Politics*. Santa Fe, N.Mex.: School for Advanced Research.

Valle Escalante, Emilio del, ed. 2010. *Uk'u'x kaj, uk'u'x ulew: Antología de poesía maya guatemalteca contemporánea*. Pittsburgh, Pa.: Instituto Internacional de Literatura Iberoamericana, Universidad de Pittsburgh.

Varese, Stefano. 2006. *Witness to Sovereignty: Essays on the Indian Movement in Latin America*. Copenhagen: International Work Group for Indigenous Affairs.

Varese, Stefano, Guillermo Delgado, and Rodolfo Meyer. 2008. "Indigenous Anthropologies Beyond Barbados." In *A Companion to Latin American Anthropology*, edited by Deborah Poole, 375–98. Malden, Mass.: Blackwell.

Vogt, Evon Z. 1994. *Fieldwork Among the Maya: Reflections on the Harvard Chiapas Project*. Santa Fe: University of New Mexico Press.

Volpi Escalante, Jorge. 2004. *La guerra y las palabras: una historia intelectual de 1994*. Mexico City: Ediciones Era.

Warren, Jonathan W. 2001. *Racial Revolutions: Antiracism and Indian Resurgence in Brazil*. Durham, N.C.: Duke University Press.

Warrior, Robert Allen. 1995. *Tribal Secrets: Recovering American Indian Intellectual Traditions*. Minneapolis: University of Minnesota Press.

Warrior, Robert Allen. 2005. *The People and the Word: Reading Native Nonfiction*. Minneapolis: University of Minnesota Press.

Warrior, Robert Allen. 2008. "Organizing Native American and Indigenous Studies." *Modern Language Association* 123 (5): 1683–91.

Weaver, Jace, Craig S. Womack, and Robert Warrior. 2006. *American Indian Literary Nationalism*. Santa Fe: University of New Mexico Press.

Womack, John, Jr. 1999. *Rebellion in Chiapas*. New York: New Press.

Worley, Paul M. 2013. *Telling and Being Told: Storytelling and Cultural Control in Contemporary Yucatec Maya Literatures*. Tucson: University of Arizona Press.

Worley, Paul M., and Rita M. Palacios. 2019. *Unwriting Maya Literature: Ts'íib as Recorded Knowledge*. Tucson: University of Arizona Press.

INDEX

ABOUT THE AUTHOR

Dr. Silvia Soto is an assistant professor of Chicano and Latino studies at Sonoma State University. She earned her doctoral degree from the University of California, Davis, in Native American studies. Her research focuses on the contemporary Maya literary movement of Chiapas, Mexico, more specifically on concepts of identity formation, gender relations, and Maya cosmovisions. Soto has been the recipient of the postdoctoral research fellowship at the University of Illinois at Urbana-Champaign in American Indian studies.